Myra Moore
1301 SW Highland
J.S. Mo 64081
524-8976

1095

S0-BOO-431

Demon
Possession
& the
Christian

Demon Possession & the Christian

C. Fred Dickason

CROSSWAY BOOKS • WESTCHESTER, ILLINOIS
A DIVISION OF GOOD NEWS PUBLISHERS

Demon Possession & the Christian. Copyright © 1987 by C. Fred
Dickason. Originally published by the Moody Bible Institute of
Chicago. This edition published by Crossway Books, a division of
Good News Publishers, Westchester, Illinois 60153.

All rights reserved. No part of this publication may be reproduced,
stored in a retrieval system or transmitted in any form by any means,
electronic, mechanical, photocopy, recording, or otherwise without
the prior permission of the publisher, except as provided by USA
copyright law.

First Crossway printing, 1989

Printed in the United States of America

Library of Congress Catalog Card Number 88-63692

ISBN 0-89107-521-6

Selected quotations from Kurt Koch, *Occult Bondage and Deliverance*
(Grand Rapids, MI: Kregel, 1970) are used by permission of Kregel
Publications.

The excerpt on page 305, taken from Frederick Crews, "The Future of
an Illusion," *The New Republic,* January 21, 1985, pp. 28-33, is reprinted
by permission of *The New Republic,* © 1985, The New Republic, Inc.

All Scripture quotations in this book are from the *New American
Standard Bible,* © 1960, 1962, 1963, 1968, 1971, 1972, 1973, 1975
and 1977 by the Lockman Foundation, and are used by permission.

Contents

Foreword

"Pastor Bubeck, when I read your first book a number of years ago, I thought you were moving into dangerous extremism. I have called to ask your forgiveness. In my pastoral ministry I am facing increasing numbers of people who seem to be troubled by the powers of darkness." Those words were recently spoken by a pastor in a southern state who called me for some encouragement and counsel. If the increasing numbers of telephone calls I am receiving are a partial measure, one must conclude that the demonization problem in the Christian church is experiencing a dramatic upswing. Since completing my second book on spiritual warfare, it is not unusual to receive as many as six or eight calls each day from people who are seeking help in their spiritual battle.

C. Fred Dickason is a humble Christian and a well-trained theologian. Though having traveled separate roads in our study of the problems encountered in the believer's battle with darkness, our conclusions are remarkably similar. That is as one would expect. Those who hold tenaciously to the final authority of God's inerrant Word will usually arrive at common understanding concerning the basics of what that Word teaches. The subject of spiritual warfare is one that Satan has sought to cloud with much emotional charge and subjective prejudice. Many Christian people are fearful of the subject. They want to retreat into a belief about their safety from demonic encounter that is not only unbiblical but terribly dangerous. As the battle between light and darkness intensifies in these last days, believers need as never before to be equipped with a sound, doctrinal understanding of their victory. This book provides opportunity for such equipping.

Dr. Dickason makes a much needed contribution to a solid, biblical study of what God's Word teaches about demonology. He approaches the study with thoroughness, fairness, and integrity. His scholarly preparation is obvious. As he systematically unlocks the teaching of relevant biblical passages, one is impressed by his efforts to reveal what is said and not to prove his personal prejudice. Dr. Dickason does not, however, limit his approach to academic understanding. His teaching on the subject has been tested in the laboratory of life. Over the last several years, he has personally counseled more than four hundred counselees who have experienced the spiritual struggle of the believer's warfare.

When the Lord first led me into a study of spiritual warfare, I was chagrined by the lack of preparation I had received through my academic training. Though having graduated from Bible college and seminary, my understanding of the believer's warfare with Satan's kingdom was almost nonexistent. I have discovered that I was not alone. In talking to numerous missionaries through the years, one discovers that most of them were sent out to the mission field with very little, if any, training in spiritual warfare. The resulting wounding has sometimes been disastrous. Praise God that many missionaries on the field have learned from other veteran missionaries concerning the nature and victory of the battle. Pastoral leadership in our country is equally lacking in training and understanding of the believer's warfare. How often I hear telephone callers lament, "My pastor has no understanding of the fearful struggle I am facing." It ought not to be that way.

There is desparate need for Bible colleges and evangelical seminaries to equip leaders who can fearlessly help the spiritually oppressed. This book by Dr. Dickason should become a standard text and required reading for everyone aspiring to spiritual leadership. Pastors, missionaries, professors, teachers, elders, deacons, and Christian parents need to work through this study. Satan will tremble and God will be glorified as these truths set forth in this book are assimilated and applied. I commend it as "must" reading for the Christian public.

MARK I. BUBECK

Preface

"I can't believe my ears! I thought no one in the twentieth century still seriously believed in such things! I suppose that if we were back in the time of the Salem witchcraft hunts, you would have me burned at the stake!" The concerned gentleman complained to me after I had preached on the topic "Christ Came to Destroy the Works of the Devil."

This outburst reflects the general unbelief of Western, secularized society, even in the church, regarding the reality of the spirit world. Materialism is reality. All we need to know or can know is determined by the scientific method.

I pointed out to the man that I accepted the extremes of neither the witch hunters nor of materialists. His real argument was not with me, but with the Lord Jesus, whose words about the reality of demons are recorded in the Scriptures, God's authoritative message to men.

Closely related to this form of unbelief is the attitude of another Christian man who is a psychiatrist. He stated, "I must believe that demon possession is a reality because it is taught in the Scriptures. However, I have never seen a case. I think that such things are not very common, particularly in civilized societies."

Though he accepted the authority of the Bible, this man's knowledge and experience were limited. He could not, then, draw a general statement regarding the presence or absence of demonization today in the United States or in foreign countries. Neither was there any indication that he knew what symptoms to seek or how to test for the presence of inhabiting demons within a client.

It was in 1975 that I witnessed my first case of demonization. That was the year Moody Press published my book *Angels, Elect and Evil,* which has been read popularly and used as a textbook in colleges and seminaries. I witnessed a change of personality when a colleague addressed a demon in a depressed and confused person. After twenty minutes, the counselee returned to normal and was unaware of what had happened. The demon claimed that right then the girl's aunt was involved in a seance. I was a bit startled by this new experience but also witnessed God's control of the situation as my colleague exercised his authority in Christ.

Since that time I have encountered more than 400 cases of demonization, many of whom I have counseled on several occasions. I have conferred with others who have also counseled in this area, including some psychologists and psychiatrists. There have been presentations of the reality of the demon world, the reality of demonization, and a biblical and clinical method of treating it. These presentations have been to pastors, professional counselors, and to students in formal courses taught at the Moody Bible Institute in undergraduate and graduate level courses (the latter taught in collaboration with Dr. Mark I. Bubeck).

The results have been encouraging and, I trust, honoring to our Lord Jesus Christ. Many have been permanently helped, freed from slavery to evil influence. A file of testimonies witnesses to that. There are others who are now able to help those afflicted because of training received. One pastor who took a course in counseling the demon oppressed said, "This course should be a required course of the Graduate School. It is perhaps the most urgent and significant course I have ever taken." Another wrote, "I especially appreciate the thorough biblical approach for the courses I have taken and the presentation of sound, practical insight and ways to use the material in ministry." For this we are truly grateful to our Lord and trust that He will receive the credit and the glory for any good accomplished.

I have recognized the need for a book that would treat the issue of the relation of believers to demonization from the standpoint of the biblical data and from genuine clinical investigation. With the background the Lord has given to me in theology and biblical exegesis and in counseling experience, I wondered if I should attempt to write such a book. After all, I have done a fair bit of study and teaching in the area of angels, Satan, and demons for a previous book and in the classroom. And if I were to fulfill the biblical responsibility to teach faithful persons who would be able to teach others also, then perhaps I could serve beyond my personal contacts to help meet the needs of a world suffering under the oppression of Satan and his angels. When Moody Press asked me on three occasions to consider writing a book on demonization and believers, I surmised that God was in it.

Though demonization is a controversial subject even among believers, I believe that it must be faced with objectivity and charity (much as the issue of biblical inerrancy or the millennial issue). So I have dared to tread the ground that angels know quite well. Perhaps the saints will be encouraged and equipped by the contribution of this humble attempt. I pray that they will.

I owe a great deal to those who have studied and written before me. To Dr. Mark I. Bubeck, Dr. Kurt Koch, Dr. Merrill F. Unger, Mr. Ben Johnson, and others, I am indebted. For the encouragement of my colleagues at Moody Bible Institute and at Moody Press in particular, I am thankful. I want to acknowledge the prayers and encouragements of pastors, professionals, friends, and especially my family.

I trust that this work may be a contribution to the building of Christ's universal church, against which the authorities of the unseen world will not prevail.

Introduction

The issue we undertake to study is a serious one—extremely serious. It touches upon the mental, physical, and spiritual welfare of many Christians. It affects the disciplines of biblical and theological studies and relates to the areas of psychology and psychiatry. The question is, Can a Christian be demonized?

There is a great deal of disagreement among Christians on this question. It boggles the mind of many; and emotions run high, often clouding the issue. Yet the question must be faced. Christians can no longer ignore this matter (though some may feel more comfortable to do so). It has become an issue more and more discussed in our times.

This book is directed to the serious, informed Christian, one who regards the Bible as God's authoritative Word. It is designed for those who desire to devote their lives to the Lord Jesus Christ and disciple others to do the same. It is not directed only to the scholar.

Our study will be primarily in the New Testament, though we may consider related passages in the Old Testament. We will consider the biblical evidences, the theological arguments, and the experience of counselors and counselees. This work is not a guide to counseling, though it may provide background for such. The subject of counseling the demon oppressed requires another book. In this work we are not dealing with the Christian's problems with the flesh and with the world system, but with the Christian's relationship to demonization, generally called demon possession.

There are problems to face. We must deal with the preliminary questions: (1) What are demons? (2) What is demonization? (3) What is a believer, and what is involved in salvation? (4) What is spiritual warfare (the flesh, the world, and the devil)?

We also must face some major considerations. We shall look at the biblical evidence. This involves a proper approach to biblical interpretation and the weighing of evidence. It also involves treating passages that are used for and against the idea that believers can be demonized.

A second major consideration will be that of the theological arguments for and against the demonization of believers. A third will be clinical evidence. Here we need to discuss the place of reason and experience and the type of evidence necessary. Case studies will be presented and evaluated.

Our study would not be complete without considering the dynamics of demonization, that is, what is involved in the actual relation and working of a demon with regard to his subject. We must also concern ourselves with defense against demonization. A proper approach to warfare and perspective in warfare is essential. We shall treat in general deliverance from demonization and the propriety of counsel along this line.

To complete our study we will look at the response to the issue—dangers to avoid and duties to assume.

Our basic approach to this study must be clarified. We are assuming the authority of the Scriptures as final where they are specific in matters of doctrine and practice. We shall assume, on good grounds, biblical inerrancy. We cannot allow theological or dogmatic positions to govern our approach to the exegesis of the Word of God, although they may be helpful if genuinely biblically derived. God has spoken in His Word. It is our part to submit to its authority, to interpret it properly, and to apply it to our lives (2 Tim. 3:15-17).

The Scriptures do not treat all the issues or answer all the questions we might like to ask. They do not speak specifically and clearly to all matters. But they do provide the framework in basic principles and in many particulars that help us to gain answers to some of our questions. Here we must be careful not to formulate doctrine where the Scripture is not specific. We may form opinion based upon scriptural principles and particulars and use reason and experience as supplementary evidence.

In this latter case we must be careful not to exalt our reasoning on biblical and experiential evidence to the place of biblical doctrine. Theological statements may be considered valid if based upon proper biblical exegesis and understood in the historical perspective of the progress of revelation contained in Scripture. We must revere the Scriptures as from God and treat them properly, not reading into them our prejudices or biases. We must treat them fairly and humbly stand ready to change our opinions.

What benefits should result from this study? (1) There should be the clarification of the biblical and theological contributions that may be used to answer the issue. (2) We hope there will be the cultivation of open-mindedness and the contribution of useful material for discussion. (3) We hope to stimulate concern to treat properly and considerately those under bondage to demonic oppression. We make our appeal to professionals in the fields of medicine, psychiatry, psychology, counseling, and pastoral care. We cannot ignore those deeply hurting any longer or treat them with a world view that ignores the reality of demon oppression or of demonization. We are to shepherd God's people. (4) It is our desire to ease the burden of the afflicted and to help to set the prisoners free.

We urge, therefore, open-mindedness and fair evaluation of the material presented in this book so that its presentation and the reader's response may result in the glory of God and the good of man.

PART 1

Preliminary Questions

1

What Are Demons?

There is no doubt that the Bible, interpreted in normal fashion, testifies very clearly to the reality and activity of demons.[1]

THEIR REALITY

EVIDENCE FROM THE OLD TESTAMENT

The record in the Old Testament is quite clear. Demons are real spirit beings who oppose God and man. A spirit being spoke through the serpent in Genesis 3 and caused the Fall of the human race into sin's guilt and degradation. Satan may be considered a demon, since he is named "the ruler of the demons" (Matt. 12:24). Satan seems to have motivated the first murder (Gen. 4:1-6, cf. John 8:44; 1 John 3:12). Demons may have attacked the race in Genesis 6:1-10.

Satan accused Job and accused God and brought, under God's permission and restraint, great destruction and distress (Job 1-2). A demon volunteered to be a "lying spirit" to Ahab (1 Kings 22:20-22). There were spirit beings energizing the world rulers in the time of Daniel (Dan. 10:13, 20).

No fewer than five different Hebrew words are translated by the Greek Septuagint (LXX) version of the Old Testament by the well-known New Testament Greek words *daimon* or *daimonion*. They are *shedhim* (Deut. 32:17; Ps. 106:37), *seirim*

---

1. For a larger treatment of the subject, see C. Fred Dickason, *Angels, Elect and Evil* (Chicago: Moody, 1975), pp. 150-81.

(Lev. 17:7), *'elilim* (Ps. 96:5, LXX 95:5), *gad* (Isa. 65:11), and *qeter* (Ps. 91:6, LXX 90:6).

More than one hundred references to demons sprinkle the New Testament. Four Greek terms definitely refer to demons. *Daimon* is used once in the critical editions of the New Testament (Matt. 8:31). *Daimonion* occurs 63 times, and *pneumata* (spirits) 43 times. The general term for angels, *angelos,* describes demons in several contexts (Matt. 25:41; Rev. 12:7, 9).

It is significant testimony to the reality of demons that every writer (though not every book) of the New Testament, except the author of Hebrews, mentions demons or evil angels. Even Hebrews, however, directly names the devil (Heb. 2:14).

The testimony of the crucified, risen Lord Jesus carries great weight, even among those who may question the rest of the New Testament. He is the way, the truth, and the life (John 14:6) and speaks the truth (John 8:45). Jesus accepted the fact that Satan was the ruler of an army of demons (Matt. 12:22-28). He regarded Satan and demons as morally responsible persons who were guilty and assigned to the lake of fire (Matt. 25:41).

The Lord Jesus placed His claims to messiahship partly on His miraculous ability to cast out demons from the demonized: "If I cast out demons by the Spirit of God, then the kingdom of God has come upon you" (Matt. 12:28). This necessitates the same level of reality for the demons and His identity as Messiah. He gave His disciples authority to cast out demons (Matt. 10:1). When His disciples asked why they could not cast out a certain demon, He responded, "Because of the littleness of your faith" (Matt. 17:20). Note that He did not correct their concept of a demon's inhabiting a boy. Instead He added, "This kind cannot come out by anything but prayer" (Mark 9:29). The Lord Jesus, Creator of heaven and earth, was not locked into a naive world view. He actually cast out the demon on that occasion and spoke about the reality of such in private. If He had wished to correct His followers, He certainly missed an appropriate occasion!

A large part of Christ's ministry involved the casting out of demons. The synoptic gospels record seventeen mentions of demons connected with the ministry of Christ, and in nine cases they specifically state that Jesus cast out the demons.

Even a writer who does not hold our view of the Scriptures, writing about the Bible's presentation of the picture, says regarding Peter's statement in Acts 10:38:

> The statement is clear and unequivocal. It is made by the apostle Peter during his sermon at Caesarea, and it emphasizes that the ability to release men from the power of the devil was central to the ministry of Christ. All the early preachers underscored this function as they spread the word of Christ, using it as powerful evidence to assert the authenticity of Christ as the messenger of God. The claim was a literal one and had ample foundation: in the synoptic gospels demoniacs are presented as the most frequent objects of Christ's curative powers.[2]

There is no suggestion that demons are temporary entities that ceased to exist after the time of Christ and the apostles. In fact, the New Testament witnesses to their continuing activity throughout the church age. Paul and John warn of future deception by demons (1 Tim. 4:1; 1 John 4:1-3). Demons will be extremely active in the Great Tribulation period (Rev. 9:3-11; 12:7; 16:13-14). They continue their terrible work until Christ comes to place them into the abyss (Rev. 20:1-3; Isa. 24:21-23). Though bound completely during the millennial kingdom, afterward they along with Satan are released for a short time to deceive the nations. Then they with all unbelievers are cast permanently into the lake of fire (Rev. 20:7-10).

The evidence from the New Testament for the existence of demons is overwhelming. We cannot profess to believe the Bible and deny the reality of demons, either in the day of Scripture or now.

THEIR ORIGIN

There is a problem concerning the exact origin of demons, since it is not precisely stated in the Bible. We can say a few things with certainty. They are not the product of an overactive imagination or the disembodied spirits of a supposed race of men before Adam. Neither are they the monstrous offspring of

2. Roger Baker, *Binding the Devil* (New York: Hawthorne, 1975), p. 35.

angelic cohabitation with women before the Flood (Gen. 6:1-4). There is no evidence for these views.

STATEMENT OF POSITION

There is good evidence, however, that demons are fallen angels aligned with their leader and chief demon, Satan. In his original rebellion, Satan drew with him a great number of lesser angels, perhaps a third of all created (Ezek. 28:18; Rev. 12:4).[3] They may now be classified as either confined or free. The free have their abode in the heavenlies and have access to earth and its inhabitants (Eph. 3:10; 6:12).

Others are confined in one of several places. Some are in the abyss, or pit (Rev. 9:1-11), a place to which Christ cast many (Luke 8:31). This is the place where Satan will be confined during the future kingdom (Rev. 20:1-3). Others are bound in the earth. Four great angels, and perhaps their armies, who will destroy one-third of mankind are confined at the river Euphrates (Rev. 9:14). Jude 6 describes a particularly wicked group of demons as "kept in eternal bonds under darkness [reserved] for the judgment of the great day." This is the same group that Peter describes as in tartarus (2 Pet. 2:4).

SUPPORT FOR POSITION

Support for the fact that demons are fallen angels is sufficient. First, they have a similar relation to Satan as do Satan's angels. The parallel expressions "the devil and his angels" (Matt. 25:41), "the dragon and his angels" (Rev. 12:7), and "Beelzebul the ruler of the demons" (Matt. 12:24, 26) support this.

Second, when Satan is designated "ruler of the demons," the term that is used is *archonti,* which has the basic meaning of "first." "As 'first among demons' he is their ruler."[4] This same relationship may be seen in that demon-locusts, released from the pit during the Tribulation, have over them an angel named Abaddon or Apollyon (destroyer), who may be Satan (Rev. 9:11).

Third, demons and angels have similar essence. Angels are

3. For support that Ezekiel 28 and Isaiah 14 speak of the original sin of Satan and his angels, see Dickason, *Angels,* pp. 127-37.
4. Charles R. Smith, "The New Testament Doctrine of Demons," *Grace Journal* 10 (Spring 1969):32.

termed "spirits" (Ps. 104:4; Heb. 1:14), and so are demons (Matt. 8:16; Luke 10:17, 20).

Fourth, they carry out similar activities. Demons seek to enter and control men (Matt. 17:14-18; Luke 11:14-15). So also may evil angels such as Satan (Luke 22:3; John 13:27). Evil angels, just as demons, join Satan in war against God and man (Rev. 12:7-17; Mark 9:17-26; Rev. 9:13-15).

Fifth, the ranks of angels and demons are similar, if not identical (Rom. 8:38-39; Eph. 6:10-12; Col. 1:16; 2:15).

The above reasons seem quite sufficient to identify demons as fallen angels subservient to Satan, carrying out his plans. If that is not the case, then we have no biblical evidence for determining the origin of demons.

THEIR NATURE

Since we may quite certainly identify demons as fallen angels, we can predicate about demons what is also true of angels.[5]

PERSONAL BEINGS

They are persons, originally created in the image of God (inference from personality); but having rebelled against God, they fell and remain irreversibly in estrangement from God and in the depravity of sin.

Evidence of their personhood may be seen in that personal pronouns are applied to them by Christ and by the demons to themselves (Luke 8:27-30). They may assume personal names, such as "Legion" (Luke 8:30). They use intelligent speech (Luke 4:33-35, 41; 8:28-30). They recognized the identity of Christ (Mark 1:23-24) and of Paul (Acts 16:16-17). In this case they also divined the future. It is an encouragement to the saints that the demons exhibit the emotion of fear, trembling at their judgment (Luke 8:28; James 2:19). It is also obvious that they exercised their will in rebelling against God and later in appealing to Christ not to cast them into the pit (Luke 8:32). However, they had to obey the will of Christ when He cast them out (Mark 1:27).

5. For further description of the nature of angels, see Dickason, *Angels,* pp. 26-27.

SPIRIT BEINGS

As angels are spirit in nature, so are demons. They are contrasted with flesh and blood, that is, beings with bodies (Eph. 6:12). They are among the invisible creatures of God (Col. 1:16), though they may, as angels, take upon themselves visible form at times. When they appear, they may appear as if they were angels of light (2 Cor. 11:14) or as hideous and fearsome beings (Rev. 9:7-10, 17; 16:13-16).

POWERFUL BEINGS

Demons have the powers of supernatural intelligence and strength. Satan has vast intelligence (Ezek. 28:12). Demons are capable of creating a network of information and carrying out strategems on the local or worldwide scene (Eph. 6:11-12; 2 Cor. 2:11). They may control men and overpower men. An evil spirit moved a man over whom two unbelieving Jewish exorcists sought to use the name of Jesus in magical fashion; and he "leaped on them and subdued both of them and overpowered them, so that they fled out of that house naked and wounded" (Acts 19:14-16). The demoniac of the Gerasenes was controlled by many thousands of unclean spirits, "and no one was able to bind him any more, even with a chain" (Mark 5:1-4). The power of this "Legion" forcibly arrested the attention of those who saw the effect of demons leaving the man and entering two thousand swine to drive them down the hill into the sea (Mark 5:12-13).

Their powers are used in terribly wicked fashion. Their murderous action torments men to the point of preferring death (Rev. 9:1-11). Some demons spew fire from their mouths to slay one third of mankind during the Tribulation (Rev. 9:13-19).

Demons can produce deceptive miracles. Like Satan they may interfere with the laws of nature to produce "all power and signs and false wonders" (2 Thess. 2:9). God limits what they can do, however. Pharaoh's court magicians seemed to be able to duplicate some of God's miracles through Moses but could not match others (Ex. 8:5-7 and 8:16-19). Furthermore, all they could do was add to Egypt's misery, not relieve it. Modern "miracles" and "magic" may not be mere human fakery. They could be the product of counterfeiting demons.

Just as angels move swiftly in space and are not limited by material bodies or barriers, so demons may use this ability to promote their schemes. They are, however, creatures limited in time and space, power, and knowledge. Since there are seemingly millions,[6] their combined intelligence and powers may be felt in many places near the same time. Their deception and powers may be very efficient and effective. We are comforted by the fact that our sovereign Creator and Defender limits the devastation they might design.

THEIR ACTIVITIES

In general demons are Satan's untiring and devoted henchmen organized to accomplish their common unrighteous purpose.

PROMOTING SATAN'S PROGRAM

Because he is limited in time, space, and power, Satan must extend his influence through his many angels. He is their forceful dictator who demands and secures their allegiance. There is no opportunity for a divided army (Matt. 12:24-26). They are constantly at work, needing no rest as do humans. Combining their resources of information and power, they scheme powerfully and have millennia of successful history in the promotion of evil. They seek to control individuals (Eph. 2:1-2), political governments (Dan. 10:13, 20), and the whole world's philosophy and course of history (John 12:31; Eph. 6:11-12; 2 Thess. 2:8-10).

OPPOSING GOD'S PURPOSES

Demons promote rebellion against God among men. When Satan asserted, "I will make myself like the Most High," he introduced a creature-centered philosophy among angels (Isa. 14:14; Ezek. 28:16, 18). He came to man with the same lie: "You will be like God" (Heb., *elohim*, mighty one or ones). The results were the same: guilt, death, and degradation. Satan's Antichrist will be the epitome of rebellion, "the man of lawlessness . . . displaying himself as being God" (2 Thess. 2:3-4). He will gather men to warfare against God and Christ in the Tribula-

---

6. Demons account for about one-third of the innumerable angels. See ibid., pp. 85-86.

tion (Rev. 16:14) and after his release from millennial confinement (Rev. 20:7-9).

Demons delight in slandering the character of God. They want us to believe that He isn't loving, kind, considerate, fair, or faithful—that He is restrictive and harsh and protective of His own position (Gen. 3:1-5).

Demons drive men to idolatry and keep them deceived by displaying supernatural powers, as in the case of the gods of Egypt. The plagues were against Egyptian idols (Ex. 12:12) and prevailed against the Egyptian magicians (Ex. 7:12-13; 8:18-19; 9:11). The Old Testament considered the worship of idols to be the worship of demons (Ps. 106:36-38).

In opposing God, wicked spirits promote false world religions and a maze of cults of Christendom. Whether it be in animistic religions where superstition, magic, and the worship of spirits bring men into bondage, or whether it be in attractive philosophical systems seemingly promoting good, the dynamic is the same—demons distracting from the only true and living God and from His unique Son, the only Savior for the whole world.

OPPRESSING MANKIND

Deception and degradation are their means, and destruction is their goal. Demons hate God and those made in the image of God. They want to drag as many as possible into the lake of fire. They keep them from enjoying true life and God's grace. They are antagonistic and malevolent.

Demons sometimes afflict men through nature (Job 1:12-19; 2:7). To degrade men made in the image of God, they lead them into the creature-centered philosophy of humanism (Rom. 1:18-32; Eph. 2:1-3). This leads to perversion and corruption of God-given powers in religion, society, and sex.

They distract men from the truth. They may promote obvious evil, but they often promote what seems good to man's blinded mind to accomplish their evil ends. Demons hate the grace of God and the doctrine of salvation by grace through faith alone in Christ. To this they seek to blind men's minds (2 Cor. 4:3-4). They promote legalism (Gal. 3:1-3; 1 Tim. 4:1-8) and loose living (1 John 3:8; Jude 4).

Some of their destructive activities include attacking men's bodies with dumbness (Matt. 9:32-33), blindness (Matt. 12:22), deformity (Luke 13:11-17), and convulsive fits (Matt. 17:15-18). The Bible does not label all illness as demonic, but clearly distinguishes natural ailments from the demonic (Matt. 4:24; Luke 7:21). They may drive men to self-inflicted injury (Mark 5:5; 9:22) or to destroy others (Rev. 18:2, 24). They may directly slaughter men (Rev. 9:14-19).

Certain mental disorders stem from the activity of demons. Some appearances of insanity, such as withdrawal, nudity, moroseness, filth, and compulsive behavior characterize some cases of demonization (Luke 8:27-29). Some suicidal manias come from their treachery (Mark 9:22). Such mental distress may be human in source, but we cannot rule out the demonic if we assume a truly biblical world view. Alfred Lechler records a few modern demonic cases of mental distress.[7]

We must mention the phenomenon this book will seek to treat, that of demonization, or demon inhabitation. Through this power, demons seek to control certain persons to promote their own schemes. Sometimes the humans are very cooperative, and other times they are opposed to the things they are led to do. This we will treat in the next chapter.

OPPOSING BELIEVERS IN CHRIST

Make no mistake about it. Satan's main target is the Christian. He hates believers because they are on the side of his archenemy, Jesus Christ. "The activity of demons is so intimately and inseparably bound up with their prince-leader that their work and his is identified rather than differentiated."[8]

Satan's evil forces are arrayed against the believer, seeking to carry out their schemes (Eph. 6:10-12). They attack his confidence in God and His Word (Matt. 16:22-23; 1 Tim. 4:1). They tempt him to sin (1 Chron. 21:1-8; Rev. 2:12-14). They promote immorality (1 Cor. 7:2, 5). They love to break up Christian marriages. They can cause physical maladies (Job 2:7-9; 2 Cor. 12:7).

7. Alfred Lechler, "Distinguishing the Disease and the Demonic," in *Occult Bondage and Deliverance,* by Kurt Koch (Grand Rapids: Kregel, 1970), pp. 133-98.
8. Merrill F. Unger, *Biblical Demonology* (Wheaton, Ill.: Scripture Press, 1957), p. 69.

Demons would divide and defeat genuine unity in the church, locally or universally. They use doctrinal divisions through false teachers or faddists (1 Tim. 4:1-3). They question the genuine deity, genuine humanity, or the very historicity of Christ (1 John 4:1-4; 2 Tim. 3:5; 2 Pet. 1:16). They use practical divisions through jealousy, selfish ambition, arrogance, and personality cults (James 3:14-16; 1 Cor. 3:1-4). They create harshness and lack of forgiveness (2 Cor. 2:5-11; Eph. 4:26-27).

Countering the gospel ministry is their delight. They hinder communication and incite misunderstanding (1 Thess. 2:2-18). Local and national governments may be influenced to resist the spread of the truth (2 Thess. 3:1-2). They incite persecution and imprisonment (Rev. 2:8-10) and even murder of true believers (Rev. 18:2, 24).

LIMITED BY GOD

The activities of Satan and demons are controlled and often overruled by God. He accomplishes all His good pleasure and will bring justice and grace to triumph in the end.

God may use demon powers to correct defection (1 Tim. 1:19-20) or immorality (1 Cor. 5:1-5). Through difficulties inflicted by them, the believer may grow in discernment (Job 40:1-3; 42:1-6) and learn to trust God more thoroughly (2 Cor. 12:7).

God has used demons to defeat the ungodly. He may have used demons as "a band of destroying angels" ("a deputation of angels of evil," NASB marg., Ps. 78:49) to judge Egypt. God judged Ahab by death as he was led by a lying spirit in the mouth of a false prophet (1 Kings 22:20-38).

When demons are cast out, God's power over evil and rebellious creatures is demonstrated (Luke 10:17-19). Christ is shown to be the strong deliverer from Satan and demons (Matt. 12:28-29). His miraculous deliverances substantiated His claims and authority (Mark 1:27). God will demonstrate His justice and the wretchedness of evil when Satan and his angels are cast into the lake of fire (Rev. 20:10).

Despite the awesome powers of Satan and demons, believers may confidently rest in their sovereign Creator and Savior. He defeated Satan's hosts at the cross, controls all things, and guarantees in His wisdom, love, and faithfulness that He will never leave us or forsake us. Neither can any demon separate us from the love of Christ (Col. 2:15; Heb. 13:5). The demons believe and tremble (James 2:19). Believers may believe and trust.

CONCLUSION

The Bible presents overwhelming evidence that such beings as demons actually exist and are active in the present world scene. The Old and New Testaments agree in this. The testimony of the Lord Jesus Himself is conclusive as He recognized their reality, faced their opposition, and cast them out as proof that He is the Son of God and Messiah.

Demons are actually fallen angels under the leadership of Satan, the first among demons. Satan and demons are personal spirit beings, powerful and perverted. They oppose God and mankind, especially believers in Christ. Demons extend Satan's influence and promote his destructive program. Often they do this by invading humans to accomplish their schemes.

Powerful and fearful as they are, they are no match for the Savior, their creator and judge. Christ limits them, uses them despite their intentions, and will finally cast them into the lake of fire for eternal punishment. So we may confidently rely upon Christ to protect our salvation, to guide our lives in victory, and to keep us from demonic plots and practices as we walk with Him in obedience to His Word.

2

What Is Demonization?

Demonization is a reality despite the rationalistic Western mind-set. The New Testament and current events demonstrate the truth of demon invasion and control of humans.

Humanism has done the human race a great disservice. It has degraded man into a mere natural creature, the product of a chance environment. Though it accords him the highest station among evolved forms of life, it denies him the dignity of being created in the image of God. It denies him the tremendous worth found in personhood that reflects God's Person. It denies him the privilege of facing sin for what it is with its guilt, condemnation, and depravity. It makes him think he has no needs before God but leaves him destitute, deprived of the fellowship of God and destined for the lake of fire.

Humanism also denies the reality of demons and demonization. In doing so it cannot properly diagnose or relieve the problems attendant to demonization. Humans have been sold a false bill of goods and are reaping the tragic consequences.

M. Scott Peck, a psychiatrist, has caught the public eye with his book *People of the Lie*. In it he challenges the traditional scientific approach that excludes evil and the supernatural:

The concept of evil has been central to religious thought for millennia. Yet it is virtually absent from our science of psychology—which one might think would be vitally concerned with the matter. The major reason for this strange state of affairs is that the scientific and the religious models have hitherto been considered totally

immiscible—like oil and water, mutually incompatible and rejecting. . . . So for the past three hundred years there has been a state
of profound separation between religion and science. . . . The very
word "evil" requires an a priori value judgment. Hence it is not
even permissible for a strictly value-free science to deal with the
subject. . . . There are many compelling reasons today for their
reintegration—one of them being the problem of evil itself—even
to the point of the creation of a science that is no longer value-free.
In the past decade this reintegration has already begun. It is, in
fact, the most exciting event in the intellectual history of the late
twentieth century.[1]

It is high time that Christians shake off the shackles of scien-
tism. We must face the reality of God's world as it really is to
deal with the stark realities of satanic oppression and demonization. How else will we help this world for which Christ died?
The Scriptures say, "The Son of God appeared for this purpose,
that He might destroy the works of the devil" (1 John 3:8). The
Lord Jesus Himself said in His first sermon in Nazareth:

> The Spirit of the Lord is upon Me, because He anointed Me to
> preach the gospel to the poor. He has sent Me to proclaim release
> to the captives, and recovery of sight to the blind, to set free those
> who are downtrodden. (Luke 4:18)

Since demons have not gone out of business, we should join our
Lord and Savior in the business of proclaiming the gospel and
setting men free from Satan's bondage. The apostle Paul was
sent "to open their eyes so that they may turn from darkness to
light and from the dominion of Satan to God" (Acts 26:18).

We would do well, then, to consider the frequency, definition, symptoms, degrees, and relief of demonization as presented in the New Testament.

FREQUENCY OF DEMONIZATION

Though there may be several cases in the Old Testament, the
New provides us ample evidence of the phenomenon of demonization. As mentioned before, there are seventeen occa-

---

1. M. Scott Peck, *People of the Lie* (New York: Simon & Schuster, 1983), pp. 39-
40.

sions on which demonization is mentioned in the gospels. Some of these references state that Christ treated many who were demonized (Matt. 8:16; Mark 1:32; Luke 4:41).

The Lord Jesus treated nine specific cases of demonized persons, according to the synoptic record. A brief noting of the cases follows:

1. Mark 1:21-28 (Luke 4:31-37). A man in the synagogue at Capernaum had an unclean spirit. "He cried out, saying, 'What have we to do with You, Jesus of Nazareth? Have You come to destroy us? I know who You are—the Holy One of God!' And Jesus rebuked him, saying, 'Be quiet, and come out of him!' . . . The unclean spirit cried out with a loud voice, and came out of him." The onlookers were amazed at His authority.

2. Luke 8:2 mentions "some women who had been healed of evil spirits and sicknesses: Mary who was called Magdalene, from whom seven demons had gone out." These were some of those who accompanied Jesus' group and supported them.

3. Matthew 12:22-29 records the case of the demonized man who was blind and dumb, whom Jesus healed. This is the occasion when the Pharisees said, "This man casts out demons only by Beelzebul the ruler of the demons." But Jesus claimed to cast out demons by the Spirit of God, showing He was Messiah.

4. Matthew 8:28-34 (Mark 5:1-17; Luke 8:26-37) records the unusual case of two Gadarene men who were demonized, living in the tombs and exceedingly violent. Upon this occasion they recognized Him as their judge and pleaded to be sent into a herd of swine. The whole herd rushed into the sea and perished. The incident showed the tremendous power of the Lord Jesus.

5. Matthew 9:32-34 records a case in which demons inhabiting a man caused dumbness. The reaction of the crowd to Jesus' healing the man is significant: "And after the demon was cast out, the dumb man spoke; and the multitudes marveled, saying, 'Nothing like this was ever seen in Israel.' " This is not to be confused with a similar case of a blind and dumb man in Matthew 12.

6. Mark 7:25-30 presents the case of the Syrophoenician woman whose little daughter had an unclean spirit. After instructive conversation, the Lord healed her daughter from a distance. She returned home to find the child free of the demon.

7. Matthew 17:14-20 (Mark 9:14-28; Luke 9:37-42). Coming down from the Mount of Transfiguration the Lord found a man beseeching Him to heal his son, who was "very ill; for he often falls into the fire, and often into the water." The disciples had not been able to cast out the demon, but Jesus "rebuked him, and the demon came out of him, and the boy was cured at once." Jesus answered their question in private that their lack of faith prevented their casting it out.

8. Luke 11:14 presents a third case of Jesus' casting out a demon that caused dumbness so that the man then spoke and the multitudes marveled. This is not to be confused with the similar situation in Matthew 12, though on this occasion Christ's enemies also accused Him of casting out demons by Beelzebul.[2]

9. Luke 13:10-21 presents the tragic case of "a woman who for eighteen years had had a sickness caused by a spirit; and she was bent double, and could not straighten up at all." The Lord Jesus freed her from her sickness, and she became erect again and began glorifying God. In answering the criticism of the synagogue official who recognized that Christ had healed a demonized person on the Sabbath, Jesus answered, "You hypocrites. . . . This woman, a daughter of Abraham as she is, whom Satan has bound for eighteen long years, should she not have been released from this bond on the Sabbath day?"

The above instances of Christ's healing demonized persons demonstrate forcibly that Christ used such miracles to prove His claims to be the Messiah, the King of Israel, the Son of God. And it is quite clear that the Jewish rulers and people understood those claims well. So instead of denying the miracles—which they could not do, since they were done in front of all and the cases were well attested—they denied that Jesus had done them by the power of God. On several occasions they accused Him of being in league with Satan. Of course Jesus answered this quite forcibly as the record shows in Matthew 12:25-29.

James Kallas in one of the SPCK Biblical Monographs takes all the miracles of Christ as evidence of the kingdom in the hand of Christ, who reclaims man and nature from Satan. Al-

2. Robert L. Thomas and Stanley N. Gundry, eds., *A Harmony of the Gospels* (Chicago: Moody, 1978), p. 139.

though to regard all the miracles in such fashion may be a bit strained, it is worth considering.[3]

The reality of demonization is evidenced by the great frequency of the record of such cases in the synoptic gospels. Jesus recognized demonization as real and, with the authority He had from God, healed those afflicted.

DEFINITION OF DEMONIZATION

At this point we need to look at the etymology and usage of the terms for demonization and their equivalents in the New Testament.

ETYMOLOGY

Etymology deals with the meaning of a word by analyzing its elements, considering its root and derivation. When we look at the word for demonization, improperly translated "demon possession," it is highly instructive to notice its root and structure. The verb *daimonizomai* means "to be possessed by a demon."[4]

The participle from the same root, *daimonizomenos,* is used twelve times in the Greek New Testament. It is used only in the present tense, indicating the continued state of one inhabited by a demon, or demonized. This participle has components to its structure. First there is the root, *daimon,* which indicates the involvement of demons. Second is the causative stem, *iz,* which shows that there is an active cause in this verb.[5] Third is the passive ending, *omenos.* This conveys the passivity of the person described as demonized.

Putting it all together, the participle in its root form means "a demon caused passivity." This indicates a control other than that of the person who is demonized; he is regarded as the recipient of the demon's action. In other words, demonization pictures a demon controlling a somewhat passive human.

---

3. James Kallas, *The Significance of the Synoptic Miracles.* SPCK Biblical Monograph Series (Greenwich, Conn.: Seabury, 1961), pp. 77, 81. This book is a protest against the demythologizing of New Testament miracles and world view.
4. William F. Arndt and F. Wilbur Gingrich, *Greek-English Lexicon of the New Testament* (Chicago: U. of Chicago, 1952), p. 168.
5. William Douglas Chamberlain, *An Exegetical Grammar of the Greek New Testament* (New York: Macmillan, 1957), p. 15.

Confusion has been introduced by translating this participle as "demon possessed." The word *possession* implies ownership. Actually, demons own nothing. The New Testament regards them as squatters or invaders of territory that does not belong to them. In reality God owns *them,* for He is their Creator and their Judge. Such a faulty translation, then, misleads people regarding the state of the demonized person and causes undue consternation and terror in the hearts of the afflict and those concerned for him.

In my book *Angels, Elect and Evil,* published in 1975, I quoted Unger's definition of demon possession with some approval: "Demon possession is a condition in which one or more evil spirits or demons inhabit the body of a human being and can take complete control of their victim at will."[6] Six years after this quote Unger wrote another book in which he modified his definition. He then wrote:

> Unfortunately, the term "demon possession" has been commonly used, not to refer correctly to *all* cases of demon invasion, but incorrectly to refer *only* to the basest and most enslaving forms, such as those represented by the demoniac of Gadara. (Mark 5:1-20)[7]

It is much better to use the term "demonization" or "demonized." To this Unger agrees and further describes the term as meaning "under the control of one or more demons."[8]

USAGE

The use of the word *daimonizomenos* in its various contexts confirms the meaning derived from its etymology as above. In Matthew 8:28 the term is used of two demonized persons. Their abnormal behavior indicates supernatural control, particularly supernatural knowledge, strength, and the use of the voice by the leader of an inhabiting group of demons. All of this indi-

---

6. C. Fred Dickason, *Angels, Elect and Evil* (Chicago: Moody, 1975), p. 182, quoting Merrill F. Unger, *Demons in the World Today* (Wheaton, Ill.: Tyndale, 1971), p. 102.
7. Merrill F. Unger, *What Demons Can Do to Saints* (Chicago: Moody, 1977), p. 87.
8. Ibid., p. 86.

cates a demon caused control with passivity on the men's part. It is noteworthy that when Jesus healed one of the men, he had his right mind, was properly clothed, and was sitting with Jesus (Luke 8:35).

In Matthew 9:32 they brought to Christ a dumb man who was demonized. In this case the demon had caused a passivity of his speech. He was unable to use his voice, not because of an injury or a genetic or an endogenous problem, but because of the demon who was controlling his speech mechanism. This is confirmed by the fact that when the demon was cast out, the dumb man could speak. There was no recuperation time or learning indicated. The demon control was gone; the man was in control.

The same situation pertains in the case of the blind and dumb man of Matthew 12:22. In this situation, not only his speech but also his sight was impaired by the action of a demon. Again there was nothing of physical or psychological impairment. The cause of both maladies was due to the control of a demon. When Christ cast the spirit out, the man was able to use his sight and speech normally.

The usage in all these contexts indicates that *daimonizo menos* means "demon-caused passivity," or control by one or more demons with various results in the life of the person including the physical and the psychological.

EQUIVALENT TERMS

A common parallel expression in the New Testament is "to have a spirit," such as in Luke 4:33, where the Greek phrase is actually "having the spirit of an unclean demon" *(echōn pneuma daimoniou akathartou)*. The same general expression is used in Acts 8:7 regarding many who came to Philip to be freed of spirits. This occurred in Samaria. In Acts 16:16 when Paul was in Philippi of Macedonia, he had to confront "a certain slave-girl having a spirit of divination," literally "having a python spirit" *(echousan pneuma puthōna)*. This spirit caused her to bring her masters much profit by fortune-telling.

Other parallel expressions occur. Mark 1:23 presents a man with an unclean spirit *(en pneumati akathartō)*. In Luke 6:18 we read that Jesus cured "those who were troubled with unclean spirits" *(enochloumenoi apo pneumatōn akathartōn)*.

Peter, in Acts 10:38 speaking for the first time to Gentiles, speaks of Jesus and His credentials, including His going about doing good "and healing all who were oppressed by the devil" *(katadunasteuomenous hupo tou diabolou)*. In Acts 5:16 the people from around Jerusalem brought those "who were sick or afflicted with unclean spirits" *(ochloumenous hupo pneumatōn akathartōn)*. A particularly grievous case is described by the mother when she says her daughter is "cruelly demonized" *(kakōs daimonizetai;* Matt. 15:22).

Demonization is always presented as a spirit's inhabiting a human. This is evidenced by the expressions such as "for many demons had entered him" *(eiselthen . . . eis auton)*. Here the spirit who is external to the man is seen as invading his body, most likely the control centers of the brain that affect his mind, behavior, and physical strength (Luke 8:30).

Christ clearly describes the phenomenon and the attendant activity of demonization in Matthew 12:43-45:

> Now when the unclean spirit goes out of a man, it passes through waterless places, seeking rest, and does not find it. Then it says, "I will return to my house from which I came"; and when it comes, it finds it unoccupied, swept, and put in order. Then it goes, and takes along with it seven other spirits more wicked than itself, and they go in and live there; and the last state of that man becomes worse than the first.

The Lord regards the demon as residing in the man as its home, a place where it lives by choice. He may leave, and he may return. Note also that more than one demon may invade and reside in a human.

It seems quite clear that we may define demonization as demon caused passivity or control due to a demon's residing within a person, which manifests its effects in various physical and mental disorders and in varying degrees.

Some writers refer to four stages of demon control: (1) simple subjection, (2) demonization, (3) obsession, (4) demon possession by an indwelling spirit. The Bible knows no such differentiation; it merely classifies the demon's working as either external or internal. If it is internal, it is demonization, the proper term for the commonly misused "demon possession."

SYMPTOMS

Symptoms in general. What are the characteristics of demonization? "The chief characteristic of demon possession . . . is the automatic projection of a new personality in the victim."[9] Demonization is not merely an old-world term for schizophrenic illness, which many agree is caused by a chemical imbalance in the brain and is aggravated by circumstances so as to lead to abnormal thinking, emotions, and behavior. Genuine schizophrenia may be relieved by the application of proper drug therapy. But we are not talking about a human illness. In demonization the personality of the demon eclipses the personality of the person afflicted. The demon displays his personality through the human's body to a greater or lesser degree. The control may be overt or covert. In fact, there is no indication that the human must be aware of demonization in order to be so classified. The control of the thought processes and emotions seems to be the primary characteristic.

Specific symptoms in Scripture. We may note a variety of symptoms from the New Testament. Kurt Koch analyzes the story of the demoniac in Mark 5. He suggests eight symptoms of possession:

1. Indwelling of an unclean spirit (Mark 5:2). This is really the cause of the symptoms.
2. Unusual physical strength (v. 3).
3. Paroxysms or fits of rage (v. 4).
4. Disintegration or splitting of personality (vv. 6-7). The man ran to Jesus for help, yet retreated in fear.
5. Resistance to spiritual things (v. 7). He asked Jesus to let him alone.
6. Hyperaesthesia, or excessive sensibility, such as clairvoyant powers (v. 7). He knew immediately, without previous information, Jesus' identity.
7. Alteration of voice (v. 9). A legion of demons spoke through his vocal faculties.
8. Occult transference (v. 13). The demons left the man and entered the swine with destructive effects.[10]

9. Unger, *Demons in the World Today,* p. 102.
10. Kurt Koch, *Occult Bondage and Deliverance* (Grand Rapids: Kregel, 1970), pp. 57-58.

We cannot classify the last four symptoms as results of a psychiatric illness. As Koch states:

> For example, clairvoyance itself is never a sign of mental illness, and a mental patient will never be able to speak in a voice or a language he has previously not learned. Yet this is exactly what has happened and still does happen in some cases of possession.[11]

Strictly speaking, transference cannot be classified as a symptom of the demonized. It is a result of the casting out of demons or the treatment received from a demonized person.

The symptoms noted in Mark 5, however, do not exhaust scriptural indications of demonization. There are others of varying severity. We have noted the cases of those who were *dumb* or *blind and dumb*. There was a case of experiencing *seizures*, which some incorrectly identify as epilepsy. In that case the seizure threw the person into the fire or into the water for the purpose of destruction (Mark 9:22). Then there is the case of the woman who seemed to have a very severe case of *scoliosis* so that her back was bent double. This was said by Jesus to be caused by a satanic spirit (Luke 13:11-17).

Those involved in occult practices that are enabled by wicked spirits undoubtedly perform their arts energized by indwelling spirits. Consider the supernatural effects produced by the court magicians of Pharaoh as recorded in Exodus. The Samaritan magician Simon, who practiced magic, astonished the people, "claiming to be someone great; and they all, from smallest to greatest, were giving attention to him, saying, 'This man is what is called the Great Power of God' " (Acts 8:9-10). His own concept was that he could tap into outside power as evidenced by his offering the apostles money for power that they could give (Acts 8:18-20). Notice also the fortune-telling ability of the slave girl inhabited by the spirit of divination (Acts 16:16).

Symptoms noted by counselors. Those who counsel the demonized have noted some of the above and agree upon other symptoms. Unger lists several: projection of new personality, supernatural knowledge (including ability to speak in unlearned languages), supernatural physical strength, moral depravity; in addition there may be deep melancholy or seeming

11. Ibid., p. 58.

idiocy, ecstatic or extremely malevolent or fero
spells of unconsciousness, and foaming at the
some of these in Luke 9:39, 42.)

Koch lists the following symptoms noticed
ing: resistance to prayer or Bible reading, fallin
during prayer, reaction to the name of Jesus, exhi ___ ... ...-
voyant abilities, and speaking in unlearned languages. He warns
those who put much stress on speaking in tongues that Satan has
his counterfeits.[13]

German psychiatrist Alfred Lechler lists these symptoms:
passion for lying and impure thoughts, restlessness and depression and fear, compulsion to rebel against God or blaspheme,
violence and cursing, excessive sexual or sensual cravings, resistance and hatred of spiritual things, inability to pronounce or
write the name of Jesus, appearance of mediumistic or clairvoyant abilities, inability to act on Christian counsel, resistance to a
Christian counselor, inability to renounce the works of the devil,
seizures or spells of unconsciousness, speaking in unlearned
languages, extraordinary physical strength, molestation with
pain unrelated to illnesses or injuries. He advises that some of
these marks may stem from mere subjection or affliction rather
than actual demonization, since their marks have much in common.[14] The entire second section of Koch's book is written by
Lechler to treat the problem of the relationship and differentiation of the psychological and the demonic.[15]

We note that the above symptoms listed by counselors of
present-day demonized persons are similar to symptoms found
in biblical cases. We also note that some symptoms of demonization overlap with psychological illness, and others extend
beyond what can be reasonably explained by that designation.

Demons may also enter animals to take control of them in
some way. This was the case with the swine, who were obviously
driven by demons into the water to destroy them. The same
terms are used of the swine as were used of humans; "the
demons came out from the man and entered the swine" *(exel-*

12. Unger, *Demons in the World Today,* pp. 102-8.
13. Koch, *Occult Bondage,* pp. 64-67. See also Koch, *Strife of Tongues* (Grand
    Rapids: Kregel, 1969).
14. Alfred Lechler, "Distinguishing the Disease and the Demonic," *Occult
    Bondage and Deliverance,* by Kurt Koch (Grand Rapids: Kregel, 1970), pp.
    136-53.
15. Ibid., pp. 133-98.

...onta de ta daimonia apo tou anthropou eiselthon eis tous choirous). Similar cases have been reported by modern counselors.

Counselors would do well to take into account the biblical and clinical data suggested by the foregoing information.

DEGREES IN DEMONIZATION

To some extent we have already discussed the degrees of effects in demonization; however, a few observations might be added at this point. Unger comments:

> It is evident, then, *all* demonic invasion is demonization of whatever degree of mildness or severity. To call it "demon possession" rather than demonization is biblically permissible, but *only* insofar as the usage does *not* attempt to differentiate it from demonization in general or limit it to some cases (the milder forms) rather than all cases (including the more severe forms). . . . While cases of severe demonization are indeed a far cry from very mild forms, they are nevertheless mere variations in degree of the same supernatural phenomenon. Both involve demonic invasion and both involve a degree of satanic control.[16]

To what may we attribute the varying degrees of expression in demonization? First, there is the matter of the degree of wickedness of the character of the spirits. Jesus spoke of a spirit's returning to its house (man's body) from which it came; it "takes along with it seven other spirits more wicked than itself, and they go in and live there; and the last state of that man becomes worse than the first" (Matt. 12:44-45).

Second, it logically follows that the more demons inhabiting, the greater the hold the spirits have upon a person. This could result in more control and possibly more violent manifestations. Consider the case of the demonized man who had a spirit called "Legion." By using such a name, this spirit claimed to have thousands of demons with him. In that day a Roman legion involved generally 6,000 troops. Whatever the case, there were enough demons in the one man to enter 2,000 swine and drive them to destruction. We are not told how the demons divided up to control the swine, but it is likely that there were

16. Unger, *What Demons Can Do to Saints,* p. 87.

several in each of them. This, by the way, indicates that demons are not crowded by a small space. Since they are spirit beings, they have no dimensions or weight.

A third observation related to the degree of severity is the matter of organization. Since angels and demons have ranks,[17] it seems that the higher-ranking demons exercise more power and use the organization of the armies under them to greater effect. It may also be that the better organized and tightly run organizations function more effectively.

We cannot deduce from biblical examples that the symptoms of demonization were present at all times. There were many who were oppressed by inhabiting spirits. We are given the record of outstanding manifestations. Jesus treated these outstanding cases so that people could see that Christ performed miraculous deliverances that could not be denied. These cases of casting out demons stood as effective proof of His deity and messiahship. Some cases may be more unnoticed and perhaps even unknown by the person demonized.

RELIEF FROM DEMONIZATION

There is deliverance from demonization. That deliverance is found in Christ and by delegated authority in genuine believers in Christ.

DELIVERANCE BY CHRIST

His personal ministry. Christ delivered the demonized by casting out the demons by His own authority over the spirit world (Matt. 8:16, 32; 9:33; 12:28; Mark 1:27). The relief came immediately and seemed to be lasting (Mark 5:15).

His delegated ministers. Christ delegated to His disciples authority over demons (Matt. 10:1; Mark 3:14-15). The seventy realized that He had given to them, as well, authority over demons, for demons were subject to them in Christ's name (Luke 10:17-20).

His redemptive work. By His cross Christ stripped evil spirits of their weaponry, paraded them in public display, and Christians walk in the train of His triumph (Col. 2:14-15). He Himself said that Satan was judged through the cross (John 12:31-33;

17. Dickason, *Angels,* pp. 85-89.

16:11). Through His death He defeated the devil and delivered those who were subject to fear of death and to bondage from Satan and his demons (Heb. 2:14-15).

Today the resurrected Savior is exalted far above all angelic beings, and they are subject to His name (Phil. 2:9-11; 1 Pet. 3:22).

Christ is victor over Satan and demons, and He delivers those who trust Him. It is only by coming to Christ that men can be freed from demonization.

DELIVERANCE THROUGH BELIEVERS

The Lord Jesus promised, "I will build My church; and the gates of Hades [authorities of the unseen world, including demons] shall not overpower it" (Matt. 16:18). Members of the Body of Christ, His church, who are qualified and walk in fellowship with Him, may help others find deliverance from demonization.

By Christ's authority. If believers are to be involved in freeing people from the domination of demons, they cannot do so by their own power or wisdom; it is only through the authority granted them by Christ. Whether it was the disciples accompanying Him or the apostles and their followers casting out demons, as in the book of Acts, deliverance was only through the delegated authority of the risen Lord Jesus.

All Christians are involved in a spiritual struggle (Eph. 6:10-18). All Christians have the delegated authority of Christ to carry on His ministry of making disciples (Matt. 28:19-20). Though we are not working miracles to prove the deity of Christ or to back the gospel message, we do have all the authority we need to face the host of Satan. We need to note that casting out demons is not a spiritual gift or the peculiar ability of a few unusual believers.[18]

We need not live in terror of demonic power as if Christ had not defeated them and as if they were not subject to Him and to us because of our position in Christ. Christ has been raised and exalted to the right hand of God, and we legally share in that position (Eph. 1:19-21; 2:5-6). Where there is need for deliverance, the church of the exalted Lord must not fail to meet that need or to do His works (Matt. 16:18; John 14:12-14).

18. Unger, *Demons in the World Today,* p. 189.

By biblical principles. We may apply the principles of Scripture in the process of treating those demonized. Proper diagnosis according to biblically presented symptoms is important so as to properly and considerately help those who are afflicted. We must speak the truth in love, sometimes confronting persons with the possibility that demons are involved in their plight. Here we need to use care that we do not attribute all unknown phenomena to demonic agencies. But on the other hand we must not fear to face the truth or fear to face the power of wicked spirits. We are in Christ, far above the enemy in authority. The demons believe this with trembling.

The Lord Jesus encouraged prayer for deliverance (Mark 9:29). Lack of prayer may indicate lack of faith (Matt. 17:18-20). Counselors need to pray with their clients and Christians with Christians about this matter. The more specific praying we do, the more we shall learn of spiritual warfare and of the Lord's deliverance.

Sometimes deliverance demands a direct command to the inhabiting demon. The Lord Jesus and the apostles spoke to demons directly (Matt. 8:32; Mark 5:8; Acts 16:18). They commanded them to depart, and the demons had to obey the authority of Christ. Again we stress that believers today are not working messianic miracles, and the immediate relief in the case of Jesus' miraculous deliverances may not always be the case today. Nevertheless, it is within our prerogative to command in the name of Jesus and to put demons under duress to obey. In this Christ will support us (Matt. 18:18-19), and in this we must take a firm stand (Eph. 6:10-20).

CONCLUSION

Not only does the Bible present demons as a living reality, but it treats demonization as a tragic reality too. It is not superstitious misconception or a religionist's description of phenomena we can explain today in scientific and psychological terms. The phenomenon of demonization surpasses scientific and psychological explanation. It is marked by the influence of a demon personality within a human with certain rather well-defined characteristics—a demonic syndrome obvious in Scripture and in case studies today.

We must be ready to recognize this reality, not as the last thing to be suspected in treating people with questionable symptoms. But taking a biblical world view and a proper wholistic approach, we should investigate all possible causes. We must stand in the authority of Christ and treat demonization realistically and compassionately.

3

What Is a Believer?

We are addressing believers, but sometimes the term *believers* requires an explanation. Is everyone who calls himself a Christian a genuine believer in Christ? What does salvation involve? What place has faith in salvation? What does salvation provide? How secure is the believer? These are basic questions we must answer in treating demonism and believers.

SALVATION PROCURED IN CHRIST

We must consider here the Person of the Savior and the procurement of His salvation.

THE PERSON OF THE SAVIOR

His deity. A believer in Christ in the biblical sense is one who believes in a Christ who is biblically defined. He is a historic person, not merely an ideal personage. He is genuine, eternal deity, equal in person with God the Father and Creator of all things (John 1:1-3). He created all things visible and invisible, including all ranks of angelic beings (Col. 1:16).

His humanity. The Bible also presents Christ as genuinely human with all features of humanity except for sin. He was born of a virgin so that He might remain one eternal Person when taking on humanity, which He joined to His divine nature (Luke 1:35; John 1:14). He lived a sinless life (Heb. 7:26; 1 Pet. 2:22). He died for our sins and rose again bodily from the grave (John 10:15, 17; 1 Cor. 15:3-4). He ascended into heaven where He now intercedes for us as our great High Priest (Heb. 4:14; 7:25). He will come again to judge all men when He raises the dead (John 5:25-29).

THE PASSION OF THE SAVIOR

The Bible presents the salvation accomplished by the Savior in several aspects.

Objective and legal. God designed His Son's death to stand before Him and His law as an objective, historical accomplishment that paid the penalty for man's sin. It appeals to the heart and mind of man, but it is valuable apart from individual response. Repentance and faith do not lend it any worth. It stands entirely valuable before God as the basis on which He saves man. It is a satisfaction of all that God's righteousness requires (Rom. 3:25-26).

Substitutionary and complete. When Christ died, He shouted, "It is finished!" (John 19:30). He had paid in full all that God required so that He might forgive and grant right standing to those who believe in Christ (Rom. 5:9). He died as a legal substitute for sinners (Matt. 20:28; 2 Cor. 5:21). His death dealt finally with the sin problem and procured a perfect salvation (Heb. 9:12, 26; 10:12, 14).

Conditioned upon faith. Though Christ's death paid the penalty for our sin in full, God still requires a genuine trust in Him and what He has said about His Son and His death. There must be a reception of the provision (Rom. 3:25; 5:1). Only upon trusting Christ is an individual personally right with God.

SALVATION PERSONALIZED BY FAITH

We have introduced the condition of faith, but this needs further explanation. What is faith, and what makes it effective?

DEFINITION OF FAITH

Insufficient faith. Some hold that believing in a supreme being makes one a believer. Actually, that would qualify demons as believers. The New Testament says, "The demons also believe and shudder" (James 2:19). That type of faith will not save a person, that is, bring him into a right relationship with God.

Some hold that a sincere person, no matter what his religion, is accepted before God. The Lord Jesus would not accept that. He said, "I am the way, and the truth, and the life; no one comes to the Father, but through Me" (John 14:6). Even Unitarians, who hold to one God similar to that presented in the Bible but do not regard Christ as genuine God, cannot claim to be genuine believers in the biblical sense. Jesus made Himself equal with God (John 5:18). He claimed all honor was due Him as it was due the Father (John 5:23). This forceful claim cannot come from a good man if He is not God-man! The one who believes in Christ as God-man "has eternal life, and does not come into judgment, but has passed out of death into life" (John 5:24).

Some hold an orthodox or biblical doctrine of Christ—that He is genuine God and genuine man in one person and that He died for our sins and rose again. That is good, but that is not enough! John wrote his gospel that we might understand those facts, but John did not stop there. He continued in the same breath: "and that believing you may have life in His name" (John 20:31).

Proper faith. Believing in Christ is more than just believing facts or holding to true teaching. It involves personally receiving Christ so as to be born of God: "But as many as received Him, to them He gave the right to become children of God, even to those who believe in His name, who were born . . . of God" (John 1:12-13). Throughout the gospel of John, which was written specifically to present the Savior and what man must do to be saved, faith means receiving Christ and what He offers. It is illustrated by verbs such as "eat" (John 6:51) and "drink" (John 6:54; 7:37). Receiving is not giving. Salvation is not conditioned upon living for Christ but upon receiving the life of the living Christ. One who has received Christ has exercised the proper faith that God requires for salvation (Eph. 2:8-9).

A genuine believer, then, is one who has personally received the Person of Christ upon the basis that Christ is God-man who died to pay in full the penalty for our sins and rose again to grant forgiveness and eternal life to those who trust Him. This is what we mean whenever we use the term *believer* in this book.

NECESSITY OF FAITH

For several reasons faith is required by God to apply salvation to the individual.

To obey God. There is a moral submission that involves the repentance that faith contains. Faith involves a repentance that means we turn from trust in our hopes to trust in God's Word about His Son. This is the "obedience of faith" required of all (Rom. 16:26). God has commanded that all everywhere should repent and trust His Son, whom He raised from the dead (Acts 2:30-31).

To avoid judgment. God did not spare His own Son when it came to paying for sin (Rom. 8:32). (Of course, the Son willingly gave Himself, Rom. 8:34; Heb. 10:5-7.) He will not spare any who refuse His Son (Ps. 2:12; Heb. 2:1-4; 10:26-27). Jesus warned of the judgment He would bring upon those who do not know Him (John 3:36; 5:29; 8:24). Without personal faith in Christ, there is no salvation. Jesus declared, "He who does not believe has been judged already" (John 3:18), and, "The wrath of God abides on him" (John 3:36). We must trust that our Substitute took our judgment for us and receive Him, or we must take our judgment personally.

To appropriate salvation. Faith is the condition by which we morally agree with God and receive His benefits (Heb. 11:6). This moral alignment means honoring God's righteousness and His Word. He has properly provided at awful cost the complete payment for our salvation. To neglect or reject such a gracious gift is to do insult to God, His Son, and the Holy Spirit (Heb. 10:29; 12:25).

SUFFICIENCY OF FAITH

True faith in Christ saves and saves completely.

Faith is effective. Since proper faith is in the eternal Savior and in His perfect salvation, the one who believes is trusting the proper source of salvation. It is only the grace of God that saves man, and that grace is completely appropriated by faith (Eph. 2:8-9). It is grace that moves us to trust the Savior, and it is grace that will bring us to glory (Acts 18:27; Eph. 2:4-7). God justifies us when we trust Christ; and as a result we have settled peace (not truce) with God, we stand in His grace, and we are confident of arrival in glory (Rom. 5:1-2).

Faith is enough. No additions to faith are required—not rites of religion, or obedience to a law (Rom. 4:13-16), certainly not a perfect life (Rom. 7:14-15; 8:1-4). Paul says forcibly: "But to the one who does not work, but believes in Him who justifies the ungodly, his faith is reckoned as righteousness" (Rom. 4:5). If faith is not sufficient, then Christ died needlessly (Gal. 2:21). Not as a condition to be saved, but as a normal result, there will be life changes in the one trusting Christ. This results from the grace of God acting in the person (Eph. 2:10). If a person does not show some evidence of new life, we may question the authenticity of his faith.

THE ASSURANCE OF FAITH

If faith is what God requires and faith is sufficient, then we who trust the Savior may have the full assurance of a right relationship to God (Heb. 11:1). We have confidence to enter the very presence of God by the blood of Christ (Heb. 10:19), we have confidence to come to the throne of grace for all we need (Heb. 4:16), and such confidence has great reward (Heb. 10:35). God's grace was granted to us in Christ before the creation of the world, and that grace will see us through to glory (John 6:37; Rom. 8:28-30).

SALVATION'S PROVISIONS

The salvation that Christ provides for us has a great content and a great certainty. All the forces of Satan and demons cannot diminish our eternal relationship with God even in the slightest. When we speak of spiritual warfare, oppression, and demonization, the believer need not fear a separation from God now or ever.

CONTENT

Three aspects of the grace of God in salvation come to us by faith.

Positional grace. Great and unchanging, perfect and complete are the works of the Trinity accomplished for us the very moment we believe in Christ. These cannot be improved or removed by man or demons or even God, since they are His eternal provisions.

The finished work of the Son of God includes:

1. Redemption, the ransom from sin (1 Pet. 1:18-19)
2. Propitiation, the satisfaction of God's righteousness (Rom. 3:24-25)
3. Reconciliation, the restoration to God (2 Cor. 5:18-21)

The finished work of the Father includes:

1. Forgiveness, the erasure of guilt (Col. 2:13)
2. Justification, the provision of right standing before God (Rom. 5:1)
3. Adoption, the placing as full sons and heirs of God with Christ (Gal. 4:4-6)

The finished work of the Spirit includes:

1. Regeneration, the creation of new life through new birth (John 3:3-6)
2. Indwelling, the permanent presence of the Holy Spirit within the believer (John 14:26)
3. Sealing, the Spirit's presence which guarantees our acceptance by God and our arrival in glory (Eph. 1:13-14)
4. Baptizing, His placing us into Christ and into His Body, the church (Rom. 6:1-10; 1 Cor. 12:13)

Progressive grace. Second Peter 3:18 commands us to "grow in grace." Certainly this cannot mean to gain further favor with God, since Christ has purchased for us all the favor and standing possible (Gal. 2:21; Heb. 10:14). What this does mean is that we are to appropriate God's grace for living the Christian life. God alone creates our new life in Christ (Eph. 2:4-6; James 1:18), but the good works that He designed for our lives result from our cooperation with His present working in us (Phil. 2:13). Since God has granted us the gift of life in Christ, we are to be diligent to develop that life in accord with His revelation (2 Pet. 1:3-7). The virtues mentioned in this passage are to make us useful and fruitful in the true knowledge of our Lord Jesus (2 Pet. 1:8).

Growth starts with dedication to the will of God (Rom. 12:1-2). We must allow God to deliver us from former ways of worldly thinking to transformed minds and hearts expressing the wonderful and pleasing plan of God.

Growth continues as we appropriate the means of growth.

We have the Word (1 Pet. 2:1-2), prayer (John 15:7-8), fellowship with believers (Eph. 4:7-16), and the experiences of life with opportunities for service (Rom. 5:3-5; James 1:2-4). Even the opposition of men and demons may be occasions for growth and development of insight and strength (Rom. 8:35-37).

This does not mean we do not fail to grow as we should, nor does it exclude the possibility of sinning. John says that if we are to have fellowship with the Father and the Son, we must walk in the light, the truth of the Word of God (1 John 1:6-7). If we sin, then we must confess that sin to be restored to God's fellowship and again walk with Him in the light (1 John 1:9). We should not deny involvement in sin, as if acknowledgement would overwhelm us or interfere with our relationship with God (1 John 1:10). Instead God points out sin so that He might restore us and enjoy us and we enjoy Him (Ps. 32:5-6; 130:4) Even before we confess our sins, however, the Savior stands as God's appointed defense lawyer for His people. His sacrifice satisfied God once for all for sin, and He guards us against the accusations of the devil or of men (1 John 2:1-2). We need to keep short accounts with God, judging our own sins by confessing them quickly. Otherwise our loving Father may chastise us (child-train, *paideuo*) to bring us back to Himself and the joy of our salvation (Ps. 51:12; Heb. 12:10).

The enemy will tell us that chastisement is an evidence that God has rejected us and is hard on us. Nonsense! We cannot afford to listen to such a lie. We are to take His dealing with us as an evidence of our genuine sonship and of His great love and desire for our good (Heb. 12:8; 10). We are not to disregard it or faint under it, but to submit and be exercised by it to learn to walk with God in close fashion and keep on growing in grace (Heb. 12:5, 9).

Prospective grace. There is a future grace that all believers can expect with certainty. Peter speaks of that as a living hope, an inheritance imperishable and undefiled, which does not fade, "reserved in heaven for you, who are protected by the power of God through faith for a salvation ready to be revealed in the last time" (1 Pet. 1:4-5).

In view of the struggles and battles of life here and now, we are told, "Gird your minds for action, keep sober in spirit, fix your hope completely on the grace to be brought to you at the revelation of Jesus Christ" (1 Pet. 1:13). This speaks of our inheritance at the return of our Lord Jesus. What encouragement!

The forces of Satan promote the doctrine of insecurity. From the beginning Satan caused man to doubt God's character, God's work, and God's sufficient supply for life and well-being. To combat the forces of evil and to understand the problems of the demonically oppressed or demonized, we must be assured of our security and be able to assure others. Assured victory in the battle allows no place for lack of assurance in salvation.

The believer's security. The gracious and eternal accomplishments of the Triune God, as outlined before under "positional grace," guarantees that no one can remove us from the grace and love or from the control of our heavenly Father (John 10:27-30). Works of man or angels do not gain our salvation, nor can they lose it. It is the work of God's grace from start to finish. Every one of the above gracious works of God would have to be reversed. Such a situation is unthinkable and has no foundation in the Bible.

The security of the genuine believer in Christ is guaranteed by the eternal purpose of God to rescue us from sin and Satan and deliver us to His eternal kingdom (Col. 1:13). God's purpose and His providential control are active on behalf of

> those who are called according to His purpose. For whom He foreknew, He also predestined to become conformed to the image of His Son. . . . and whom He predestined, these He also called; and whom He called, these He also justified; and whom He justified, these He also glorified. . . . If God is for us, who is against us? . . . Who shall separate us from the love of Christ? . . . For I am convinced that neither death, nor life, nor angels, nor principalities, nor things present, nor things to come, nor powers, nor height, nor depth, nor any other created thing, shall be able to separate us from the love of God, which is in Christ Jesus our Lord. (Rom. 8:28-39)

Assurance of the believer. Assurance is the confidence that genuine believers may have that they are in right relationship to God. This confidence is not presumption on our part. God expects us to believe His Word and rejoice in the security of His love and grace (Rom. 5:1-2). This is the basis for joy and prosperity in Christian growth and warfare. Without such confidence, there is little spiritual and psychological basis for personal well-being or effective service for God.

The basis for knowing our personal salvation is threefold:

1. The clear statements of the Word of God such as we have mentioned above. Note also 1 John 5:10-13.
2. The witness of the Holy Spirit assuring us that we are genuine children of God (Rom. 8:16; Gal. 4:4-6).
3. The new-life experiences of the believer speaking of new life implanted and enjoyed. There is new understanding and hunger for God's Word (1 Pet. 2:1-2), new love for believers (1 John 3:14), real answers to prayer (1 John 5:14-15), a desire to share the gospel with others (1 John 1:3-4), a new desire to please God and Christ (John 14:21).

Security is God's keeping of the genuine believer in Christ. Assurance is the believer's confidence of a right relationship to God. Security is unchangeable; assurance may vary in a person's experience. Some may be uncertain at times of their salvation because they don't know the Word of God or they are confused by men or demons. But God is not confused. "The firm foundation of God stands, having this seal, 'The Lord knows those who are His,' and, 'Let every one who names the name of the Lord abstain from wickedness' " (2 Tim. 2:19).

When we face spiritual warfare, we must keep these things straight in our thinking. We are in a mind-control battle. The armor of God (Eph. 6:10-18) indicates that demons attack confidence and commitment. Experiences and emotions must not be allowed to determine what we think is God's truth. We must know the truth as found in the Scriptures and stand firm in the gracious and perfect provision of Christ's salvation.

CONCLUSION

We have defined a believer as a person who has placed his personal trust in the Lord Jesus Christ, the God-man, for forgiveness and right standing before God. The Christian has recognized that Christ died to satisfy God for his sins and rose again, and he has received Christ by faith. That faith is more than intellectual assent to these truths. It involves an active trust in Christ alone and the rejection of all other hopes of salvation. Without such faith, there is no certainty of acceptance before God or being a member of His family.

Simply, uncomplicated faith in the Savior and His finished redemption is sufficient genuinely to save a person. The believer may enjoy from Scripture the assurance that he is completely accepted and will never lose his relationship to God in Christ. We would normally expect that there will be evidences of new life in Christ that follow trusting Him for salvation.

The believer's salvation includes ten marvellous and unimproveable works of the Triune God as positional grace: the Son's redemption, propitiation, and reconciliation; the Father's forgiveness, justification, and adoption; and the Spirit's regeneration, indwelling, sealing, and baptizing. Progressive grace includes all the factors of growth and service in the Christian life. Prospective grace involves resurrection to glory and inheritance with Christ.

Though Satan and demons may seek to confuse and accuse, the certainty of the believer's salvation is secured by the grace of God apart from human works. God saves and keeps the believer with His power on the basis of the blood of Christ and His faithfulness. This confidence is a fortress against the onslaughts of demonic forces and against teachers who promote his concept of insecurity and uncertainty. Nothing shall separate the genuine believer from the love of Christ. Even in the battle with demons, we may be more than conquerors through Christ.

4

What Is Spiritual Warfare?

We need some perspective at this point on the kind of battle in which we, as Christians, are engaged. The situation is complex, and the battle rages on several fronts. We must be able to define the fronts, know our resources, and channel our energies properly and forcibly against our enemies.

Christians generally recognize three major enemies: the flesh, the world, and the devil (with his demonic armies). We need a brief look at each of these and their interconnections.

THE FLESH

The biblical word *flesh* has several connotations, depending on the context in which it is used. When we speak of our enemy called "the flesh," we do not mean our human nature, mankind, or the covering of our bones. There is a special and limited meaning to that term.

DEFINITION OF THE FLESH

Characterizing expressions. Our enemy the flesh is that evil spiritual capacity within each human. Ever since Adam sinned, all men are born in a state of sin (Ps. 51:5) and are "by nature children of wrath" (Eph. 2:3). This is related to depravity. It means that man is totally affected by sin in his intellect, emotions, and will (Rom. 3:10-18; Eph. 4:17-19). The flesh is that part of a human person that is in rebellion toward God.

The flesh has several titles. The title "flesh" *(sarx)* is found in Romans 8:3-4 and Galatians 5:16-19. It is called "sin in the flesh" (Rom. 8:3). It is "our old man" *(ho palaios hēmon anthrō-pos)* that was crucified with Christ (Rom. 6:6; Eph. 4:22). Romans 7 calls it "sin which indwells me" *(hē enoikousa en emoi hamartia,* v. 17), "sin which dwells in me" *(hē oikousa en emoi hamartia,* v. 20), "the evil present with me" *(emoi to kakōn parakeitai,* v. 21), "a different law [than the law of God] in my members" *(heteron nomon en tois melesin,* v. 23), "the law of sin which is in my members" *(tō nomōi tēs hamartias tō onti en tois melesin mou,* v. 23), and a combination of terms, "with my flesh the law of sin" *(tē sarki nomō hamartias,* v. 25). Paul presents all this in present-tense verbs in 7:11-25, contrasted with aorist tense verbs in 7:7-13. The clear indication is that Paul considers this a continuing force within his own person, a force that only Christ can conquer.

Continued existence. Some teach that the "old man" is "dead" because it was crucified with Christ (Rom. 6:6); and by "dead" they mean removed completely by annihilation. Some teach that this is a special experience or "second blessing" that completely takes away our bent toward sinning. Others hold that there remains a bent toward sinning, but it is merely a part of our bodily capacities and habits. We must answer these positions by noting that "dead" as used in the New Testament never means annihilation. It means separation and lack of normal functioning. This is so whether it refers to spiritual death (separation from God and lack of ability to function with God, Eph. 2:1), physical death (separation of the spirit from the body, James 2:26), or eternal death (lasting separation of the sinner from God, the second death, Rev. 20:14). The death of the sin nature, or flesh, is a legal judgment that separates it from dominating us that we might not operate in our former natural function as sinners.

DYNAMICS OF THE FLESH

Selfish activity. The power of the sin nature functions in the realm of rebellion against the law of God (Rom. 7:21-25). It seeks to forbid the practice of spiritual good in the life of the believer (Rom. 7:14-20). The flesh, whether in unsaved man or saved man, cannot begin to please God (Rom. 8:6-8). It produces actions of self-gratification, whether it appears bad or good. Some obvious products of the flesh are mentioned in Galatians 5:19-21:

> Now the deeds of the flesh are evident, which are: immorality, impurity, sensuality, idolatry, sorcery, enmities, strife, jealousy, outbursts of anger, disputes, dissensions, factions, envyings, drunkenness, carousing, and things like these.

The flesh is capable of all sorts of evil. The first three listed above are deeds of self-satisfaction, the second two involve spiritual defection, and the rest express social sins.

Satanic use. The devil uses the flesh as a tool to gain control in our lives. Paul warns, in the context of putting off the old man, that we must beware of not giving place to the devil (Eph. 4:27). Mark I. Bubeck rightly states regarding the Christian who practices fleshly sins:

> He gives place—literally claim or practical ground—to Satan's activity in his life. Giving way willfully to practice sins of the flesh gives occasion for Satan to have his way in a believer's life. Although all legal claim of Satan against us was canceled at the cross, a believer's willful indulgence in fleshly sins gives the enemy a place or a claim against us which he will be quick to exploit.[1]

DEFEAT OF THE FLESH

By Christ. Romans 6:1-10 declares that the flesh was defeated legally at the cross through our co-crucifixion with Christ. Because we were baptized into Christ by the Holy Spirit upon our trusting Christ, we were placed into union with Christ in His death and resurrection. This legally judged the flesh and removed its right to rule our lives constantly.

By Christians. Our responsibility is to apply this truth. We do it by (1) *recognizing* the fact of the defeat of the sin nature (Rom. 6:6), (2) *reckoning* ourselves dead to sin but alive to God (6:11), (3) *refusing* to let sin rule us (6:12), and (4) *relinquishing* the control of our lives to God, as those alive from the dead, and of our members to Him for righteous living (6:13). In this we have the promise that grace (not the law) will enable us for victory (6:14).

When we give God control of our lives, we are actually open

---

1. Mark I. Bubeck, *The Adversary* (Chicago: Moody, 1975), p. 34.

to being *filled by the Holy Spirit.* To be constantly filled with the Spirit is a command for all believers (Eph. 5:18). This involves obeying the Spirit's Word (Col. 3:16). When we yield control of our lives to the Spirit, He will help us in gaining victory over the flesh. The flesh and the Spirit are in constant battle, never agreeing (Gal. 5:17). Walking in the Spirit means depending upon Him for power to live for Christ (Gal. 5:16) and obeying the particulars of His Word (Gal. 5:25; Col. 3:16), not grieving Him through unconfessed sin (Eph. 4:30) or quenching Him in resisting His will (1 Thess. 5:19).

THE WORLD

The Bible clearly pictures the world as an active enemy of God and of the Christian. Again, to understand the foe and the battle in which every believer is engaged we must define *the world,* assess its power, and know how to overcome it.

DEFINITION OF THE WORLD

The world involves a philosophy and an organized system to express that philosophy.

Philosophy. Satan's title "the god of this age" ("world," KJV*; 2 Cor. 4:4) pictures him as the originator of a creature-centered philosophy. The Greek term, *aion,* refers in its various contexts to a spirit of the age that rejects the true God and sets up a counterfeit life and substitute religion with the creature at the center.

Organization. Another Greek word, *kosmos,* is used of the world. This pictures an ordered system of which Satan is the ruler. Jesus referred to him as "the prince of this world" *(ho archōn tou kosmou,* John 12:31; 16:11). Satan rules an organization of fallen men and angels who are separated from God and are His natural enemies. This world is the counterfeiter's counterpart to God's rule and kingdom. It includes individuals and nations.

DYNAMICS OF THE WORLD

Sinful culture. Men walk according to the course *(aion)* of this world *(kosmos).* They are governed by and enslaved to it.

*King James Version.

Since it partakes of its leader's characteristics, it is called "this present evil age" *(ainos . . . ponerou,* Gal. 1:4). This word for "evil" *(poneros)* is used of Satan by Christ (John 17:15) and by John when he states, "The whole world lies in the evil one" (1 John 5:19). This word speaks of a pernicious evil that is not content to remain alone but must extend its corrupting and malevolent influence to involve others.[2] This was demonstrated by Cain who "was of the evil one, and slew his brother. . . . Because his deeds were evil" (1 John 3:12). This evil, creature-centered spirit of the age may vary in its expressions from period to period of history, but its core is the same. It is the ground in which newborns are planted, then nourished, breathing in and out the polluted air of corrupt creatures with their ideals, standards, and hopes. A present expression of that age-spirit is humanism, in which man is the center and standard of all things.

John describes the dynamics of the *kosmos* in 1 John 2:16-17: "For all that is in the world, the lust of the flesh and the lust of the eyes and the boastful pride of life, is not from the Father, but is from the world." It is evident that the world extends the dynamic of the flesh, as noted in John's threefold description: desire for pleasures, desire for possessions, and desire for recognition—from among those of the same philosophy and system.

Satanic control. Satan desired to be like God in control, not in character; and his sin caused his expulsion with his followers (Isa. 14:14-15). He sold his rebellious philosophy to man, and now he rules over all who have fallen into sin. He promotes with a vengeance and by multiplied means His concept of creature-centered living. James speaks of the wisdom of the world that promotes "bitter jealousy and selfish ambition" that leads men to "be arrogant and so lie against the truth." He declares, "This wisdom is not that which comes down from above, but is earthly, natural, demonic" (James 3:14-15). The rulers of this world, following the wisdom of this world, crucified the Lord of glory (1 Cor. 2:4-8).

The demonic use of the flesh and the world is obvious. Satan rules the world system and influences the flesh, his toehold in man's heart, to accomplish his rebellious and destructive pur-

---

2. Kenneth S. Wuest, *In These Last Days* (Grand Rapids: Eerdmans, 1954), p. 151.

poses. He wants to rule as a god. He desires the worship that only God deserves. He is a governmental and religious counterfeiter. So this world involves false religionists (John 8:44; 1 John 4:1-6) and threatens to defeat the true children of God (John 16:1-3; 1 John 5:19).

Daniel uses the titles "the prince of Persia" and "the prince of Greece" to refer to demonic agencies influencing world governments (Dan. 10:13, 20). Satan offered the kingdoms of this world to Christ in exchange for His worship. Christ refused his offer but did not correct his claim to current rulership (Matt. 4:8-10). Satan would control the kingdoms of the world to carry out his schemes in opposition to God and the church of Christ. We could expect demonic forces to seek to control human governments to oppose the spread of the gospel and the growth of Christ's Body.

The Christian must beware of the world's philosophy and organization in order to stand against it in battle.

DEFEAT OF THE WORLD

There is a bright side to this battle. Christ has overcome the world, and the Christian can apply this victory to his own life.

By Christ. "In the world you have tribulation, but take courage; I have overcome the world" (John 16:33). These words of Christ give us hope. But how did He defeat the world? Through the judgment of the cross. By His cross He judged the prince of this world (John 12:31; 16:11). When the general is defeated, so is the whole army. Satan's power to control is limited, and his time is limited. Now Christ has robbed him of his captives and led many captive to Himself (Eph. 4:8). Satan's judgment is evident through Christ's death and resurrection (Heb. 2:14-15). His final judgment will come in proper time. Satan's final and greatest political and religious ruler, Antichrist, with his false prophet (Rev. 13; 2 Thess. 2:3-9) will be cast into the lake of fire at Christ's return to rule on the earth (Rev. 19:20). Satan himself will be permanently confined to the lake of fire after his short release from millennial imprisonment (Rev. 1-3; 7-10).

By Christians. Though the world seeks to overcome us through appealing to our flesh, enticing with its offers, shaming our faith, and seeking to conform us to its standards (John 15:18-19; Rom. 12:2), yet we can overcome the world by practical attitudes and actions.

First, we must take our victory stand in faith. We are to lay hold of the truth John expresses, "And this is the victory that has overcome the world—our faith" (1 John 5:4). This refers to the commonly shared doctrine that the Son of God has defeated Satan and has overcome the world. We are not overcome, but we are on the victory side! We do not have to give in. This enemy has been soundly defeated.

Second, we must daily walk in victory as our birthright. John also declares, "For whatever is born of God overcomes the world" (1 John 5:4). We do this by choosing not to love the world. John commands, "Do not love the world, nor the things in the world. If any one loves the world, the love of the Father is not in him" (1 John 2:15). After all, the world is not worth our pursuing. It can offer us nothing of lasting value. "And the world is passing away, and also its lusts; but the one who does the will of God abides forever" (1 John 2:17). We must take sides as did Joshua and choose for God (Josh. 24:15).

We do this also by obeying the Word of God, "and His commandments are not burdensome" (1 John 5:3). The worldly attitude says that God is hard and restrictive, but our faith knows that God is good and gracious, leading us into His pleasures and spiritual prosperity.

We walk in victory, then, by realizing that the world has been defeated; it need not dominate us. We walk in victory by taking the perspective of the Word of God and walking in obedience to the Word of God. We must remember that the world's philosophy and organization is a spiritual enemy that Satan and demons use effectively in the battle. We must stand against it!

SATAN AND DEMONS

We have treated the reality and activity of wicked spirit beings in chapter 1. But here we must face the reality and specifics of their attack upon Christians.

REALITY OF DEMONIC WARFARE

Our need to know. Many believers recognize our warfare with the flesh and the world; but when it comes to direct warfare with demons, they consider that rather remote or unreal; "Personal combat with demons? Isn't that going too far? Pretty soon you will be looking for demons behind every bush!"

Other believers are afraid to study what the Bible says about it, lest they come under demonic influence. How tragic! God did not reveal the great amount of information He did in His Word to have it ignored or considered unimportant or harmful. A good teacher, such as Paul, should not shrink from declaring the whole purpose of God or anything that is profitable (Acts 20:20, 27). Paul would not have his disciples ignorant of Satan's schemes (2 Cor. 2:11). But there are those who think that ignorance is bliss and protection. They thereby leave themselves and their Christian friends open to demonic wiles. But all Scripture is inspired by God and is profitable to teach us, to correct us, to instruct us in proper living that we might be personally mature and have a profitable ministry (2 Tim. 3:16-17). We must know what the Bible teaches on this subject to stand victoriously in the battle.

Mark I. Bubeck, pastor and counselor in this area, agrees:

> It is a very human and natural response of man to fear the unknown. For a believer to keep himself in the dark about Satan's person and work is a dangerous mistake. If this enemy with whom we personally have so much to do in battle remains to us some mysterious, foreboding, awesome power we are afraid to oppose, we are indeed at a disadvantage. From a biblical perspective, we should know all we can about Satan's tactics and his methods of attack against us. We must also know the biblical basis of our victory over Satan and his world of darkness.[3]

The evidence. Actually there is not a person in this world that is not affected indirectly or directly by demonic influence. All men are found sinners through the sin that Satan enticed Adam to commit (Rom. 5:12-21). We are all influenced by the flesh, which is related morally to the devil (John 8:44). We all live and breathe surrounded by the satanic world system. Demonically influenced individuals and governments impinge upon many lives. No one can totally escape the influence of demons.

What evidence is there that Christians actually face demonic influence and their direct opposition? There is much in the statements, warnings, and directions of Scripture and in God's provisions for warfare.

3. Bubeck, p. 30.

We have already seen much of the activity of demons in the gospels as treated in the previous chapters of this book. It is significant that Luke thought it important to record eleven instances of confrontation with demons in the book of Acts (5:3, 16; 8:7, 9; 13:6-11; 16:16-18; 19:12, 13-17, 19, 24-36; 26:18). We list these with the understanding that idolatrous activity is energized by demons. Their general work as described by Luke involves the rejection of the gospel and opposition to its spread.

A casual survey of the rest of the New Testament reveals at least sixteen passages that deal specifically with satanic or demonic effects upon believers. Many Christians would not have guessed there are that many. Actually there may be more. We shall briefly look at some of them and define some categories.

1. Demons oppose reception of the gospel that Christians are to spread. They are used by Satan to prevent understanding of it (Luke 8:12), to blind the minds of unbelievers (2 Cor. 4:3 4), and to hinder progress of Christian workers (1 Thess. 2:18).

2. Demons wage direct warfare with believers, described by Paul as hand-to-hand combat ("wrestling," *he pale,* Eph. 6:12). The opponents are not "flesh and blood" (human), but are spirit beings described as rulers, powers, world forces of this darkness, and spiritual forces of wickedness. These are demons, not men. These terms are found in other listings of the ranks of demons (Col. 1:16; 2:10, 15; Eph. 1:21; 3:10; Rom. 8:38). "This reference to hand-to-hand combat emphasizes the personal nature of this struggle. Each believer has his own struggle to face."[4]

3. Demons accuse and slander in several ways. Satan slandered God before Eve. He accuses believers before God (Rev. 12:10), and it appears from the breastplate of righteousness provided in our armor that he inserts accusing thoughts in the believer's mind (Eph. 6:14). He obviously must extend his power through demons to do this.

4. Demons plant doubt about God's truth, His goodness, and His concern about us and our welfare (Gen. 3:1-5). This seems to be the reason for the "shield of faith" (Eph. 6:16).

5. Demons promote rebellion and defection (Gen. 3:1-5).

4. Homer A. Kent, Jr., *Ephesians.* Everyman's Bible Commentary (Chicago: Moody, 1971), p. 114.

6. Demons tempt to specific sins, such as hypocrisy and lying (Acts 5:3), illicit sex (1 Cor. 7:5), occupation with worldy values and pursuits (1 John 2:15-16; 5:19), dependence upon human wisdom and strength (1 Chron. 21:1-8; Matt. 16:21-23), pride in spiritual matters (1 Tim. 3:6), and overconcern and discouragement (1 Pet. 5:6-10).

7. Demons incite persecution (Rev. 2:10).

8. Demons seek to weaken the church of Jesus Christ through false teachers (1 Tim. 4:1-5). These teachers pose as "angels of light" but are in reality messengers of Satan (2 Cor. 11:13-15). They promote erroneous doctrine, denying that Christ is the God-man (1 John 4:1-4), and distract to false life-styles (Col. 2:18-23). They also weaken the church through false followers. The enemy has his tares in the same field with God's wheat (Matt. 13:38-39). These hinder the working of the Body of Christ and confuse its true nature and testimony.

9. Demons promote division in the church. When there is serious difference of opinion, Satan has an opportunity. Paul warned about the lack of forgiveness to a truly repentant brother. This, he stated, is one of "his schemes" (2 Cor. 2:10-11). It is obvious that Paul knew of Satan's methods but the Corinthians did not.

10. Demons take advantage of anger unresolved and developing into bitterness. We are warned in this regard, "And do not give the devil an opportunity" (Eph. 4:26-27).

11. Demons would lure us away from pure devotion to Christ (2 Cor. 11:3). Satan hates Christ and cannot tolerate our love for Him.

12. Demons would lead us into compromising situations and actions that involve actual fellowship *(koinonia)* with demons (1 Cor. 10:20). This may involve participating in heathen ceremonies or investigating the secrets of the occult.

13. Demons discourage us in battle, telling us that we are weak and losers and that they are strong and will win. This is lying propaganda, but it will work if we believe it. This seems to be the reason for "the helmet of salvation" (Eph. 6:17), which in 1 Thessalonians 5:8 is termed "a helmet, the hope of salvation." This refers to that hope or confidence in the Savior's deliverance from judgment and the effects of evil. We are on the winning side, and we must keep this in mind.

RESOURCES

How can we face such formidable foes? At this point we will consider the answer briefly, for we will treat this in some detail later.

Receive scriptural teaching. We must face the reality of the battle and expect opposition as presented in the Bible. We cannot afford to be surprised or overwhelmed by such concepts (Eph. 6:10-12; 1 Pet. 4:12).

Recall scriptural perspective. Satan should be respected, but we should remember that he is limited, a creature under God's control and already judged, headed for the lake of fire (Matt. 25:41; Col. 2:15). Christ has purchased our victory and freedom, and He cares for us in our present difficulties. We have a position of victory far above the enemies of our souls (Eph. 1:19-21). God uses struggles to make us strong (Rom. 8:35-39).

Resist Satan and demons. James 4:7 says, "Submit therefore to God. Resist the devil and he will flee from you." We must take sides with God and stand in His truth. We must put on the whole armor of God (Eph. 6:12), and we must walk in God's truth depending upon Christ and the Holy Spirit to enable us. We must develop strong Christian lives, not depending upon our own thoughts, emotions, or experience but upon the true teaching of God's Word.

Conclusion

We cannot escape reality. We are in mortal combat with the flesh, with the world, and with demons. To survive and to prosper we must know the truth about our enemies, how they work, and how to battle them successfully. This means casting away fear, casting our concerns on our risen Lord and Victor, and trusting Him for the victory as we stand in the truth of His Word and appropriate His provisions, which are adequate for the conflict.

PART 2

Major Considerations

5

Demonization of Believers: Approach to Biblical Evidence

Having considered some necessary preliminary questions, we now turn to the major considerations we must treat to answer the question, Can genuine believers be demonized? Here we will consider three lines of evidence: biblical, theological, and clinical.

Before we actually look at the biblical evidence, we must clarify how we should approach it. This involves our presuppositions regarding Scripture, proper hermeneutics, and the logic of proof and disproof.

PRESUPPOSITIONS REGARDING SCRIPTURE

Everyone has certain basic concepts of the Bible, but they do not all agree. We must define some of these so that we may have common understanding as to the approach taken here.

AUTHORITY

In approaching biblical evidence on this question, we want to make clear that the Scriptures are considered the revealed Word of God with final authority. We refer to the Old and New Testaments contained in the sixty-six books of canonical writings. There are good reasons for this stance, which many readers know. We want to mention a few.[1]

---

1. For a thorough treatment of the authority, revelation, and inspiration of the Bible, see Norman L. Geisler and William E. Nix, *A General Introduction to the Bible*, rev. and exp. (Chicago: Moody, 1986).

The claims of Scripture. There is no doubt that the Bible claims authority from God. The Old Testament prophets proclaimed 3,808 times, "Thus says the Lord."[2] They knew they were delivering the message of God to men. In many instances, prophets recognized the authority of other prophets, as Daniel did concerning Jeremiah (Dan. 9:2-3). The unity and harmony of the Bible, written over a period of about 1,600 years by forty different authors in various cultural settings, testifies to the fact that God was superintending the process.

The New Testament continues the same claims. Paul writes that all Scripture is God-breathed and authoritative (2 Tim. 3:16). This agrees with Peter (2 Pet. 1:19-21) and with John (1 John 1:1-5; Rev. 1:1-2). We must pay attention to its authoritative message.

The statements of Christ. The Son of God had the highest confidence in Scripture as God's authoritative Word. He constantly relied upon it, whether with friends or opponents (John 5:39; 10:34-35). In facing Satan himself, the Lord resisted him with confidence that every word of Scripture came from God as the ultimate source (Matt. 4:4). He held that Scripture was sure and inviolable (John 10:35) and that it must be fulfilled in detail, down to the smallest letter and part of a letter (Matt. 5:18).

Such confidence of the risen Savior should also be ours as we come to the Bible. We may regard the Bible as totally inspired in all parts and details and as inerrant. It is thoroughly reliable in all its statements and is the only proper guide to doctrine and life.

We cannot put on the same level of authority any church dogma or creed or any human opinion, conviction, experience, or bias. Reason and emotion cannot rule over God's Word.

REVELATION AND INSPIRATION

Revelation. The Bible claims to be a revelation from God. It discloses the truth of God, which men could not otherwise know (1 Cor. 2:9-11). Peter warns that we should heed the Scriptures—even more than one utterance from heaven—because no prophetic utterance of Scripture ever came into being

2. Ibid., p. 69.

by human origination; for the prophets were not self-starters. Instead they spoke only as they were carried along in the process by the Holy Spirit (2 Pet. 1:16-21).

Inspiration. The Bible claims to be inspired by God. God superintended its authors so that, writing in their own language and style, they composed without error their records in the original languages (1 Cor. 2:12-13; 2 Tim. 3:16). The source of the Scriptures is God; they are "God-breathed" *(theopneustos),* the product of God's creative and superintending work. This includes "all Scripture" *(pasa graphē)* without exception. The purpose of God's granting us the Bible is that we may know the truth (doctrine) and be conformed to the truth in practice. The product in view is that Christians may be personally mature and be completely outfitted to have a profitable ministry (2 Tim. 3:17).

HERMENEUTICS

Hermeneutics deals with the science and art of interpretation. It forms the basis on which we derive meaning from the written Word of God. Everyone has some system of interpretation, whether it is formal or informal; but not all approaches are equally valid. We will take an approach that is widely held by those who regard the Bible as God's Word.

OUR SYSTEM

We shall take the approach to interpretation described as literal, cultural, critical.[3] *Literal* means we take the words and statements in their normally understood meaning, not seeking to read in some hidden or mystical concept. By *cultural* we mean that all must be understood in the history and culture of the day in which the author wrote. We are not to strip the terms down to match our peculiar world view and culture, but we must understand the mind-set and historical setting of the author and the meaning understood by the original writers and readers. The term *critical* indicates that we must submit our interpretation to evaluation from the pertinent evidence, whether from the Bible or from external sources. The interpretation

---

3. For further explanation, see Bernard Ramm, *Protestant Biblical Interpretation,* rev. ed. (Boston: W. A. Wilde, 1956).

we assign, then, must fit harmoniously with the context and with the rest of the Bible and its setting.

OUR METHOD

In harmony with the above system, we should then consider the evidence presented in the Bible before coming to conclusions. We should not *eisegete,* or read into God's Word what we might want the passage to say. Instead we should *exegete,* or lead out the meaning as far as we are able to determine the author's intent.

To do this we must consider key factors that are common to any proper interpretation. *Words* must be considered in their etymology and usage along with their synonyms. We must notice the details of *grammar,* which involves the parts of speech and their connections. This governs the logic and emphasis of the words in their setting. *Context* is a major consideration. The immediate context presents connections and flow of thought. The book with its purpose and development of theme must be taken into account. The whole testament and then the Bible in total must be used to see that setting. Then the context of the historical, cultural setting puts things in proper perspective. Another key factor is the matter of *cross references.* Here we do not mean passages that have a mere appearance of speaking to the same topic, but we mean genuine parallel passages where the same topic is treated and the words are used in similar connotations.

All of this is to guide us as we consider the evidence for any interpretation and to guard us from presumption and precipitous conclusions. We have a responsibility to God and to God's people in interpreting and teaching His Word. Personal or group positions should not allow us to slant or twist the Scriptures. The honor of God and the good of man is at stake.

To illustrate the importance of choosing a consistent system and method of interpretation in the matter of Satan and demon oppression of believers, consider the difference of opinion on the binding of Satan. Revelation 20 says that Christ has Satan bound during the millennial kingdom. If we were to understand the millennial kingdom in the allegorical sense, such as does the amillennialist, then the kingdom would be now—spiritual and in effect between the first and second comings of Christ.

Since Christ now reigns from heaven over the church, there would be no future thousand-year kingdom. In that case, Satan would now be bound in some serious sense and could not seriously affect the Christian.

On the other hand, if we are to take the picture in Revelation 19-20 in normal fashion, it is only upon the second coming of Christ to earth, when He defeats His enemies and sets up His kingdom, that Satan (and demons) are bound. This fits the normal use of the terms, the sequence of events in the passage, and agrees with the parallel passage in Matthew (24:15-31 and 25:31-46), not to mention the hopes of the Old Testament and gospels of the Messiah's ruling in righteousness upon the earth over a restored nation of Israel. In this case Satan is now free and actively continues his destructive work with all men, saved and unsaved, and we must be presently on guard (1 Pet. 5:8-10).

THE LOGIC OF PROOF

Human logic is a good tool if properly used and governed by the Word of God, but it cannot take precedence or even equal position with the Scriptures and their proper interpretation. We will discuss this further in chapter 9, where clinical considerations in determining the possibility of the demonization of Christians require that we consider the place of reason and experience.

NATURE OF PROOF

The concept of proof is actually the adducing of evidence for support of a particular statement. Proof may take various forms and may be of varying degrees of strength. Proof does not always mean that a definite and accurate conclusion has been reached. That depends upon the accuracy and completeness of the facts and the proper logical handling of the information.

APPROACH TO PROOF

Inductive method. This approach starts with the particulars and moves toward a general statement as conclusion. This fits the concept of the scientific method of investigation of facts, classification of facts, organization of information, presentation of conclusions, and evaluation. This is also the way to build a biblical doctrine.

Deductive method. Starting with a generally accepted or previously proved general statement, this approach moves toward a statement regarding a particular. A form of this approach is the syllogism, a three-part series of related statements. This form includes a major premise, a minor premise, and a conclusion drawn from the two premises. Here proper statement and definition of terms is important. We might illustrate in this manner:

1. Angels are limited in time and space.
2. Demons are fallen angels.
3. Therefore demons are limited in time and space.

PROBLEMS OF PROOF

Argument for a positive statement. To support a positive assertion there must be sufficient evidence. If varying types of known evidences agree and contrary statements have been properly rejected, then there is a good measure of support. The validity of the conclusion depends upon the weight of the support. We have used this type of argument regarding the reality of Satan and demons in chapter 1.

Argument for a negative statement. Again, as with the positive statement, the validity of a negative argument depends on 'ts support. However, the proof of a universal negative may be more difficult. For instance, to support the fact that a genuine Christian cannot be lost requires a clear universal statement to that effect, or good general support with all contrary statements shown to be false or weak. We have used this type of argument in treating the security of the genuine believer in chapter 3.

When one states that a genuine believer can never be demonized, he must produce a clear statement from the Bible that says so specifically. If he does not have such a statement, then he is in a predicament. Now he must produce all the evidence from all sources through all history to show that no Christian under any circumstances has ever been demonized. That is obviously impossible.

CONCLUSION

We have briefly and informally treated the matters of the authority of Scripture, approach to interpretation, and the use of human logic at the outset because it deals with evaluating the evidence, whether biblical or clinical. Too many who have treated this subject have merely quoted a Bible verse or two, which did not directly or even indirectly deal with demonization, to prove their point. Even some who sought to deal in more depth with the scriptural evidence have strayed beyond proper hermeneutics and logic. Theological arguments on both sides need to be evaluated, for here again, many reason imperfectly. We need more objectivity in approaching this vital issue.

6

Biblical Evidence Against Demonization of Christians

We are now ready to approach the biblical passages that are used as evidence that genuine believers cannot be inhabited by demons. Not all carry equal weight, but we will seek to analyze the evidence passage by passage.

We must remember that the passages must speak for themselves. We are not to read into them our presuppositions. We must let them say what they actually were intended to say. Any meaning in them for us today must be the genuine result of (1) applying the proper rules of exegesis and interpretation and (2) deducing the proper principles to apply to our questions.

Nor are we to fear what is actually written in Scripture. God did not give us truth to cause us fear but to create and support faith. The more clearly we understand the whole truth of God, the more firmly we may stand in the faith by our faith.

PASSAGES ON THE DEFEAT OF SATAN

These passages are construed to mean that since Christ has defeated Satan, he is bound from seriously affecting the Christian and certainly not free to demonize him.

JOHN 12:31; 16:11

Jesus said, "Now judgment is upon this world; now the ruler of this world shall be cast out." He also said later that the Holy Spirit would convict the world of judgment "because the ruler of this world has been judged." Both statements speak of the judgment upon Satan (and his demons) accomplished by the death of Christ, as easily noted by the context of each. The argument that may be offered here is that the cross has bound Satan from ruling over those in Christ's kingdom, those who are genuinely His.

We should notice that Christ refers to the legal judgment of Satan, not to his detainment in the abyss or lake of fire. This judgment allows Christ to draw all from among mankind to Himself (John 12:32-33). This also allows the Holy Spirit to convict the world, under Satan's control and blinding, of judgment upon its system and members, since the leader of the system is judged (John 16:8). This is a provision even at this present time when Christ is absent and Satan is still blinding men to the gospel (2 Cor. 4:3-4). This judgment, then, deals with the effects upon the unsaved world, who need to have presalvation enlightenment so that they might possibly believe Christ and be saved. We cannot understand this as a statement that Satan has no serious influence upon the believer. Even after Christ made these startling declarations, Satan very seriously affected Peter, leading him to deny the Savior (Luke 22:31-32).

REVELATION 20:1-3

"And I saw an angel coming down from heaven, having the key of the abyss and a great chain in his hand. And he laid hold of the dragon, the serpent of old, who is the devil and Satan, and bound him for a thousand years, and threw him into the abyss, and shut it and sealed it over him so that he should not deceive the nations any longer, until the thousand years were completed."

Some, notably amillennialists, take this to be a reference to the binding of Satan through the judgment of the cross. The thousand years refers in symbolic fashion to the kingdom age, which is present now in the church. There is no literal future millennial kingdom. The resurrection of the saints who "came to life and reigned with Christ for a thousand years" (20:4) is considered to be a reference to the new birth. In this case, Satan and demons (also bound) have no ability to seriously attack the believer, let alone invade him.

There are several problems with this view. The first is that a normal interpretation of Revelation 20:1-3 and its context presents the binding of Satan occurring at the second coming of

Christ in great glory and power with the destruction of His foes (Rev. 19:11-21). This is immediately followed by the kingdom, which is designated as one thousand years long, both in the vision (20:1-5) and in the interpretation of the vision (20:6). The resurrection of the saints refers to "those who had been beheaded because of the testimony of Jesus and because of the word of God." This can not be their new birth but a bodily resurrection for those who had previously believed and had been martyred by the Antichrist, whom they resisted during the Great Tribulation (20:4).

Neither can the second resurrection after the thousand years be considered spiritual. It likewise is a physical resurrection this time for those who were unbelievers and are destined for the lake of fire (20:11-15). The sequence of the events described is in the order found in the flow of the context, noted by such phrases as "And I saw" (19:11, 17, 19; 20:1, 4, 11), "until the thousand years were completed" (20:3, 5), and "when the thousand years are completed" (20:7). This cannot be, according to normal interpretation of the words and flow in the context, a reference to the present age. It must be a future binding of Satan during the reign of Christ and believers on earth. To this agrees the flow of events described by the Lord Himself in Matthew 24-25.

The second problem with the view that Satan is now bound is that the New Testament presents him as dangerously active along with his demons at the present time (2 Cor. 11:13-15; Eph. 6:10-12; James 4:7; 1 Pet. 5:8). Some seek to answer this obvious difficulty by saying that Satan is "not totally bound or destroyed as yet. His doom is sure; his back is broken and he is in his death throes. Still his wrath is great and he 'prowls about like a roaring lion . . .' (1 Pet. 5:8)."[1] Though Grayson H. Ensign and Edward Howe do not totally agree with Satan's limitations so described, they offer this explanation: "The binding of Satan is limited in its scope during this present age and that limitation is stated, 'so that he should not deceive the *nations* any longer' (Rev. 20:3). Thus Satan is bound in reference to the nations, the

---

1. Grayson H. Ensign and Edward Howe, *Bothered? Bewildered? Bewitched? Your Guide to Practical, Supernatural Healing* (Cincinnati: Recovery, 1984), p. 148. This has proved to be a valuable resource. This and subsequent quotations are used by permission of Recovery Publications, Amarillo, Texas.

state governments, and nothing is said to indicate that the devil is bound as regards individual Christians."[2] In support of this position, they cite George Eldon Ladd, who says that "binding Satan is a symbolic way of describing a curbing of his power and activity."[3]

This explanation does allow for the obvious present activity of demonic forces, but does not do justice to the context. As pointed out, the binding of Satan is future. He is certainly now deceiving the nations, involving both governmental leaders and other individuals. How is it possible to deceive groups without deceiving individuals? Deception involves individual minds. Further, the Greek word *ethnē* can mean nation, Gentile, or pagan[4] and is best taken in this context to mean all nationalities of mankind as individuals. This is the sense of its use in Revelation 20:8, where the nations (Gentiles) number more than the sand of the seashore (hardly governments).

We cannot properly understand, then, that Revelation 20 refers to a binding of Satan and demons today such that they cannot harass or invade Christians. It does not speak to that matter.

HEBREWS 2:14-15

"Since then the children share in flesh and blood, He Himself likewise also partook of the same, that through death He might render powerless him who had the power of death, that is, the devil; and might deliver those who through fear of death were subject to slavery all their lives."

It might be argued that Satan and demons were judged by Christ's incarnation and death, so that he is powerless over Christians. Again, we note some of the same answers. Satan's judgment is legal, as was ours at the cross. Our judgment was executed in Christ our Substitute, and we are freed by faith in the substitute. (Demons were not the objects of substitution; Christ died for "flesh and blood"—humans.) Our sinful capacity, the "old man," also legally judged (Rom. 8:3), is not powerless;

---

2. Ibid., p. 149.
3. George Eldon Ladd, *A Commentary on the Revelation of John* (Grand Rapids: Eerdmans, 1972), p. 262.
4. William F. Arndt and F. Wilbur Gingrich, *A Greek-English Lexicon of the New Testament* (Chicago: U. of Chicago, 1952), p. 217.

Satan is not really "powerless" either. The Greek word used here, *katargeō,* does not mean to destroy or reduce to no power. It rather means to make ineffective, nullify, set aside, doomed to perish.[5] The same word is used of the judgment of our old man in Romans 6:6. Few would argue that our sin nature has no possibility of controlling our lives.

Proper understanding of this passage leads us to say that demonic forces have been judged by the cross and have been rendered inoperative in having the rule over death and the bondage that results from fear of death. Satan's domination of believers through this fear has been broken. His stranglehold has been removed judicially, and believers who lay hold of this truth are released to live without this dread of death. This passage cannot be construed to say that Christians cannot be demonized, for it does not speak to that topic.

COLOSSIANS 2:14-15

"When He had disarmed the rulers and authorities, He made a public display of them, having triumphed over them through Him" (or, through it, the cross).

This passage speaks of the triumph of Christ through His cross over wicked spirits. Its terms graphically describe God's conquering Leader, true God with human nature, dying and rising from the dead to forgive all our sins (2:12-13), removing all condemnation of God's law (2:14), and by the same act defeating Satan's hosts. The picture is of an invading general defeating the enemy and then stripping them of their weapons and armor, publicly embarassing them, and leading them in His triumphal march among the populace.

If Christ has so routed and stripped the enemy of weapons, how could the Christian ever expect the enemy to attack, let alone invade a believer's body?

We must understand this passage as portraying a positional, legal victory over Satan and demons ("rulers and authorities," NASB; "principalities and powers," KJV). Paul did not intend to convey that we need not stand guard against them or that they could not seriously affect our lives as Christians. Of course they

5. Ibid., p. 418.

cannot dislodge us from our perfect position in Christ; for as the context says, "In Him you have been made complete, and He is the head over all rule and authority" (v. 10). Our complete and perfect position before God is secured by the grace of God in Christ. But this context also warns those of such a perfect position that they must be on guard against the attacks from false teachers who would lead them captive through man's wisdom and deception (2:8). This deception involved Jewish legalism (2:16-17), mystical visions regarding angelic intermediaries (2:18), and ascetic practices (2:20-23). They were in danger of being defrauded of Christ's approval and use of their lives (2:18).

It is one thing to have a perfect, legal standing before God through being "in Christ"; it is quite another to walk in obedience to the Word and to keep one's self from being led astray through demonic deception. In facing Gnostic heresy, the Colossian believers had to realize Christ had defeated principalities and powers, and no angelic intermediary could contribute to their acceptance before God. Christ was not just an intermediary among others; He was the fulness of deity in bodily form. He was all they needed (Col. 2:9-10).

Some may argue that Christ stripped demons of their weaponry, so that they have no strength against us. However, the judgment is legal and breaks their claim to rule. Demons are still active and dangerous; so says the same author in Ephesians 6:10-13. Note the parallel in Colossians 3:9 where the same Greek word for stripping the weapons *(apekduomai)* is used of the defeat of the old man, or flesh. The flesh is not absent or without strength. It is, however, judged by the cross, removed from ruling over us; and we are to count on that and oppose its attempt to rule. The same holds true regarding demons. Practically we must face them by faith and in the authority of Christ and His Word.

This passage, then, does not give any support to the contention that a believer cannot be invaded by demons. In fact it warns against openness to their attack upon genuine believers.

The above passages are representative of those that may speak of the judgment of Satan and demons through the cross. None of them make any genuine contribution to the question as to whether Christians can be inhabited by wicked spirits.

PASSAGES ON DELIVERANCE FROM SATAN'S DOMAIN

One Bible college counselor expressed her dismay: "If Christians can be so affected by Satan, then I don't understand what salvation is all about!" She stated what many might say in considering if Christians can be demonized. The Bible does say that we have been delivered from Satan to Christ. What does that mean, and how does it affect our problem question?

COLOSSIANS 1:13

"For He delivered us from the domain of darkness, and transferred us to the kingdom of His beloved Son."

This may support the position that we are removed completely from the activity, at least the serious attack, of demonic forces. "Darkness" certainly does speak of the realm of Satan, sin, and error; and "delivered" and "transferred" do speak of a completed work of rescue and removal.

Again the passage must be understood in the positional and legal sense. We are no longer citizens of the kingdom of Satan. We have been redeemed and forgiven of sins (1:14); redemption and forgiveness are legal possessions of those in Christ. We are now citizens of the Son's kingdom. However, we are in a battle, as noted in the treatment of Colossians 2:15. Paul speaks of that struggle in the context (2:1) and of the battle for their minds (2:8, 18). They must know their participation in the victory of Christ over the spirit world (2:10, 15) and stop listening to false teaching regarding spirit beings who give special revelation about the supposed truth and wisdom (2:18). Christ is the wisdom of God in total (2:2-3), and they need no secret wisdom from demonic sources (2:8, 18).

Once again we see that this passage does not state anything about the believer's freedom from demonic influence or invasion but instead is set in a context of warning against demonic deception through false teachers.

ACTS 26:18

Paul recounts his conversion experience and commission in Acts 26:18. Christ sent him to the Gentiles "to open their eyes so that they may turn from darkness to light and from the dominion of Satan to God, in order that they may receive forgiveness of sins and an inheritance among those who have been sanctified by faith in Me."

Here is another statement of deliverance from darkness and from the dominion of Satan to God's truth and rule. Does it mean that Satan has no power of attack and that Christians cannot walk in darkness?

What has been said above applies here also. This is positional truth, but the practical walk and battle continue. In fact, as Paul was uttering these words, he had not been delivered from the Gentiles as might be presumed from the words of Christ's commission (26:17). He was in a Gentile court, defending himself before King Agrippa and Festus (25:23–26:1). He had been forced to appeal to Caesar because of continued persecution from the Jews and the threat of improper judgment from local Roman authorities (Acts 25:9-11). The deliverance from the dominion of Satan and demons must be understood in the same legal sense as the forgiveness of sins and the inheritance also mentioned. We could note that after that commission and after the statement of deliverance of believers from Satan, Paul himself had battle with Satan, who prevented his service (1 Thess. 2:18) and was allowed to cause some bodily illness (2 Cor. 12:7).

This passage fails to support the concept that Christians cannot be seriously affected by Satan or invaded by demons. It does not speak to the point. The same is so of all the passages above in this category.

PASSAGES ON CHRIST'S DEFENSE OF SAINTS

Certain passages forcibly speak of Christ's keeping genuine believers from the power of Satan. How shall we understand their meaning and contribution to whether demons can invade believers?

JOHN 10:22-29

The Lord Jesus said, "My sheep hear My voice, and I know them, and they follow Me; and I give eternal life to them, and they shall never perish; and no one shall snatch them out of My hand. My Father, who has given them to Me, is greater than all;

and no one is able to snatch them out of the Father's hand."

Some ask, "In view of such a promise, how could we ever begin to think that a believer could be demon possessed?"

Again, the term *possessed* is misleading. We saw in chapter 2 that this is an improper term. It suggests ownership, a concept not involved in the Greek word *daimonizomai*. The real concept is invasion and control to some degree, lesser or greater; but never ownership. The possession of eternal life and Christ's keeping of the genuine believer until glory is never at question. That is the real point of the statement of Christ here in John 10.

This passage, then, speaks of the Savior's keeping His sheep in eternal relation to Himself: "They shall never perish." It does not deal with demonic attack or invasion.

JOHN 17:15

Christ prayed, "I do not ask Thee to take them out of the world, but to keep them from the evil one."

Protection from Satan *(tou ponērou)* is the request. What does this involve? The predicate asks for a preservation from even entering the sphere of the evil one *(tērēseis autous ek tou ponērou)*. If this means no opposition or influence, then the prayer was not answered, for the apostles and all Christians (17:20) have suffered opposition. If it means no invasion should ever be possible, it is not too clearly stated. Why would the Lord Jesus suddenly introduce that peculiar request at this point? Where is there any such suggestion of that subject in the context that this matter should rise to consideration?

The most acceptable understanding of this verse is that Christ is not praying that believers be kept from the influence of Satan, for that would certainly be encountered (and was) from the world, out of which the Lord did not pray for deliverance. He *is* praying for their preservation from becoming completely engulfed in Satan's destructive power and devastation. Some may think Christ is praying that believers would never be lost again. That is possible but unlikely at this point. That seems to be requested later in the prayer in verse 24.

There is too little evidence to say that Christ prayed for preservation from demonization. We cannot fairly construe this verse to mean that.

MATTHEW 6:13

Included in the requests of our Lord's pattern prayer is this one: "And do not lead us into temptation, but deliver us from evil" (the evil one).

The same term, *tou ponērou,* used in John 17:15, is used here as well. Believers would do well to obey Christ and pray this prayer daily, as for their daily bread (6:11). What is the meaning of this request and how does it affect our question of demonization?

First, we should note that this is a responsibility laid upon believers. What would happen if the believer did not pray this or walk closely with the Lord? Why did the Lord teach that this was a necessary prayer? Is there some danger involved? It seems there is. It is best understood in connection with the phrase "And do not lead us into temptation." Believers are allowed to encounter temptation. James says this is common and expected (James 1:2-4). To this Paul agrees (1 Cor. 10:13) and adds that God will help us in the temptation by granting strength. But the immediate connection seems to give this meaning: "Do not allow us to fall into such temptation that would lead to ensnaring by Satan." Understood in this fashion, we see that the Lord was not ruling out the possibility of temptation, but warning us to pray to be kept from that serious type of temptation where we would fall into direct influence and possible domination, to some degree, by demons.

Second, we should note that Christ recognizes the reality of direct opposition of Satan to believers and the distinct possibility of his direct action against believers. So He teaches us to pray against such inroads that would capture us in his snare and make us unfruitful. Again the issue of security of salvation is not in view, but productive practice in our lives.

This passage does not contribute any guarantee of safeguard of all believers against demon influence or demonization.

2 THESSALONIANS 3:3

"But the Lord is faithful, and He will strengthen and protect you from the evil one."

How shall we understand this promise and its implications? Paul is writing to a young church that has just been severely upset by a false teaching that may even have been promoted by wicked spirits (2:2). The members had been suffering affliction and persecution (1:4), and some had not been behaving responsibly (3:6). But their faith was virile and spreading (1 Thess. 1:2-10). After instruction and encouragement, Paul asked them to pray for his deliverance, since he often faced perverse and evil men (3:2). Then he made this general statement about the Lord's faithfulness in giving strength and protection.

We cannot take this as an all-inclusive promise for all Christians at all times. Certainly the Lord is faithful. He has a plan and will keep us from evil and use us when we walk with Him. But there are conditions for walking with the Lord, and some believers do not meet those conditions, even as the two letters to these churches demonstrate. Further, Paul knew the attack of Satan in his ministry and in his body (2 Cor. 12:7; 1 Thess. 2:18) and warned all Christians to put on the whole armor of God so that they might be able to stand against demonic wiles (Eph. 6:10-12). It is to be expected that those who do not stand in the power of the Lord and the armor of God will not be able to stand in the battle. The command and provisions are not in vain. Some of those Paul knew in the ministry had made shipwreck of the faith. Paul, in the attitude of discipline, had turned them over to Satan for their correction (1 Tim. 1:19-20).

This promise, then, is for those who walk in obedience to the Lord. Satan will not be able to take them unaware and render them weak, unfaithful, and unproductive in Christian life and service. It is a great promise for the obedient and watchful Christian, but is not a blanket protection promised to all. It does not promise that no Christian will ever be attacked or seriously affected by demonic forces. It does not address the matter of demonization.

1 JOHN 4:4

"You are from God, little children, and have overcome them; because greater is He who is in you than he who is in the world."

This, perhaps, is the verse most quoted by those who hold that the Christian cannot be demonized. It is a very encouraging statement to back a command. It is not cast in the form of a promise. What does it actually mean, and can it be used to support the position that Christians cannot be demon invaded?

Some construe this statement to be a guarantee that believers cannot be seriously affected by demons or have demons resident in their bodies. It is taken to mean that the Holy Spirit resides in the Christian (though we cannot exclude the Son and the Father) and that He will prevent the presence of wicked spirits within. The indwelling of the Spirit of God is also mentioned in 1 John 2:20, 27. We will treat in chapter 8 the theological question of whether the Holy Spirit and an evil spirit may reside in the same person, but here we want to evaluate this verse in context.

First, we must note that there is no direct statement about a demon resident in a believer. If there is inhabitation (and there seems likely to be) in the false teachers, that is exhibited in demonically energized doctrine denying the Person and work of the God-man, our Savior.

Second, we observe that John is warning against possible deception promoted by false teachers influenced by a spirit or spirits not from God. Believers must not be deceived by a Gnostic doctrine that denies either the true deity or true humanity of Christ and His substitutionary sacrifice that satisfied God for our sin (1 John 4:2, 10).

Third, we note that John gives two tests that believers are to apply to those who claim to be teachers of God's truth. Believers are not to be gullible or nondiscerning. We do not offend the Holy Spirit if we test those who claim to be speaking under His influence; instead we are obeying His command. The first test: Does the teacher confess "Jesus Christ has come in the flesh?" (4:1-3). This acknowledges the preexistence of the Son as eternal God and His taking upon Himself genuine humanity to become our Redeemer. The second test: Do the teachers continue to abide by the apostles' doctrine (2:5-6)? If they fail these tests, they are to be rejected as energized by a spirit of error.

If believers apply these two tests, then the indwelling Holy Spirit will give insight and prevent deception, "for greater is He who is in you than he [the false teacher] who is in the world." If they do not apply these tests, they are open to deception and the influence of the wicked spirits energizing the false teacher. These are the spirits of antichrist (4:1-3).

Instead of 1 John 4:4's promising no serious demonic influence or inhabiting by a demon, the verse states that God's Spirit will enable the discerning and obedient believer so that he will not be taken in by false teaching. It cannot be used to refute the possibility of demonization of a believer.

Just as I was writing these paragraphs, a thirty-five-year member of the Jehovah's Witnesses came to my door to speak about the name *Jehovah*. When I asked him if he knew that Philippians 2:9-11 applied the name to Jesus, he denied that it did. I reminded him that that was a direct quotation from Isaiah 45:22-23 and that it identified Jesus as Jehovah. He said, "Then you believe in the Trinity?" I responded, "I certainly do!" He countered, "But the word Trinity is not used in the Bible." "That is true," I responded, "but the evidence is widespread. Have you considered the baptizing formula of Jesus' Great Commission that commands baptizing in the singular name of the Father and the Son and the Holy Spirit? That cannot be taken as in the name of God, a human, and an influence." He sought another diversion, but we ended the conversation. Here is an example of applying the tests that John commands we should apply regarding the Person and work of the Lord Jesus.

1 JOHN 5:18

"We know that no one who is born of God sins; but He who was born of God keeps him and the evil one does not touch him."

This might at first glance seem a very forceful statement to the effect that Satan cannot seriously affect the believer; certainly a demon would not invade him or even be allowed to reside in him from a condition prevailing before his conversion.

There are several problems of interpretation of this verse. We must consider them to gain insight to its meaning. The first part of the verse along with the context indicates the connection of this verse. It deals with the professing believer and the problem of sin. Verse 16 deals with prayer for the restoration of a sinning brother and mentions the extreme case of discipline by God that brings death upon a constantly sinning brother. The use of the term for sin without the article *(hamartia)* indicates that no particular sin is in mind, but God is dealing with the individual and his sin problem. Probably this refers to "not a single act but acts which have the character of sin unto death."[6] Verse 17

---

6. Charles C. Ryrie, "The First Epistle of John," in *The Wycliffe Bible Commentary,* ed. Charles F. Pfeiffer and Everett F. Harrison (Chicago: Moody, 1962), p. 1477.

clarifies that no sin is acceptable, even if it is not met with such severe chastisement as death. Verse 18 states the norm for the true Christian: "The one born of God does not keep on habitually sinning."[7]

Now whom does "He who was born of God" describe? Some point out that this seems to refer to the Son of God. This may be supported by the change of tenses in the Greek language. The first phrase, "No one who is born of God," is in the perfect tense and refers to the state of one who has trusted Christ. The second phrase, "He who was born of God," is in the aorist tense and is said to refer to the Son of God.[8] If this is the case, then John is saying that Christ guards the believer, and Satan does not touch him.

The word translated "touch" *(haptō)* means to take hold of, to grasp, and carries the idea of injury in this case.[9] Some could take it to mean that Satan could not seriously affect the life of a believer. That has been shown not to be the case in our previous treatment of other passages. It could mean that Christ keeps the believer secure in his salvation, and the believer can never be returned into the kingdom of Satan. Or, as we pointed out, John could mean that Christ keeps us from coming under the devastating influence of Satan lest we be completely defeated and brought in the sphere of his control. If this is the case, John could be recalling a similar expression of the Lord Jesus that he recorded in John 17:15, where the Son prayed that we would be kept (same verb, *tērēsō)* from the evil one (same title, *ho ponēros).*

If, however, "He who was born of God" refers not to Christ but to the believer, then we have a different meaning. The differences in the tenses previously mentioned do not rule out that both phrases could refer to the believer. In this case we are to understand that the believer does not habitually practice sin, but instead he guards himself so that Satan does not grasp hold of him. The phrase "keeps him" could be translated "guards himself." This is an allowable reflexive use of the Greek pronoun *auton*[10] and fits the context when John warns them to

7. Kenneth S. Wuest, *In These Last Days* (Grand Rapids: Eerdmans, 1954), p. 182.
8. Ibid., p. 182.
9. Arndt and Gingrich, p. 102.
10. H. E. Dana and Julius R. Mantey, *A Manual Grammar of the Greek New Testament* (New York: Macmillan, 1948), pp. 124, 131.

guard themselves from idols (5:21). There is, then, an implied condition. It is the believer who guards his person carefully who will not be caught by Satan and dragged into sin and more of his control.

Both of the above interpretations have support from the context and from other sections of John's writings and from the entire New Testament. However, only one meaning is allowably the intent of John. The weight falls on the side of the second. But in neither case does this verse say that no believer can be seriously affected by demons or demonized. Certainly the believer will not *become* demonized if he avoids habitual sin and guards himself by walking in obedience to the Word, avoiding the wiles of the devil. But what happens if the believer does not take these safeguards? Why the statement about guarding, and why the command to keep ourselves from idols? The danger seems clear. We may open ourselves to Satan's particular attacks.

Neither this nor any of the passages in this category provide any sure basis for saying that believers cannot have resident demons.

PASSAGES ON DENIAL OF PARTICIPATION WITH DEMONS

There are certain sections of Scripture that deny the possibility of partaking of demonic evil and fellowshiping with Christ. These are often used as support that no Christian could have a demon resident in his body, that is, be demonized.

PSALM 5:4

We must consider this Old Testament passage because it seems to state a principle clearly: "For Thou art not a God who takes pleasure in wickedness; no evil dwells with Thee."

At first glance the statement seems quite clear and could be a forceful statement that a demon, who is evil, cannot dwell in a believer's body where God resides. However, we must note the connection between the two stichs of Hebrew poetry. As in synonymous parallelism, the two have the same or similar meanings. That is, *God does not take pleasure in wickedness* is the same concept as *God does not dwell with evil*. The main idea is not mutual exclusion of the presence of God and evil but the lack of pleasure or fellowship of God with evil. Presence and fellowship are certainly different.

This understanding of the verse is supported by the meaning of the Hebrew word for "dwell," which means to sojourn, as noted in the margin of the *New American Standard Bible* (Ps. 5:4). This speaks of fellowship along the road or in the house. Evil cannot have fellowship with God. God can call Satan into His presence (Job 1:6; 2:1) and even talk to him, but He has no fellowship with him. Presence and fellowship must be distinguished.

The statement, then, denies the possibility of evil's having fellowship with God. One could speculate that a demon might be present in a believer's body but certainly not have fellowship with God. The believer, if he were inhabited by a demon, still could have fellowship with God by standing against evil and siding with God. Psalm 5:4 does not exclude a demon from inhabiting a believer.

1 CORINTHIANS 10:21

"You cannot drink the cup of the Lord and the cup of demons; you cannot partake of the table of the Lord and the table of demons."

Does this statement of impossibility exclude the presence of a demon from any believer's body? It is a strong statement of exclusion. What does it exclude? Several observations are in order.

First, Corinthians 8-10 deals with the question of food offered to idols. Could believers properly eat such food? Paul answers according to the situation. The believer has liberty to do so under certain conditions. He is not to cause a brother to stumble by encouraging him to eat in spite of his conscience against it (chap. 8). A Christian has undeniable liberties in the Lord, but he is to voluntarily limit the exercise of his rights for the sake of others and the promotion of the truth (chap. 9). Chapter 10 points out that privileges received from God do not exclude the possibility of falling into temptation and sin, thus becoming unfruitful and perhaps inviting the chastisement of God. This is the setting of this verse. It is a warning, not a promise.

More immediately, verse 12 warns, "Let him who thinks he stand take heed lest he fall." Verse 13 promises that God will not allow the obedient one to be tempted beyond ability to resist.

But verse 14 commands, "Therefore, my beloved, flee from idolatry." Christians evidently were in danger of being involved or were already involved in idolatry, just as they were in immorality (1 Cor. 6:18). Paul reminds the readers that they share in the blood and the body of Christ. He means that they fellowship with Christ and other believers at the Lord's Table on the basis of the sacrifice of Christ. This sharing, or fellowship, is the Greek word *koinōnia* (v. 16). It means to share in common and, in this case, in a spiritual, moral oneness.

Next, Paul denies that idols are really gods (v. 19), but he affirms that demons promote idolatry and in a sense receive worship (v. 20). (This agrees with Ps. 106:36-38, which equates sacrifices to idols as sacrifices to demons.) His concern is expressed pointedly: "I do not want you to become sharers in demons" (v. 20). The Greek word has the same root as the one used earlier for fellowship with Christ *(koinōnous)*. In other words, if they sat at table at an idolatrous feast and partook of the food dedicated to idols, they would be fellowshiping with demons! This is a great defection and involves great danger.

Paul points out the sharp incongruity in verse 21: "You cannot partake *(metechein)* of the table of the Lord and the table of demons." This partaking means to participate, to have a part in. This unfitting combination does not rule out the possibility that some may try to partake of both tables. But did they not know that fellowship with demons excludes fellowship with the Lord?

Paul is really warning about the actual possibility of such sin. He also warns against the resultant chastisement of the Lord: "Or do we provoke the Lord to jealousy? We are not stronger than He, are we?" (v. 22). This connects to God's jealousy expressed against idolatry in the second of the Ten Commandments (Ex. 20:4-5). God rewards idolatry and the worship of demons with visiting these sins upon the third and fourth generation of those who in this way hate Him.

Instead of excluding the presence of demons from believers, this passage is a stern warning about the possible sin of fellowshiping with demons by participating in idolatrous actions.[11]

---

11. For a good explanation of the terms, the warning, and the danger, see E. G. Findlay, "St. Paul's First Epistle to the Corinthians," in *The Expositor's Greek Testament*, ed. W. Robertson Nicoll (Grand Rapids: Eerdmans, 1951), pp. 863-66.

2 CORINTHIANS 6:14-16

"Do not be bound together with unbelievers; for what partnership have righteousness and lawlessness, or what fellowship has light with darkness? Or what harmony has Christ with Belial, or what has a believer in common with an unbeliever? Or what agreement has the temple of God with idols? For we are the temple of the living God."

This statement of lack of agreement or harmony between Christ and evil may be used to claim that demons cannot live in the same body with Christ. What does it really mean?

The context of 2 Corinthians 1-6 deals with the contrast between the surpassing glory of the New Covenant ministry and the faded glory of that of the Old. In 6:14 Paul appeals to the Corinthians not to listen anymore to the false teachers of the law of Moses nor to support them, for they have nothing in common with them. The rest of the chapter, including the verses here under consideration, speak forcibly of the inconsistency of trying to fellowship with false teachers and with the true God, the Father of the Lord Jesus.

We must note some important details. Paul commands the Corinthians to stop being unequally yoked with unbelievers, the false teachers of Law. The present tense of the command indicates that they are in the process of listening and supporting these teachers. They were to some degree already yoked together *(heterozugountes)* with a different kind of moral entity. His argument for separation builds upon the incongruity of light and darkness, Christ and Belial, a reference to a pagan deity, sometimes to Satan in Jewish literature.[12] This shows that it is possible for a Christian, the temple of the living God, to have fellowship with unbelievers, even to participate in the works of Satan. It is obvious that Paul again sees evil spirits energizing these false teachers and that cooperation with them is cooperation with demons (compare 1 Tim. 4:1-3; 1 John 4:1-3).

Note also the five terms used for cooperation between these believers and the false teachers who are demon energized.[13] In verses 14 we find "partnership" *(metoche),* meaning a sharing

---

12. Arndt and Gingrich, p. 138.
13. Ibid., pp. 516, 439-40, 788, 506, 781, in order of text listing.

or participating. The next is "fellowship" *(koinōnia)*, which indicates a communion and close relationship, a term used of the believer's fellowship with Christ and other believers. In verse 15 there is "harmony" *(sumphōnesis)*, an agreement or working together as instruments in a symphony. The term for "what in common" is *meris*, meaning part, share, or portion. In verse 16 the last term is "agreement" *(sugkatathesis)*, which means a union or common decision by group action. Paul multiplies these terms in questions that build upon each other to show the terrible inconsistency that has overtaken the Corinthians. They are in the middle of a moral conflict. Their actions are inconsistent with their union with Christ and with their professed allegiance to His righteous cause.

Far from supporting the idea that Christians cannot have fellowship with evil, these verses confirm it and warn against it vociferously. There is no way that a principle can be drawn from these words of Paul that would mitigate against a Christian's being severely influenced by demons or being inhabited by demons.

CONCLUSION

None of the passages we have studied can with any fair treatment be construed to eliminate the possibility of a genuine believer's being inhabited by wicked spirits. As much as one might want such passages to say that, for whatever reason, there is no way that these must be understood to deny demonization of any believer. We may say definitely, however, that the believer who heeds the warnings and obeys the Scripture and walks in fellowship with Christ cannot be freshly invaded. Christ will guard him from that as the believer guards himself from evil with the provisions from God.

Two authors, who have had considerable experience in counseling believers who have been demonically oppressed, come to this conclusion:

> In vain do we search for a Scripture that grants Christians *full* immunity from the attacks or invasions of Satan. All of us know too well the external attack of Satan which Paul calls "the flaming missles of the evil one" (Eph. 6:16). Also we know that we sometimes sin grievously and that it comes as a shock to everyone

including ourselves. . . . There is no statement of Scripture to indicate that Christians are incapable of being harassed or even invaded by evil spirits *if they give grounds* to evil spirits.[14]

Though we have considered what some regard as emotional, perhaps upsetting matters, we should not let emotions cloud our objective and rational approach to the Scriptures. The Bible, not our hopes or prejudices, must be our guide. We must take courage in the battle. Demons are no match for Christ, and they will flee from the believer who submits to God and resists the devil (James 4:7). We have the authority of Christ as those in union with Him. We have the armor of God that we may be able to stand (Eph. 6:10-13). Let us stand in faith and obedience to the Word of God. He will never fail us!

14. Ensign and Howe, pp. 134-35.

7

Biblical Evidence Supporting Demonization of Christians

Certain passages of Scripture are cited as evidence that genuine believers may be inhabited by demons. We must consider some of these in the same way we treated passages against this thesis in the previous chapter.

PASSAGES INDICATING DEMONIC INFLUENCE

Chapter 1 presented the reality of demonic activity and its direction against believers. Here we would notice briefly the statements of direct influence upon believers. We must remember that demons are agents of Satan, and indications of his activity may be best understood as the work of demons for him. We should remember also that this influence is real and distinct from the enemies of the flesh and the world, though at times they may be intertwined.

2 CORINTHIANS 4:3-4

Though this passage speaks of the blinding of the minds of the unsaved so that they may not understand and receive the truth of the gospel, it indicates the opposition to evangelistic efforts of the Christian. We can expect direct demonic opposition in communicating the gospel and even personal attack when seeking to share the truth. This passage, however, says nothing about demonization either of the unbeliever or the believer.

1 THESSALONIANS 2:18

Paul says that Satan thwarted him from coming to help the believers in Thessalonica. We have no information as to exactly how this was accomplished. That demons were involved we may surmise. There may have been human agents as well. However, this passage says nothing of demonization in any clear sense.

1 JOHN 4:1-4

This passage presents demonic spirits as operating in false teachers who deny that Jesus Christ is the God-man. This was evaluated in the previous chapter as a passage that precluded the demonization of believers. But there are some who suggest that these false teachers in the assembly were also believers:

> John agrees with Paul that evil spirits will be actively working against Christians to the end of the age and can speak through the false prophets. These men appear to be Christians and maybe are or have been Christians.[1]

Here we must note first the lack of evidence that these false teachers are genuine believers. There is no statement to that effect. There is no mention of discipline for them. Believers are to reject them and regard them as aligned with the spirit of error (1 John 4:6). Note also the words "are or have been Christians." This implies loss of salvation. We have dealt with the issue of the security of the genuine believer in chapter 3.

We conclude that this passage does not present any sure evidence that believers can be inhabited by demons.

2 PETER 2:1-22

Peter warns about the influence of false teachers invading the assemblies of believers. They will be judged, just as the well-known biblical examples of sinning angels, the unbelieving world of Noah's day, and the cities of Sodom and Gomorrah (2:4-6). Then there is another group, those who follow these

---

1. Grayson H. Ensign and Edward Howe, *Bothered? Bewildered? Bewitched?* (Cincinnati: Recovery, 1984), p. 133.

false teachers (2:2). Peter describes the character and activity of the false teachers (2:10-19*a*). He then speaks of the followers who are overcome and enslaved by them (2:19*b*-22). Of the followers, Peter states,

> For it would be better for them not to have known the way of righteousness, than having known it, to turn away from the holy commandment delivered to them. It has happened to them according to the true proverb, "A dog returns to its own vomit," and, "A sow, after washing, returns to wallowing in the mire." (2:21-22)

Following a brief survey of New Testament evidence, one source refers to this passage and states, "Christians stand in real danger of being tempted, attacked, and even controlled by evil spirits *if* they are not careful to be fully protected by the whole armor of God and the blood of the Lord Jesus Christ."[2]

What does this passage say about the demonization of believers? First, we must note that direct activity of demons is implied rather than stated. Angels are mentioned in the context but are not directly connected to the false teachers or followers (2:4). Demonization is not specifically mentioned either. It may well be that demons and demonization are involved, but there is no certain evidence here.

Second, there is no clear evidence that either the teachers or the followers are Christians. In fact, the teachers are corrupt (2:10), are born as mere natural creatures (not born again, 2:12), and are reserved for punishment in the black darkness (2:17). The followers came to know the truth, evidently by previous good teaching, and then were ensnared by the false teachers who prevented them from coming into a true relationship with Christ. They knew the facts of the gospel, but never received the Savior. This is evidenced by the fact that they returned to their previous natural way of life. This is the meaning of the proverbs quoted in verse 22. The dog acts as a dog and a sow as a sow, despite all the external changes. There has never been a change of nature either with the animals or with the followers. Their reversion indicates their lack of conversion.

We conclude that there is no sure evidence of the demoniza-

2. Ibid., p. 135.

tion of genuine believers available from this passage. Where there is a reasonable doubt of the certainty of the contribution of a passage, we cannot legitimately count on it.

1 CORINTHIANS 2:11

Paul encouraged the Corinthian church to forgive and restore to fellowship (not leadership, by the way) the disciplined and repentant person "in order that no advantage be taken of us by Satan; for we are not ignorant of his schemes."

This passage may be dealing with a man who had been influenced by Satan or demons, but there is no mention of such in the context here or in 1 Corinthians 5 where the same man may be in consideration. The man's own sin is under treatment there and his personal restoration here. There is the stern warning here, however, that Satan or demons might take advantage of the opportunity to cause difficulty of some sort. We are not specifically told what his action might be, but it may have been dividing the church over whether to restore this man involved in such a gross sin as incest. Whatever it might have been, we cannot clearly read from this passage any evidence that genuine believers can be demon inhabited. It fails to present any evidence, let alone conclusive evidence, along this line.

1 TIMOTHY 4:1

Paul warns, "But the Spirit explicitly says that in later times some will fall away from the faith, paying attention to deceitful spirits and doctrines of demons."

Some suggest this indicates that believers come under the influence of demons to such an extent that they fall away from the truth and teach demonically inspired doctrines. The statement by Unger must be seriously considered:

> These must be believers who turn and become heretics, for only such could leave true Christianity. The result is that they get involved with "seducing [wandering] spirits" and land in "doctrine of devils [demons]," denoting teaching instigated by demons (1 Tim. 4:1). Departure from the faith does not necessarily mean defection from Christ, although apostates are no more excluded from this passage than are heretics. Rather, it suggests departure from revealed truth. This doctrinal deterioration allows for the various

stages of contact with the powers of darkness in demonization depending on the severity of doctrinal lapse and the type of cult in which the victim is ensnared. Demon control is not unknown among believers who give themselves wholly to the demonic doctrines taught by the cults; witness the blindness and insulation against the truth that result.[3]

The demonic influence here described is serious. The verb used for "fall away" is *apostēsontai,* which comes from a root that indicates a departure from a professed stand and a falling away from God (Heb. 3:12).[4] It was used of the accusation by Jews that Paul was teaching men to depart from Moses (Acts 21:21). In noun form this word was used by Paul to describe the apostasy under the coming Antichrist (2 Thess. 2:3). Whether in each case this can be shown to refer to genuine believers departing from Christ or the gospel, or whether it refers only to unbelievers backing away from a professed stand for Christ, is doubtful. But the departure in 1 Timothy 4:1 is due to the direct influence of demonic forces. Here is a mind-control effort by demons on men to lead them away from the truth and to demonically influenced teaching. Whether this is control from external demons or due to invading demons, the passage does not say.

Thus we have a passage that is unclear as to whether the teachers are Christians or not and as to whether the demons involved are outside or inside the false teachers. We must conclude that this passage does not contribute clear information as to whether demons can invade Christians.

PASSAGES INDICATING DEMONIC ATTACK

There is no doubt that Satan and demons attack Christians. They seem to be special targets of the enemies of God because they are the children of God and hated as God is hated. Some do not recognize the full range of activities leveled against the children of God because they think that salvation automatically protects us from all sorts of evil. This simply is not so. The

3. Merrill F. Unger, *What Demons Can Do to Saints* (Chicago: Moody, 1977), p. 91.
4. William F. Arndt and F. Wilbur Gingrich, *A Greek-English Lexicon of the New Testament* (Chicago: U. of Chicago, 1952), p. 126.

Scriptures make it quite clear that God's children, upon entering their position in the heavenlies in Christ (Eph. 2:5-6), also enter a battle royal with the forces of wickedness (Eph. 6:10-12). Some adduce evidence from certain passages of the Bible that lead them to conclude that these attacks may include invasion of the person, or demonization. We must consider some of these passages also.

EPHESIANS 6:10-18

> Finally, be strong in the Lord, and in the strength of His might. Put on the full armor of God, that you may be able to stand firm against the schemes of the devil. For our struggle is not against flesh and blood, but against the rulers, against the powers, against the world forces of this darkness, against the spiritual forces of wickedness in the heavenly places. (6:10-12)

This classic passage presents the warfare that every believer must face soberly in the real world. Does it present any evidence of invasion of believers? The question arises, What happens to the believer who does *not* avail himself of the Lord's strength and does not put on the complete armor? Paul does not specifically say, but the passage gives some indications.

The battle seems to have mental as well as physical and external dimensions. There are obviously enemies on the outside of the Christian. But there is a sin nature within through which Satan can attack the believer. The terms in the passage indicate a mind-against-mind struggle—the mind of demons against the mind of the believer. The general term "schemes" *(methodeias)* indicates demonic craftiness or stratagems designed to deceive, defraud, and pervert.[5] Here demonic minds are presented as seeking to lead human minds into error and sin so as to trap and defeat them. Some specifics of how this may be accomplished come to light in the rest of the passage. The armor includes the belt of truth, the system of truth in Christ to be mentally apprehended and morally applied (v. 14). The breastplate of righteousness seems best understood as mentally standing in the righteousness that Christ provided through His

5. Ibid., p. 500.

merits when we trusted Him and were justified. Trusting in the peace that God established through the blood of Christ seems to be the provision of the sandals of peace that prepare us for battle. These pieces of armor are also mentally perceived and applied.

The remaining three pieces of armor are also mental and moral concepts to be applied in battle. The shield of faith is confidence in God. The helmet of deliverance seems to speak of keeping in mind that we are on the winning side, remembering that if God be for us no one can be successfully against us. The sword of the Spirit refers to the appropriate sayings *(brēma)* of Scripture, which are remembered and perceived as applying to the particular aspect of the battle at hand. These, too, are battles involving the mind.

The question remains: Are the thoughts that seek to intrude upon believers' minds from external sources or internal sources? Demonic forces seek to propagandize from whatever station they may take. Do these terms above speak of solely external mind-control games or internal also? Obviously the enemies desire some internal response from the believer. It may well be that some of the battle takes place from within the believer, but the passage does not specifically state the location of the demonic forces that seek the mind control. It is true that the same word used in Ephesians 6:11 for *schemes* is used also in Ephesians 4:14 to describe the devious means that human errorists use against believers, but that does not exclude its use of demons possibly within a person.

We conclude that though the passage speaks of attempted mind control by demonic forces, there is no definite evidence as to the location of the demons themselves. As far as we know at this point, they might be outside or inside. Evidence other than just this passage must be considered.

EPHESIANS 4:26-27

Paul warns believers, "Be angry, and yet do not sin; do not let the sun go down on your anger, and do not give the devil an opportunity."

This is representative of several passages that speak of Satan or demons taking advantage of believers due to some weakness or sin. Anger is an internal, mental attitude often expressed externally. Satan obviously takes advantage of unresolved anger, according to this passage. What does that mean? Again, Paul does not specifically state exactly how or where demonic forces would operate. They may aggravate the mind of the angry believer to lead him to hate and bitterness, perhaps even to seek revenge. They may lead to division of brethren and interruption of fellowship, the hurt of relationships, and the hindering of God's work. But again we must limit our conclusions regarding the invasion of believers by demons. There is no specific evidence that this is the case in this passage or in similar passages, some of which we will yet observe.

1 TIMOTHY 3:6-7

Paul specifies some qualifications for the elders of the church: "not a new convert, lest he become conceited and fall into the condemnation incurred by the devil. And he must have a good reputation with those outside the church, so that he may not fall into reproach and the snare of the devil."

The condemnation incurred by the devil refers to disqualification and dismissal from the place of fellowship and privilege. It does not refer to the loss of salvation. Satan never was saved by the grace of God and accorded the righteousness of Christ in which to stand blameless before God. His pride caused his fall into sin from which he could never be redeemed. Redeemed men can never be found in that condition. This passage speaks of reduction to uselessness for the office of elder.

The reproach and snare of the devil refers to that condition that Satan and demons seek to bring upon leaders of the church to disqualify them in the eyes of the public. The leaders of Christ's church must be blameless in the eyes of all (1 Tim. 3:2).

Just how all this is brought to bear by Satan is not specifically stated. Pride is a matter of the mind, and it can originate in the human mind, for all believers still possess an evil sin nature. Satan can seek to cultivate pride through various means. But this passage does not specifically state the exact influence or location of demonic forces who would attack the Christian leader.

We conclude that this passage does not support the concept that a believer may be inhabited by demons.

1 PETER 5:6-8

> Humble yourselves, therefore, under the mighty hand of God, that
> He may exalt you at the proper time, casting all your anxiety upon
> Him, because He cares for you. Be of sober spirit, be on the alert.
> Your adversary, the devil, prowls about like a roaring lion, seeking
> someone to devour.

Peter connects, by close mention, anxiety and the lack of
casting our concerns upon the Father to the possibility of attack
by Satan. He does not specify the exact type of attack. It may
again be related to the furthering of overconcern and anxiety to
the point of great depression and despair of life itself. Some are
driven to suicidal thoughts and actions through such anxiety. It
is just like the one who is called "the destroyer" ("Abaddon" and
"Apollyon," Rev. 9:11) to seek to lead a person to suicide. (In my
counseling of the demonically oppressed, I have found this to
be so.)

What does Peter mean by the term "devour"? The Greek
word is *katapinō* and refers to drinking down or swallowing,
such as an animal does his prey. It was used in translating the
Hebrew of the Old Testament when referring to the fish's swallowing Jonah (Jonah 1:17) and when describing the sinking of
Pharaoh's army in the sea (Ex. 15:4). It is used in the metaphori-
cal sense of a man overwhelmed by extreme sorrow (2 Cor. 2:7)
and of the mortal being swallowed up in life (2 Cor. 5:4).[6] Peter,
then, may be using the word here of physical hurt or spiritual
depression. How this is done is not specified. But the devil does
seek to do it. The warning is not against something unreal or
impossible. It could involve outward or inward attack, but the
passage does not clarify.

Unger comments on this warning:

> Certainly this conveys the idea that the powers of darkness are able
> to make a very serious encroachment upon the life of a child of
> God. In fact, they go so far as to kill the body (Matt. 10:28). How
> dare a believer ignore this warning or naively tone down its terrify-
> ing implications?[7]

6. Ibid., p. 417.
7. Unger, *What Demons Can Do to Saints,* p. 92.

We conclude that though the enemy seeks a ravaging of the believer's life, the form is not specifically stated. This passage does not give sufficient evidence to conclude anything about the possible demonization of a believer.

2 TIMOTHY 2:26

Paul instructs Timothy to correct with gentleness those who oppose the truth so that they might come by the grace of God to repent, "and they may come to their senses and escape from the snare of the devil, having been held captive by him to do his will."

In this passage, it is the unbeliever who has been snared by demonic forces. He needs the liberating grace of God that leads him to repent and recognize the truth. He has not previously known the truth (2:25). So we are not considering the case of a believer. This snaring involves blinding to the gospel of Christ (2 Cor. 4:3-4) and leading into a false life-style. It could involve idolatry and invasion by spirits, but the passage does not specify all that is involved.

Some understand verse 26, as in the *New American Standard Bible,* to refer to the devil's taking men captive at will. If it refers to the action of Satan, it merely states that they have been taken captive. The idea that Satan can capture them whenever he wishes is not stated here. Whenever he is allowed to do so, he captures them to get them to do his will. Others understand this verse to refer to God's setting men free from the devil so that they may do God's will.

We must conclude that this passage does not contribute evidence that believers can be demonized.

PASSAGES THAT MAY INDICATE INVASION OF BELIEVERS

The passages treated above indicate influence or attack upon believers, but the passages to be investigated here may possibly indicate demonization of believers. Some have taken them in such a fashion. Some passages imply invasion. Others speak of invasion as definite or nearly so. In the latter, we must consider whether the persons invaded were actually believers. All these portions of God's Word must be faced as objectively as possible to determine the contribution they make.

We will first treat passages that imply the possibility of believers' being demonized.

GENESIS 31:19, 34-35

Here we have the story of Rachel, Jacob's wife, stealing her father's household idols when Jacob fled secretly from Laban. The story tells of her theft and her subsequent deceit in hiding the idols and lying to her father to keep him from them. We will not dispute whether Rachel was a believer in God, but we can question whether the motivation to steal and lie was caused by inhabiting demons. We know that demons energize idol worship (Ps. 106:35-38; 1 Cor. 10:20), but we do not know if Rachel was externally or internally influenced by demons in this matter. Evidence is lacking for any sure conclusion here. What is clear is that it is difficult for those engaged in idolatry to break family and cultural influences and habits.

NUMBERS 22-24

The case of Balaam presents some people with evidence of demonic invasion of believer. Says Unger,

> The career of Balaam (Num. 22-24) offers a strange mixture of occultism and the worship and service of God. As a pagan divine of repute, Balaam of necessity was energized as a clairvoyant and soothsayer by demon power, as are all occultists who operate in the realm of evil supernaturalism.
>
> Yet, despite the fact that he was contaminated by occult religion and an enemy of Israel, God raised him up at least temporarily to the status of a true prophet of the Lord. "The spirit of God came upon him" (Num. 24:2).
>
> Balaam illustrates the fact that the Spirit of God may work in believers who are weak in faith and deficient in sound doctrine.[8]

Some hold that Balaam was a believer in the true God. He was visited by God (22:20), he sought the Lord's permission (22:8), he recognized he had sinned (22:34), and he was used of God to bless Israel (23:7-10). But he had so many questionable attitudes and actions that it is difficult to claim that he was a

8. Ibid., p. 119.

true and regenerate believer in God. He continued to seek loopholes so that he could make money in prophesying against Israel. He did not outrightly reject the monetary offer from Balak (22:8). God spoke to him, and he was afraid to continue (22:13), but he again sought some compromise (22:19). God's anger with him is obvious. As he sought to go up the mountain to curse God's people, God caused his donkey to speak and drew his attention to the angel of the Lord who came out against him because his way was against God (22:32). Balaam is never commended by God and is always the example of a prophet out for his own good and against God (Rev. 2:14). In Jude 11, ungodly teachers who are headed for destruction and darkness are said to have "rushed headlong into the error of Balaam."

It may be true that Balaam was energized by demons and was given special powers by inhabiting demons, as are many in the occult; but it is difficult to prove that this ungodly man was a true believer. He was not necessarily a believer just because the Spirit of God came upon him. This is a case of God's overpowering him in sovereign fashion to keep his mouth from cursing Israel and to direct him to bless Israel.

We cannot allow this as good evidence that a believer may be inhabited by demons.[9] Unger makes reference to other Old Testament cases which he considers as evidence for the demonization of believers, but the cases have too many assumptions and speculations to be of any great weight.[10]

MATTHEW 8:16

"And when evening had come, they brought to Him many who were demon-possessed; and He cast out the spirits with a word, and healed all who were ill."

This text says there were many demonized, and He healed all who were ill. Are we to suppose, state some, that none of these who were treated by Christ were genuine believers? Did He minister only to unbelievers? Such could hardly be the case. Many would allow that believers could be sick but not among the demonized. The text makes no such division. Another point to be made here is that illness is not automatically relieved at

---

9. Ibid., pp. 119-21. Unger develops a contrary case with some practical insights on how God may use errant believers in some limited ways.
10. Ibid., pp. 118-19, 124-27. The case of Saul is more substantial (pp. 120-23).

salvation and never to be experienced thereafter. Why should we suppose that such is the case with demonization?

This argument is from inference, and not from direct statement. It may be classified as an argument from silence. That is, since the text does not exclude believers from these groups, it must include believers in them. Such an argument is weak. Though the presence of believers might well be expected among those treated, we do not have explicit evidence to that fact. We must again say that the weight of the facts does not bring us to an inescapable conclusion.

ACTS 5:1-3

The case here is of Ananias and his wife, Sapphira, who sold their land to bring in money for the Christian community. They had seen how Barnabas was recognized for such a generous deed. But they lied by saying that what they gave was the full price, keeping back some of the sale money. Peter by God's wisdom said: "Ananias, why has Satan filled your heart to lie to the Holy Spirit, and to keep back some of the price of the land?"

Unger presents this as a case of "satanic inworking":

> The sin of Ananias and Sapphira (Ac 5:1-11) furnished an inlet for the powers of darkness. But it is not easy from the data presented to define theologically precisely what took place. . . . Satan, the "liar, and the father of lies" (Jn 8:44, NASB), "filled" their hearts "to lie to the Holy Spirit" (Ac 5:3, NASB). The same word used of the believer who is "filled with the Spirit" *(pleroō)* is employed here of Ananias, whom the power of darkness "filled" (Eph. 5:18).[11]

The least this can mean is that Satan (or demons) influenced the hearts of these believers to lie. The filling would be with the suggested scheme of self-glorification and deception. The most it could mean is that inhabiting demons controlled them, as they gave themselves to the scheme, to seek to deceive men and God. But as Unger states, the data does not allow us to define exactly what took place. The use of the same word for "fill" does not guarantee that it has the same connections or type of cause. The Holy Spirit does reside in the New Testament believer and can fill or control as the believer allows and cooperates with the

11. Ibid., p. 116.

Spirit's enabling. There is no definite indication that Satan or demons resided within either Ananias or Sapphira. This may be similar to what Jesus saw in Peter's remonstrance concerning His death. Peter was influenced by Satan and in a sense took his philosophy and gave it expression (Matt. 16:23). Would someone suggest that Peter was demonized? There is not a shred of evidence for that, nor did Christ ever seek to cast a demon out of the leader of the apostles.

We must again conclude that there is not sufficient evidence to determine if this is a case of believers being demonized. But it does show the terrible consequences of giving Satan room to work in one's life. Believers are not immune to his direct attacks, especially if they are living in sin.

ACTS 8:9-24

Here is the unusual case of Simon the magician. His power and reputation had been well established for a long time among the Samaritans. He was called "the Great Power of God" (8:10-11). When the people believed the gospel preached by Philip, so did Simon. He, along with the group, was baptized. He continued listening and observing and being constantly amazed (8:12-13). The problem enters when Simon, observing the miraculous giving of the Spirit by the authority of Christ operating through the laying on of the apostles' hands, offered them money to obtain that power. The story continues:

> But Peter said to him, "May your silver perish with you, because you thought you could obtain the gift of God with money! You have no part or portion in this matter, for your heart is not right before God. Therefore repent of this wickedness of yours, and pray the Lord that if possible, the intention of your heart may be forgiven you. For I see that you are in the gall of bitterness and in the bondage of iniquity." But Simon answered and said, "Pray to the Lord for me yourselves, so that nothing of what you have said may come upon me."

Here is an apparent believer under the influence of sin and perhaps demonic control left over from his preconversion activity in demonically empowered magic (comparable to the magical activity of Pharaoh's court magicians, who obviously worked by power other than illusion, Ex. 7-8; see also 2 Thess. 2:8-9).

Some take the word of Peter regarding Simon's sinful attitude to indicate that his faith was not real and that he was still in the bondage of the unconverted heathen magician that he was.[12]

But there are reasons to think that he was a real believer who was still thinking in terms of his occult world view. There is little reason to believe that Luke wants us to think that Simon's faith was unreal. The same terms used of other believers are used of him. The construction of the Greek text emphasizes that even Simon himself believed and was baptized, just like the other believers. He also attached himself faithfully *(proskarterōn)* to Philip.[13] We might consider that he was genuine in his repentance and asking for prayer (8:24). And it is noteworthy that Peter did not say that Simon needed to receive Christ. He centered in on the particular sin regarding this matter of seeking to buy God's power, evidently for some self-centered purpose at least in part (8:22).

We might conclude that this believer was still in the bondage of his pagan, occult world view and of his self-promoting scheming, as is the case with many former occultists we have encountered. His magic was formerly accomplished by demonic forces. But we cannot say for certain that he was still inhabited by wicked spirits, even though the attitude and actions of such bondage may be manifest here. The evidence is inconclusive, but the possibility exists that he was still demonized.

1 CORINTHIANS 5:1-13

Paul directs the church to discipline the man who is living in an incestual relationship. He calls on the congregation to judge the man by excommunication from the fellowship:

> In the name of our Lord Jesus, when you are assembled, and I with you in spirit, with the power of our Lord Jesus, I have decided to deliver such a one to Satan for the destruction of his flesh, that his spirit may be saved in the day of the Lord Jesus. (5:4-5).

Opinions differ as to whether this man was a genuine believer, but he is treated as though he were. He is judged as one

12. R. J. Knowling, "The Acts of the Apostles," ed., W. Robertson Nicoll, *The Expositor's Greek Testament* (Grand Rapids: Eerdmans, 1951), 2:215.
13. Arndt and Gingrich, p. 722.

within the church (5:12-13). He is disciplined as a brother (5:5). But the expression "that his spirit may be saved in the day of the Lord Jesus" gives some problems. If he is unsaved, why is he turned over to Satan that his spirit might be saved? That is not the New Testament norm for dealing with the unsaved. Why the reference to the future day of judgment when he could be saved by trusting Christ in repentance now? Could this be a reference to the judgment seat of Christ, where we shall give account of our life and works for Christ? This is the usual meaning of "the day of our Lord Jesus," a reference to the *bema* at which Christ rewards believers (1 Cor. 3:10-15; 2 Cor. 5:10). Perhaps this discipline is for saving his spiritual usefulness so that he will not be judged as completely unprofitable in Christ's evaluation.

The turning him over to Satan for the destruction of the flesh may refer to the overcoming of the sin nature or to the taking of his physical life, the ultimate in discipline for God's children (1 Cor. 11:30; 1 John 5:16). Some see in this the allowing of demonic invasion that would lead the man ultimately to physical death. But the fact of demonization is not mentioned, and the terms used do not demand that understanding. All we can say is that God would have employed satanic forces to be used as part of the discipline to restore this sinning man. This man may be the one Paul urged the Corinthians to restore to fellowship upon his repentance (2 Cor. 2:5-11).

The conclusion that this evidences demonization of a genuine believer is not warranted.

1 CORINTHIANS 10:14-22

We have examined this passage in the previous chapter as evidence some use to prove that demons cannot inhabit believers. We found the argument to be inadequate. On the other hand, some use this passage to prove that believers can be demonized. They appeal to the danger of which Paul warns, the danger of actual fellowship with demons:

> What do I mean then? That a thing sacrificed to idols is anything, or that an idol is anything? No, but I say that the things which the Gentiles sacrifice, they sacrifice to demons, and not to God; and I do not want you to become sharers in demons. You cannot drink the cup of the Lord and the cup of demons; you cannot partake of

the table of the Lord and the table of demons. Or do we provoke the Lord to jealousy? We are not stronger than He, are we?

Here the apostle argues against participating in idolatrous feasts because it makes them to be fellowshipers *(koinōnous)* with demons. This fellowship is considered to be a genuine possibility, not an impossibility. That is the purpose of his stern warning. The language seems clear. The sharing in common with demons is a reality, a confusion, and a testing of God that may evoke dire consequences. (Note the treatment of this passage in some detail in chapter 6.)

Some see this fellowshiping (10:20) as an evidence of the inhabiting of demons. We cannot lightly dismiss this possibility. Participation in idolatry for these Corinthians was not new. They may have been invaded by demons in their giving themselves to idolatry and immorality in their previous pagan life. That such can lead to demonization is borne out by Scripture and by observation of individuals in pagan cultures. Now these believers were involved in practices inconsistent with their relationship to Christ, and they were in terrible danger. This may have included invasion by the demons they were worshiping.

But we cannot say for certain that they were demonized or in danger of demonization from the language of this passage. Stern as it is, the passage does not speak certainly to this matter. The *koinōnia* may be sharing with demons in the worship of idols and in seeming agreement with the pagans celebrating the feast. There may be a fellowshiping that is external in this sense. Again, we must decline the certainty of the conclusion that this passage teaches the possibility of demonization of believers.

2 CORINTHIANS 11:3-4

But I am afraid, lest as the serpent deceived Eve by his craftiness, your minds should be led astray from the simplicity and purity of devotion to Christ. For if one comes and preaches another Jesus whom we have not preached, or you receive a different spirit which you have not received, or a different gospel which you have not accepted, you bear this beautifully.

It is clear that Paul is warning against satanic and demonic influence that would turn the Corinthians from loyalty to the true Savior, the true Holy Spirit, and the true apostle (11:13-15). Regarding the danger involved, Unger states:

> Christians have received "the spirit which is of God" (1 Cor 2:12). But they are in danger of receiving "another" spirit of a "different" kind (a demon spirit), especially when encountering satanic delusion working in the religious realm (1 Tim 4:1; 1 Jn 4:1-2; cf. 2 Th 2:2). This is exactly what Paul is saying in 2 Corinthians 11:4. . . . Only by another spirit, that is, a spirit "different" from the Holy Spirit (a demon spirit), could one preach another (different) Jesus and "another (different) gospel" (Gal 1:6-9). . . . The expression "receiving another" or "different spirit" therefore means more than simply believing and receiving false teachers. It denotes believing and receiving the spirit "not of [from] God" (1 Jn 4:3), who energizes *all* false teachers. . . . In such a case he receives a spirit different in kind from the Holy Spirit. The conclusion is inescapable; he receives an alien spirit.[14]

What Unger suggests must be considered. We know that demons often energize false teachers. We know that unwary believers may receive the false doctrine from the false teachers. The question, however, remains as to what it means to "receive a different spirit." Must this mean invasion by a demon in every case, or even in any case?

First, it may not be so that only by resident demons may one preach a different gospel. There is no way to assure that. Demons may promote false teaching from outside the teacher by influencing the mind. Second, to receive a different spirit may mean to receive the teacher influenced by the spirit. Yet to receive the teacher is in a sense to receive the demon influencing him. What is this receiving? Should it be directly compared with receiving the Holy Spirit? This is not specifically contrasted in the context. It could be merely the presence of the teacher in whom the spirit of a demon dwells. It seems that this may be Paul's emphasis: to receive the false teacher in the assembly may be to receive a demonic spirit into the assembly. Paul does not speak so much to the individual believer as to the assembly of believers concerning their receiving demonically inspired false teachers. In fact, Paul speaks of the Galatians receiving him into their midst (Gal. 4:14). This does not require either that Paul was internally received into the individual or that the Holy Spirit

14. Unger, *What Demons Can Do to Saints,* pp. 92-93.

was automatically received by an individual just because that one received Paul and heard his message. There is beyond that a willful giving over to the message.

We must take the warning here into consideration. Paul may be speaking of the possibility of receiving a demon to inhabit, but the evidence does not support that conclusion without doubt.

2 CORINTHIANS 12:7-8

> And because of the surpassing greatness of the revelations, for this reason, to keep me from exalting myself, there was given me a thorn in the flesh, a messenger of Satan to buffet me—to keep me from exalting myself! Concerning this I entreated the Lord three times that it might depart from me.

There are those who may consider that the "messenger of Satan" was a resident demon allowed continually to trouble Paul. They view the "thorn in the flesh" as describing the location of the demon in the body. Others see this as an external attack on Paul's body inflicted in some way by Satan himself or a demon. Bubeck sees this as an illustration of "obsession," which, in advance over "oppression," indicates "a more intense level of demonic attack which may be experienced by all believers."[15]

Actually, there are several problems of interpretation that we must consider to understand the contribution of this passage to our question of whether believers can be inhabited by demons: (1) the meaning of "thorn in the flesh," (2) the meaning of "a messenger [angel] of Satan," and (3) the meaning of "buffet."

The word "thorn" *(skolops)* means a stake, thorn, or splinter, indicating some injurious foreign body.[16] H. A. W. Meyer suggests that it is "the figurative conception of a *thorn* pressed into the flesh with acute pain" and should be understood as a Greek dative meaning *"a thorn for the flesh."*[17] If this is the case, the term does not emphasize the location as within or on the sur-

15. Mark I. Bubeck, *The Adversary* (Chicago: Moody, 1975), pp. 84-85.
16. Arndt and Gingrich, p. 763.
17. H. A. W. Meyer, *Critical and Exegetical Handbook to the Epistles to the Corinthians,* trans. David Hunter, vol. 2, *Critical and Exegetical Commentary on the New Testament,* ed. William P. Dickson and William Stewart, (Edinburgh: T. & T. Clark, 1879), p. 475.

face of the body but rather speaks of what it torments—the body. It also affected Paul's mental attitude, for it is obvious that it was God's design to prevent any spiritual pride over the great revelation God had previously given to Paul (2 Cor. 12:7). Paul knew it was allowed by God, even though instigated by Satan; for he seriously asked God three times for its removal, but God answered him three times that His grace would enable Paul to bear it and demonstrate God's power (12:8-9).

The word "flesh" *(sarx)* can mean the body or the sin nature. Meyer suggests it means "that part of my nature which lusts to sin *(in specie,* to self-exaltation)."[18] The problem here is, How can a thorn be fixed in the sin nature? Some might see this as the possibility of an angel from Satan dwelling inside the sin nature, a natural toehold for evil. (We might ask where the sin nature is located.) This seems far from what Paul is emphasizing. It seems far more natural in the context to take "flesh" as a reference to the physical body and the thorn as a physical malady brought upon the body by Satan.

The term "a messenger of Satan" *(angelos satana)* admits of more than one meaning, but there is only one that Paul had in mind. It could mean a demon sent by Satan, as he has angels who serve him (Matt. 25:41). In this case the demon could be considered as a constant or intermittent harassment to his body. The term *angelos* may also refer to Satan himself (messenger of Satan could mean the messenger Satan). However, "the *actual usage* is against it, for Satan, so often as he occurs in the N. T., is never named *angelos.*"[19] Though this is not the strongest argument, there is some strength to it. A second meaning might be that the demon actually dwelt in his body (or as some say, in his sin nature). In this case he would have been demonized. There is no indication other than this phrase that would indicate that Paul had an inhabiting demon. This would bring his apostolic ministry under suspicion.

A third and most likely meaning is that Satan or a demon caused a bodily affliction or illness. In this case, there is no inhabiting of a demon. There are many attempted explanations of what this affliction might be.[20] Two reasonable possibilities are eye trouble, such as opthalmia, or a recurrent fever, such as

18. Ibid.
19. Ibid., p. 476.
20. Arndt and Gingrich, pp. 441-42. See *kolophizō.*

malaria. It caused him such limitations that it weakened him and hindered his ministry to such an extent that he was very concerned to be relieved of it. However, the Lord said to him, "My grace is sufficient for you, for power is perfected in weakness" (12:9). We see that it is not always God's purpose to completely remove the effects of Satan's attack, but God can overrule it for good. It kept Paul humble and dependent.

The purpose of Satan, graciously overruled for good by God, was to "buffet" *(kolaphizō)* Paul. God would keep him from self-exaltation. The Greek word means "to strike with the fist, beat, cuf" or "to treat roughly."[21] The present tense of the verb indicates that this action was still continuing. It is not clear whether the action is that of the demon continuing his work or of the resultant affliction continuing to give Paul trouble. We cannot say for certain that the demon continued with Paul.

We do not have enough information to conclude what Paul had as a "messenger from Satan" for a "thorn in the flesh." We cannot say it was a resident demon. We cannot say that a demon intermittently harassed him. Most likely we can say that it was a recurrent physical malady originally caused by Satan or a demon. God continued to use it as a spiritually healthy benefit for Paul.

The above passages may be used to imply that demons may inhabit a believer, but the evidence is not all that certain. The next cases involve persons that are most likely, if not certainly, demonized. Here the question is, Are they genuine believers?

THE CASE OF KING SAUL

The book of 1 Samuel presents the strange case of Saul, who had problems with the flesh and with a wicked spirit. Though Saul started his kingly career in fairly good fashion, he deteriorated in spiritual behavior due to his self-dependence and rebellion.

Some question whether Saul was even a believer. But there seems to be sufficient evidence of this. The Spirit of God came upon him mightily, he was "changed into another man," and this was evidenced by his prophesying (1 Sam. 10:6-12). He later was empowered by the Spirit of God mightily to defend Israel

21. Ibid.

(11:6-7). God chose him as king (at insistence of the people, 10:17-24) and enabled him on occasion. Never does Samuel question his relationship to God. He received Samuel's and God's approval (12:17-18). But his fellowship and obedience were faulty (13:8-14; 15:11, 22-23). Later Saul acknowledged the providence of God and confessed his wrong to David (24:16-22; 26:21-25).

If Saul was a believer (and we have good reason to hold this), then it seems fairly clear that at least upon occasion he was invaded by a wicked spirit that controlled his behavior: "Now the Spirit of the Lord departed from Saul, and an evil spirit from the Lord terrorized him" (16:14). The demon would also depart from him when David would play his harp to refresh him spiritually (16:18-23). If the demon invaded Saul, then it also left him on ocassion or at least stopped his terrifying activity and retreated within. If the demon was merely terrorizing from outside his body, then it left his presence. The same demonic activity occurred on two or three other occasions. These were the times when Saul was so aggravated by the demon that he actually tried to pin David to the wall with his spear. Note the passages:

> Now it came about on the next day that an evil spirit from God came mightily upon Saul, and he raved in the midst of the house, while David was playing the harp with his hand, as usual; and a spear was in Saul's hand. And Saul hurled the spear for he thought, "I will pin David to the wall." But David escaped from his presence twice. (1 Sam. 18:10-11)

> Now there was an evil spirit from the Lord on Saul as he was sitting in his house with his spear in his hand, and David was playing the harp with his hand. And Saul tried to pin David to the wall with the spear, but he slipped away out of Saul's presence, so that he struck the spear into the wall. And David fled and escaped that night. (1 Sam. 19:9-10)

We must note that in the first passage, the harsh treatment from the demon caused a sustained behavioral change, introduced a murderous thought into Saul's mind, and moved Saul's body to throw the spear to kill David, God's anointed replacement for the king. This mind and body control exhibited by the demon seems fairly certain to be internal and could be compared to some of the similar characteristics of the Gerasene demoniac (Mark 5:1-5; see the treatment of this demonized case in chap. 2). The second instance shows much the same type of control. Sudden change of personality and behavior is typical of those who are subject to demonic control from within. Harassment comes from outside, but mind and body control comes from within. This is recognized by perceptive evangelicals.[22]

From the evidence it is fairly certain that Saul was invaded on one or several occasions by a demon as a chastisement from God for his rebellion, which God regards as wretched as the sin of witchcraft or divination (1 Sam. 15:23). It also is quite certain that he was a genuine though carnal believer. Here is, then, a very probable case of a believer invaded by an evil spirit.

Some will object that this could indeed happen in that age, for the Spirit of God would come upon and leave believers in accord with His purpose of enablement. That is true. The Holy Spirit did not come to dwell permanently in all believers until after the cross and the giving of the Spirit in accord with the New Covenant (John 7:37-39; Rom. 8:9). The record further states that the Spirit of the Lord departed from Saul, and the evil spirit came to Saul (1 Sam. 16:14). So with this objection recognized, some deny that such an invasion could happen in this age of grace since Pentecost. This is based upon the supposition that the Holy Spirit and an evil spirit cannot dwell in the same person. This argument will be considered in the next chapter. We briefly point out here that such an argument may not be as strong as some suppose.

THE CASE OF THE WOMAN BENT DOUBLE

In Luke 13:10-17, we read of the Lord Jesus healing "a woman who for eighteen years had had a sickness caused by a spirit; and she was bent double, and could not straighten up at all" (13:11). The Lord further describes her as "a daughter of Abraham as she is, whom Satan has bound for eighteen long years" (13:16).

22. Henry A. Virkler and Mary B. Virkler, "Demonic Involvement in Human Life and Illness," *Journal of Psychology and Theology* 5, no. 2 (1977): 95-102.

This woman obviously was incapacitated by a demonically caused disease. It might be asserted that the spirit caused the bodily illness and then retreated, but it seems more in keeping with the idea of satanic bondage for eighteen years that the spirit continued in residence to aggravate the problem. It is obvious from the term used that she was inhabited by the demon. The expression in Greek is *pneuma echous astheneias*, which actually should be translated as "having a spirit of illness." It may refer to a sickness or a weakness, but the expression "having a spirit" is equivalent to demonization. There is no doubt that the woman was demonized.

The question is, Was she a genuine believer? The following facts seem to indicate that she was. First, she was well known in the synagogue as a person plagued by demonic illness (no objection is lodged against Christ's diagnosis) and was probably a regular attender at the services (13:10-11). Second, she knew immediately that God had healed her; and she gave Him the glory (13:13), a seeming natural response of her heart.

Third, Jesus labeled her "a daughter of Abraham as she is." This expression "daughter of Abraham" could be ethnic in that she was Jewish. However, Luke's record shows Jesus applying this term to the newly converted and remade Zaccheus: "Today salvation has come to this house, because he, too, is a son of Abraham" (Luke 19:9). We cannot understand this to mean that because he was of the lineal descent of Abraham he became saved. Jesus warned men not to think in this faulty way. The Jewish opponents of Christ were Abraham's offspring but did not possess the faith of their father Abraham (John 8:37-40). The proper conclusion is that Zaccheus became a believer in Christ that day and so salvation came *(egeneto)* to him and thus he became a son of Abraham. This, then, gives us the most likely meaning of the parallel expression used of the woman, "daughter of Abraham": she was a genuine believer. Further support is found in the expression "as she is" (Luke 13:16), a clarifying and affirming phrase meaning "truly." The Greek term, *ousan*, is similar to that used of widows who were truly widows, "widows indeed" *(ontōs,* 1 Tim. 5:3, 5).

Here we have a fairly clear case of a believer who has been demonized. The cause is not stated. The cure by Christ's authority and miraculous power is the major point. Again someone may say that demonization of believers may have been possible in the day before the indwelling Spirit was given to all believers and that the presence of the Spirit forbids the presence of a demon in the same body. As mentioned before, we will treat this question in chapter 8. But it cannot be properly held that no believer before Pentecost was permanently indwelt by the Holy Spirit. There were some who had the Holy Spirit indwelling in Old Testament days. Consider David with whom the Spirit stayed after the day of his anointing by Samuel (1 Sam. 16:13). This may have been the case with Daniel (Dan. 5:14). The Spirit also dwelt in at least some of the Old Testament prophets (1 Pet. 1:11). There may be others also. So why must we assume that this dear child of God, the woman with scoliosis, did not have the Holy Spirit within?

Though we cannot come to the settled conclusion that she was a genuine believer who was inhabited by a demon, the weight seems to balance in that direction.

THE CASE OF JUDAS ISCARIOT

Judas, the betrayer of the Lord Jesus, was a disciple into whom Satan had put thoughts to betray his teacher (John 13:2). Later in the upper room, John records, "And after the morsel, Satan then entered into him" (13:27).

One source notes, "An apostle of Jesus Christ, Judas Iscariot, companied with Him up to the last night of His life, yet Satan entered into him. He betrayed the Son of God into the hands of His enemies." This same source presents this as evidence that "believers in God have been at some time invaded by evil spirits."[23] Here the writers' theology has led them to a faulty conclusion regarding the type of evidence. They seem to believe that a genuine believer in Christ can lose his salvation. This is invalid as we have shown in chapter 3, where we treat the security of the genuine believer. Besides, there is no good evidence that Judas ever really trusted Christ. The Lord Jesus called Judas "the son of perdition," the one belonging to ruination (John 17:12), who was obviously pointed out beforehand by the Scriptures to be a betrayer (John 13:18). Judas was lost, never saved, and cannot be adduced as evidence that a believer can be demonized.

23. Ensign and Howe, p. 134.

THE CASE OF THE CORINTHIAN TONGUES SPEAKER

The Corinthian believers were confused by a strange incident in their assembly. Among them came a person who under the influence of a spirit, probably claiming the power of the Holy Spirit, spoke in a foreign language saying, "Jesus is accursed" (1 Cor. 12:3). How could this person with a language supernaturally induced say such a thing? How were they to understand this in the light of the fact that God was in that day giving the gift of tongues? If the Holy Spirit gave the gift of tongues, how could this man curse Christ?

The Corinthians were not only confused, but they were also naive and presumptuous. They supposed all miraculous tongues were of God. Paul reminded them that they should have been aware of demonically induced tongues, having observed them while in their former pagan life: "You know that when you were pagans, you were led astray to dumb idols, however you were led. Therefore I make known to you, that no one speaking by the spirit of God says, 'Jesus is accursed' " (1 Cor. 12:2-3). (This supernatural phenomenon is well known today among pagan religionists.) Notice the passive verbs describing their being led astray; these indicate control from demons who energized the idolatrous worship. This question sent to the apostle by letter from the assembly in Corinth (1 Cor. 12:1) gave him the occasion to put the whole subject of spiritual gifts in perspective. The Corinthians needed this, since they were occupied with the more spectacular gifts and not the edifying gifts. Paul also concentrated on their error in overemphasis on the gift of tongues, which caused neglect of the greater edifying gifts and gave Satan the occasion to infiltrate these believers with a demonic counterfeit.

It is quite commonly accepted that the control of the mind and the voice is a symptom of demonization, as is the case of many of the demoniacs in the gospels. Such is the case today as well. Kurt Koch gives three examples of demonic tongues, and then warns us:

> These examples should serve as a warning to all those who put so much stress on speaking in tongues. There are so many possessed people, spiritistic mediums, and magicians in the world today with an ability to speak in tongues derived from demonic

sources rather than from the Holy Spirit, that seeking this gift for ourselves can be a very dangerous occupation.[24]

It seems quite clear that the Corinthians regarded the tongues speaker as a believer, for they allowed him to be in the congregation and expected him to lead them in praise to God through the gift of tongues. Here, then, is a case of a person most likely recognized as a believer who was speaking in a demonically controlled tongue.

CONCLUSION

We have considered the major passages and cases from Scripture that have been used or may be used to support the concept that genuine believers may be demonized. Most of these cases cannot be considered valid evidence for various reasons in the context or from other biblical information. However, there are some passages that present evidence that cannot be lightly dismissed but must be considered as fairly strong evidence, such as the daughter of Abraham with a spirit of illness and the Corinthian tongues speaker. However, there still may be legitimate doubts that these are genuine examples of New Testament believers inhabited by demons. Thus we cannot conclusively say that the Bible clearly presents evidence that believers may be demonized.

In the previous chapter we came to quite a definite conclusion regarding the opposing position. The Bible does not evidence that believers cannot be demonized. Thus we are left to look for other types of evidence that may contribute to answering our question: Can genuine believers be demonized?

---

24. Kurt Koch, *Occult Bondage and Deliverance* (Grand Rapids: Kregel, 1970), p. 134. See also Virkler and Virkler, p. 100.

8

Theological Considerations

Having surveyed the major passages of Scripture that have been used for and against the possibility of demonization of believers, we must now consider the major theological arguments advanced by both positions.

When approaching this matter, we must recognize that certain theological presuppositions lie behind each position, and the logic used on either side may not be proper or precise. We should seek a fair evaluation of the arguments using Scripture as the basis of truth and logical procedure as a tool in the process. Openness of mind and balance are needed as we approach these theological considerations.

ARGUMENTS AGAINST DEMONIZATION OF BELIEVERS

The theological and logical arguments presented to support this view may be grouped under the considerations of space, ownership, identity, and presence.

SPATIAL CONSIDERATIONS

Some reason that there is not room for both the Holy Spirit and demons to inhabit the same body. Since the unbeliever does not have the Spirit, he may house demon spirits. But since the believer has the infinite Spirit of God within (Rom. 8:9), there is no room for any wicked spirits.

Spatial considerations such as dimensional limitations do not apply to the spirit world. We could ask, "How may the Spirit of God and the human spirit occupy the same space?" The question is not appropriate. Spirits do not press bodily or materially against spirits, since they have no dimensions or weight (Luke 24:39). They do not crowd one another or crowd others out of room. The Bible clearly attests to the fact that the infinite Spirit of God dwells within each believer despite our limited bodies (1 Cor. 6:19). We might also consider that enough demons dwelt in the body of one maniac to enter 2,000 swine and cause them to rush into the sea (Mark 5:13). The term "Legion" may indicate as many as 6,000 to 12,000. There was no crowding or bulging of the dimensions of the demonized man.

OWNERSHIP CONSIDERATIONS

Some may ask, "But how can one who is possessed by Christ, bought with His blood, be possessed by demons?" It is clear that once we have trusted Christ, "He delivered us from the domain of darkness, and transferred us to the kingdom of His beloved Son" (Col. 1:13). Further, we are members of His body, "which He purchased with His own blood" (Acts 20:28); and we, including our bodies, "have been bought with a price" (1 Cor. 6:20).

The problem here is a matter of semantics. The term "possessed by Christ" and the term "demon-possessed" are not used in the same manner. To be possessed by Christ is to belong to Him morally and spiritually through the purchase of His blood (Eph. 1:7; 1 Pet. 1:18-19). Christ now owns us. We are his purchased possession (Titus 2:14). To take the biblical term translated "demon-possessed" in the same fashion is a grave mistake and has no support from Scripture.

We saw in chapter 2 that *daimonizomenos* does not mean owned by a demon, but simply "demonized." This basically describes the condition of a person who is inhabited by a demon or demons and is in various degrees under control with various effects. The idea of ownership is foreign to the New Testament word and its usage. Satan and demons own nothing. God owns them. They are creatures of God. He is in control of them and determines their limitations and their destiny. They are judged by the cross of Christ, defeated, and bankrupt.

The argument from contradiction in ownership holds no weight, since it is only an apparent problem due to misstatement and faulty comparison.

IDENTITY CONSIDERATIONS

Others point out that one who is chosen "in Christ" before the creation of the world (Eph. 1:4) and placed by the Spirit "into Christ" upon trusting Him (1 Cor. 12:13; Gal. 3:26-27) can never be removed from his union with Christ and His righteousness so as to fall into demon possession. God's genuine children are secure through the grace of God, so that "whom He justified, these He also glorified" (Rom. 8:30).

It is true that genuine children of God stand forever secure in their salvation. They will with no exception arrive in glory (Rom. 5:1-10; Eph. 1:13-14; 4:30). No demonic force, no creature of any sort or rank, is able to separate us from the love of God and the life of the Savior (Rom. 8:38-39). But this is not the issue with demonization.

Again we must note that *daimonizomenos* does not mean possession or ownership, and it certainly does not mean that one demonized has no salvation or has lost his salvation. We have sufficiently treated the matter of the security of the genuine believer in the last part of chapter 3. This objection to the possible demonization of a believer is based upon a faulty concept of the meaning of "demon-possession." It cannot involve a removal from union with Christ and subsequent loss of salvation.

MORAL PRESENCE CONSIDERATIONS

This is the theological argument that is most often used and seems to carry the most weight. It is based on the seeming incompatibility of the Spirit of God, who is holy, and the spirits of demons, who are evil, dwelling in the same body. It seems morally and spiritually impossible to have both present, both residing in the same person's body. This is a very serious consideration, and we must evaluate it carefully.

A more formal and a fair presentation of the argument is in the form of the following syllogism:

MAJOR PREMISE: God cannot dwell with evil.
MINOR PREMISE: God dwells in every believer.
CONCLUSION: Therefore, a demon (evil) cannot dwell in any believer.

The syllogism is well constructed. The word "dwell" is used in all three parts. The terms are well continued. "God" is used in both premises. "Evil" is used in the major premise and in the conclusion (by use of "demon"). These are simple statements.

There are problems, however—serious problems—in the syllogism. First, the term "dwell" in the major premise is ambiguous. It is true that the psalmist says, "For Thou art not a God who takes pleasure in wickedness; no evil dwells with Thee" (Ps. 5:4). Here the word "dwells" means "sojourns," and the parallel expression (according to the structure of Hebrew poetry) in the first part of the verse confirms that the concept involved is more than just presence; it means fellowship. This is the emphasis of "sojourn" and of "takes pleasure."[1] So if the major premise is designed to mean presence only, not fellowship, it fails to represent properly the general text upon which it is based.

Second, the major premise is clearly false if it means merely presence. Presence is the usual intent of those who frame this argument. The reason it is false is that it does not fit the facts as presented in Scripture. God allows, in fact calls, Satan into His presence (Job 1:6; 2:1; Zech. 3:1-2). This does not defile God or destroy Satan. There is no incompatibility of presence, though there is incompatibility of moral nature; thus no fellowship. Further, the holy Lord Jesus ate with sinners and publicans and was not defiled thereby (Luke 15:1-2).

Further, and more germane to the issue, is the fact that the Holy Spirit (in fact the Son and the Father also) lives in the believer where there is still a sinful, evil sin nature. This is clearly seen in Romans 7 and has been treated in chapter 4 of this book. It is not impossible for the Holy Spirit to live inside the same person with an evil entity. He does so to aid us and to control us in our fight against the evil fleshly nature.

The real issue, then, is not presence but control. It is a matter of fellowship and cooperation that is impossible between good and evil, between God and demons. The person who is inhabited by demons has a demon temporarily resident within, but he is not necessarily in fellowship with the demon, cooperating with the demon, especially if he may be a believer.

It is understandable, then, that a believer may be walking in fellowship with God to resist by the indwelling Holy Spirit the sin nature within. It is conceivable also that a believer might be

---

1. See the treatment of Psalm 5:4 above.

walking in fellowship with God in order to resist by the indwelling Holy Spirit a demon within.

Some might argue that a demon, however, is different and separate from the sin nature and cannot be compared. This point is granted to some degree. They are different, but both are evil. The introduction of the evidence that the sin nature and the Holy Spirit both dwell in the same believer's body is valid in questioning the major premise. Of necessity, in the nature of a syllogism, the major premise must be general, not specifying the conclusion. It is improper to start with the premise that a demon cannot dwell in the believer and conclude with the same statement. Each premise must stand on its own and lead to, not presume, the conclusion. That is "to argue the point" or presume its truth before logical proof.

Others object by saying that the sin nature has been judged, and that is why the Spirit may dwell within. Actually the indwelling Spirit baptized the believer into Christ and thus dethroned the sin nature from ruling (Rom. 6:1-14). It may also be noted that Satan and demons were also judged by the same means, the cross of Christ (John 12:31; Col. 2:15). Therefore the Spirit may dwell in a believer to control any evil within—even a possible demon.

To conclude our evaluation of this syllogism, we must declare that the major premise is invalid; and therefore the conclusion, since it is integrally based upon it, is also invalid. The argument does not prove that an evil demon cannot reside within a genuine believer.

We must note also that to disprove an argument for the negative is not automatically to prove the contrary. By invalidating this argument we do not establish that a believer can be inhabited by a demon. This requires more and substantial evidence.

MODIFIED PRESENCE CONSIDERATIONS

There are those who allow that a demon can inhabit a genuine believer but restrict the concept of possession in terms of type of inhabiting or place of inhabiting. We must note these as modifying the concept of what it means to have a believer demonized.

Ensign and Howe hold that believers may experience invasion, obsession, and oppression, but they reject the idea that a genuine Christian can be possessed, "a very strong word indicating almost complete control of a person's body, mind, and will as in the case of Legion (Mark 5:1-16)."[2] Here the authors present a faulty concept of possession. We have seen in chapter 2 that demonization does not mean either ownership or a complete overrunning of the person's will and behavior. The man in whom was Legion is not the norm, but an extreme case. The same authors allow that though sins of the flesh are not necessarily the evidence of demonization, they "when persisted in and allowed to become habitual in the life of the Christian can bring demonic control and then invasion of the child of God."[3]

Ensign and Howe, then, allow an invading presence of demons in the believer, but not possession in an all-controlling fashion. In evaluating this position, we must remember that the issue is not presence but control. This we have noted in chapter 2 and in this chapter as we treated the argument against the Holy Spirit's and a demon's inhabiting the same person.

Unger presents another position. Though he holds that believers may be demonized or inhabited, he qualifies this view.

> It must be stressed that demons cannot indwell a Christian in the same sense the Holy Spirit indwells. God's spirit enters a believer at salvation, permanently, never to leave (Jn 14:16). A demon, by contrast, enters as a squatter and an intruder, and is subject to momentary eviction. A demon never rightfully or permanently indwells a saint, as the Holy Spirit does, and no demon can ever have any influence over any part of a Christian's life that is yielded to the Holy Spirit.[4]

To this we must agree in large part. The demon does not have the legal right to reside in a Christian, though there may be a moral reason that God has allowed it. Yet the issue is not permanency or transitoriness. The demon, if invasion has occurred, does dwell within a person and seeks to control whatever area of life or whatever behavior is not controlled by the Holy Spirit. The issue is still control, as the term *demonization* means, and not modification of presence.

2. Grayson H. Ensign and Edward Howe, *Bothered? Bewildered? Bewitched?* (Cincinnati: Recovery, 1984), p. 142.
3. Ibid.
4. Merrill F. Unger, *What Demons Can Do to Saints* (Chicago: Moody, 1977), pp. 51-52.

We should clarify here that the Holy Spirit's indwelling is a personal and eternal relationship of fellowship *(koinonia)*, a commonality of moral sphere and agreement. An evil spirit's inhabitation is an unnatural and temporal invasion of antipathy, a contradiction of moral sphere and agreement. There has been some human disagreement and action that has allowed the demonic invasion to take place with the resultant control in part and in various manifestations. There is a great difference in the relationships, and removal of the demon is possible. The Holy Spirit will never leave or forsake the believer in Christ.

Bubeck also modifies the concept of possession according to the place of habitation. He writes:

> It is my conviction that no believer can be possessed by an evil spirit in the same sense that an unbeliever can. In fact, I reject this term altogether when talking about a believer's problem with the powers of darkness. A believer may be afflicted or even controlled in certain areas of his being, but he can never be owned or totally controlled as an unbeliever can. . . .

> The moment a person becomes a believer, the Holy Spirit brings birth to his spirit. . . . The spirit of the Christian is reborn, regenerated, possessed, and sealed by the Holy Spirit in a way not enjoyed by the rest of man's being as yet. The spirit of man thus reborn becomes the Holy Spirit's unique center of control and operation within man. I do not believe that any wicked spirit can ever invade a believer's spirit. The Holy Spirit's work of new birth and His sealing presence within the spirit of man seems to preclude any presence of wicked spirit control of that part of man's being.[5]

Bubeck seems to say that the spirit of man is fully developed. He holds that the "believer's soul, containing his mind, his will, and his emotions, is in the process of being transformed" by the Spirit so he grows in grace; and the soul, along with the body, will be complete only in the resurrection.[6]

Thus Bubeck holds that a demon may invade a believer's body or soul; but he cannot invade his spirit, the perfect part of man and the domain of the Holy Spirit.

Bubeck must be commended for his writings and his work in helping men to combat demonic forces. His presentation and

5. Mark I. Bubeck, *The Adversary* (Chicago: Moody, 1975), pp. 87-88.
6. Ibid., p. 88.

his counseling commend him to the student and researcher in this area of spiritual ministry and warfare. However, there are some questionable parts of his view just cited. First, his whole perspective is based upon a questionable view of the nature of man's composition. He holds the tripartite view (that man has three parts: body, soul, and spirit) Most standard theologians will say that this has very little support in the Bible. Only one place puts the three words together—1 Thessalonians 5:23. Those who hold this view say, as Bubeck, that the soul contains the rational facilities for contact with ourselves and persons around us and that the spirit provides contact with God. Nowhere does the Bible say such a thing. How shall we understand the reference by Christ to the command, "And you shall love the Lord your God with all your heart, and with all your soul, and with all your mind, and with all your strength" (Mark 12:30)? Why did He omit the supposed most important part of man in relation to God, the spirit? What are these other terms—heart, mind, strength? Are these to be taken as parts of man? It is better to take both Paul and Jesus as referring to the totality of man by multiplying the terms. They were not at the time defining the composition of man's nature. If so, then Paul omitted some parts.

We may better understand that man is two parts—body and spirit, and that his whole being is termed soul. This fits Genesis 2:7: "Then the Lord God formed man of dust from the ground [body], and breathed into his nostrils the breath of life [spirit]; and man became a living being [soul; Heb., *nephesh*]." This latter term is used also of the whole of man (Gen. 12:5; 46:15, etc.) and of animal life (Gen. 9:4). Genesis clearly presents man as material body, related to the earth, and as spirit, related to God.

Second, it is very difficult to differentiate between spirit and soul. They are both spiritual in nature according to the tripartite theory. How may there be two spiritual entities, both human, within man? But some point to Hebrews 4:12. This is supposed to see a division of spirit and soul by the Word of God. However, the Greek term *(diikneomai)* means to penetrate or pierce, as of missiles.[7] It does not mean to separate two different parts.

---

7. William F. Arndt and F. Wilbur Gingrich, *A Greek-English Lexicon of the New Testament* (Chicago: U. of Chicago, 1952), p. 194.

The idea is that the Word of God penetrates the deepest recesses of a man's being. Note the judging of "the thoughts of the heart," another reference to man's innermost being, an expansion of the same concept of penetration without any hiding of an inner secret from God.

Third, when Jesus said, "That which is born of the Spirit is spirit," He was not defining the part of man that was missing or impaired but describing the nature of the birth: it was not to be confused with the physical, or merely human. New birth is from God, not man. The new birth actually creates within the believer a renewal of the moral base of his whole person that allows him to exercise his reason, emotion, and will in harmony with God as he yields to the indwelling Holy Spirit, who created him anew. God can now work in us that we might will (rational choice) and do with God (Phil. 2:13). We have no ground for saying that man's spirit does not possess reason, emotions, or will, but that these are capacities of a separate entity called the soul. What is the spirit if it is not the reflection of the nature of God, created of God in Adam and born of God and involved in a moral renewal when a fallen man trusts Christ (Eph. 4:24)? Our whole spiritual natures are born again, not just part of our person. Scripture never speaks of just the spirit renewed and not the soul. Bubeck refers to the mistaken view of Watchman Nee for support. This view has been carried by some to logical extremes that have led to distracting and destructive practices that Bubeck would never own or support.[8]

Fourth, we cannot support from the Bible that man's spirit is nonexistent or totally inoperative before the new birth. The total man is dead with respect to God and spiritual truth in that he is separated from God and does not operate in God's moral sphere (Eph. 2:1-3). Are men less than total humans until regeneration? Neither does the Bible suggest that anything in the human being is perfect now. Our legal standing and acceptance is perfect through the provision of the righteousness of Christ, but we must be developed in the totality of our person now

8. See Watchman Nee, *Release of the Spirit* (Indianapolis: Sure Foundation, 1965) and Witness Lee, *The Key to Experiencing Christ—The Human Spirit* (Los Angeles: The Stream, n.d.). The tripartite view of man's nature has been taken to an extreme so as to deny the legitimacy of rational powers. They are considered soulish and carnal. The spirit of man must be exercised and must break through the soulish barrier to do the work of God—and this in mystical, nonrational fashion.

awaiting rapture or resurrection for the perfecting of both body and spirit (1 John 3:1-2, 5; Phil. 3:20).

Unger holds a view similar to Bubeck's regarding the trichotomous (tripartite) view of man and also says that "a demon may invade and cause upheaval and chaos in the believer through his *body* and *soul,*" but "that the new *nature* and the Spirit-indwelt human *spirit* cannot be invaded by demonic powers."[9]

We considered all this related material above, since some hold that a demon may invade a Christian's body and soul but not his spirit. This suggests a difference of location that is spatial and explained by different parts of man. Although this may seem to help some in explaining the mechanics of demonization of believers, it may confuse others. With some, such as the mystical followers of Watchman Nee, it could even give demons the opportunity to insert nonrational impulses to "the spirit," bypassing the mind and its rational use of the Bible.

Again we must be reminded that the issue is not so much presence in a certain part of the person but control of the person to some degree that evidences demonization.

CONCLUSION

None of the logical or theological arguments considered exclude the possibility of the demonization of a believer. Our emotions may dictate that we find some proof against this possibility, but scriptural and theological evidence is not sufficient to allow us to exclude it. Some seek to modify the effect, and perhaps the uneasiness and fear, by limiting the place in the believer where a demon can dwell. But the basic question we must continue to face is whether a demon can actually inhabit a believer and to some degree control his thoughts and actions.

ARGUMENTS FOR DEMONIZATION OF BELIEVERS

The arguments along this line are not well organized. They are general expressions of the possibility, often from some presumption made on grounds other than sound theology. But some have more basis for consideration than the rest. So these must be considered, since men offer them as evidence that Christians can be demonized.

9. Unger, *What Demons Can Do to Saints,* p. 77.

SALVATION LOST

It may be argued that if a believer persists in sin and if that sin leads to distrust and unbelief in Christ, this results in rejection of Christ and the loss of salvation. In the process demons may possess the person either before or after the loss of salvation.

This view stems from several erroneous concepts. First, the position that one who has once trusted Christ can ever lose his salvation is built upon a misunderstanding of the grace of God, the legal standing believers have before God, the clear statements of the Bible regarding the security of genuine believers, and the experience of believers. These are matters we have sufficiently answered in previous chapters.

Second, this view again takes demon possession to mean ownership by Satan and precludes salvation or ownership by Christ. We have shown this to be a misunderstanding of demonization *(daimonizomai),* which is basically invasion and some resultant control with various manifestations. It never means ownership. The problem is semantic as well as theological.

Third, if the person is possessed, according to this view he is no longer a Christian. Assuming that view for the sake of argument, we answer that if that is the case, we cannot have a Christian who is possessed.

SATAN'S POWER

By some Satan is pictured as so powerful that he may take people captive at his will and whim (referring to 2 Tim. 2:26). The openings afforded by a believer's sin may give Satan the opportunity to send a demon to inhabit the believer's body, such as with King Saul. Thus, believers must be vigilant at all times to guard against such a takeover.

We have treated 2 Timothy 2:26 in the previous chapter. It does not specifically say demons enter the believer, and it does not definitely refer to Satan's accomplishing the captivity. It may refer to the deliverance from Satan by God.

Further, there is no specific statement to the effect that believers must not sin lest Satan invade. Take advantage, confuse, deceive, accuse, tempt—yes; but invade? No specific Scripture may legitimately and definitely be taken along this line. If demons do invade a believer, it is not just because Satan is so powerful that God could not prevent it or that the believer could not resist it (James 4:7). As with King Saul, invasion might possibly come after persistent sin and only with God's allowing it in unusual cases. We should not live in dire fear of the power of Satan. He can make no attack without God's overall control, and he is limited in what he can do, as in the case of Job (Job 1:12; 2:6). It is understandable that if the Christian walks in the flesh and participates in activities that Satan promotes, the door is opened for Satan's oppression. But if the Christian walks in the Spirit, obeying the Word of God, and does not presume to test the Lord, then the Lord will protect him from the enemy and certainly from invasion of wicked spirits. The armor of God is the provision by which we stand against the forces of Satan in this evil day (Eph. 6:10-12). In any case, nothing can separate us from Christ or from His love (Rom. 8:38-39).

SIN'S CHASTISEMENT

Some hold that it is theologically reasonable with biblical example that God may chastise believers for their continued and blatant sinning by sending demons to invade. Such was the case with Saul, they say. We treated the case of King Saul in some detail in chapter 7. We recall that there may be some question as to whether the demon actually invaded Saul, though that seems to be the case. Some may point out that this was a special case, since he as the king was held more responsible. The real point, however, is that Saul was a believer and seems to have been inhabited, at least upon occasion, by an evil spirit from the Lord (1 Sam. 16:14; 18:10). This is obviously a chastisement from God for Saul's sin. It allows the possibility that God may use this method for disciplining other believers.

Others see the principle of disciplining through invading spirits called "tormentors." W. L. McLeod writes, "In the teaching of Jesus there is a clear indication that an unforgiving spirit may result in God delivering us over to demon powers in some degree. . . . The 'tormentors' in this case would be demon powers."[10]

---

10. W. L. McLeod, *Demonism Among Evangelicals and the Way to Victory* (Saskatoon, Sask.: Western Tract Mission, 1975), p. 106.

He refers to Matthew 18:21-35, and particularly to verses 34-35, where Jesus tells the story of the rebuke and punishment:

And his Lord, moved with anger, handed him over to the torturers until he should repay all that was owed him. So shall My heavenly Father also do to you, if each of you does not forgive his brother from your heart.

Here is a cultural way of exacting a debt from a person by handing him over to a jailer or torturer *(basanistes)* who was to exact from the debtor everything possible.[11] This word is used only here in the New Testament, so we have no biblical norm of usage to say that this was used of angels or demons. It was used in an extracanonical book, the Apocalypse of Peter, of avenging angels.[12] This is not a reliable guide to how it should be taken in Matthew's account.

It is clear that Jesus was telling an earthly story, and the tormentors were human. The question is, in the application He makes, Who were the tormentors that His Father would use with unforgiving believers? It does seem to be a believer that Jesus is describing. His great debt had been forgiven, the debt of sin's guilt. Jesus is answering Peter to illustrate the necessity of forgiveness of a brother.

We must carefully note that the Lord Jesus does not specifically say that believers are handed over to tormentors to exact the debt. He merely says, "So shall My heavenly Father also do to you." In the parable, the debt was the original weighty debt, not the debt of forgiveness. The debtor did not owe forgiveness to the master, but to the fellow-slave. There is not a direct parallel. Our original debt of sin has been fully forgiven by the blood of Christ, and we do not forgive in order to be forgiven of this guilt. That forgiveness is offered freely through trusting in the Savior and His perfect payment of our debt on the cross. We do owe others forgiveness, since we have been forgiven so great a debt. Lack of forgiveness can give Satan an opportunity (2 Cor. 2:10-11; Eph. 4:26-27). But there is no mention of demonization as the consequence. This is a great presumption.

---

11. Arndt and Gingrich, p. 134.
12. Ibid.

What is the Lord saying about the Father's treatment of believers who do not forgive one another? There is a loss of fellowship and a kind of imprisonment in isolation from that fellowship when we continue in unconfessed sin and do not forgive others. This deals with forgiveness in the family and the restoration of fellowship, just as the Lord taught in His pattern prayer: "And forgive us our debts, as we also have forgiven our debtors. And do not lead us into temptation, but deliver us from evil" (the evil one, Matt. 6:12-13). We may give the enemy an opportunity to tempt us, but there is no mention of invasion or terrible assault as if God would use demons to be tormentors. Demons are not found in the context of the parable Jesus told.

Homer A. Kent explains that this passage could not refer to the eternal ruin of a genuine believer, nor can it refer to some nonscriptural purgatory. "However, if we view the torments as temporal evils visited upon unforgiving believers by their heavenly Father, the previous difficulties are avoided."[13] He points out that the word for tormentors "is derived from the verb *basanizo,* which is used to describe sickness (Mt. 4:24; 8:6) and adverse circumstances (Mt. 14:24). . . . Such torments God may use to chasten and produce a proper spirit among his children (1 Cor. 11:30-32.)"[14]

We conclude that there is no theological or textual certainty that demons will invade as tormentors the bodies of believers who sin. It is so that God uses demons to chastise His people on occasion, but we cannot show with certainty that demons invade believers to torment them as a regular way of operating. Having said this, we must remember that Saul still stands as a very likely incident of such a case and that Paul did deliver some to Satan for the destruction of the flesh for spiritual discipline (1 Cor. 5:5; 1 Tim. 1:20). What we lack here is the *certainty,* not the possibility, of demonic invasion of belivers.

SEEKING SPECIAL GIFTS

Kurt Koch has already warned us, from his approximately fifty years of counseling the demonically oppressed, that seek-

13. Homer A. Kent, Jr., "The Gospel According to Matthew," in *The Wycliffe Bible Commentary,* ed. Charles F. Pfeiffer and Everett F. Harrison (Chicago: Moody, 1962), p. 962.
14. Ibid., pp. 962-63.

ing the gifts of tongues and prophecy may likely lead to opening one up to invasion by an evil, counterfeiting spirit.[15] Merrill F. Unger also warns against the intrusion of spirits who counterfeit spiritual gifts with mediumistic gifts:

> Mediumistic gifts that imitate the gifts of the Holy Spirit are counterfeit. This observation alone should convince the believer of the great importance of knowing *exactly* what the Scriptures teach concerning these gifts so that he will be protected from deception resulting from falling prey to the counterfeit.[16]

Unger, as well as other recognized theologians, classifies some of the original spiritual gifts as "sign gifts" or miraculous gifts that confirmed the gospel as it was introduced into an unbelieving world. He asks:

> The apostles had these gifts. But do we have apostles today? Do we need the sign gifts of an apostle now? Has not Christianity, like the infallible, inspired revelation upon which it has been founded, been authenticated by miracle and fulfilled prophecy? Have not God's people for centuries walked by faith and not by sight (2 Cor. 5:7)? Has that situation suddenly changed?
>
> Unless the nature and purpose of these gifts in the apostolic church are clearly seen from the Word of God, do we not as God's people run a grave risk of mistaking mediumistic magic for miracles by the Holy Spirit? Is it not perilous to claim that *all* the gifts in the apostolic church should be exercised in the church today?[17]

Unger refers to such gifts as tongues, healing, prophecy, a message of knowledge, and apostleship. There is strong biblical evidence that such gifts ceased with the apostolic age or very shortly thereafter.[18] Mediumistic gifts are clearly demonic as seen from their association with witchcraft and sorcery and their severe denunciation in Scripture.

---

15. Kurt Koch, *Occult Bondage and Deliverance* (Grand Rapids: Kregel, 1970), p. 134. See also chapter 4 of this present book.
16. Unger, *What Demons Can Do to Saints,* p. 160.
17. Ibid., p. 161.
18. John C. Whitcomb, "Does God Want Christians to Perform Miracles Today?" *Grace Journal* 12 (Fall 1971):3. See also Robert L. Thomas, *Understanding Spiritual Gifts,* (Chicago: Moody, 1978) and Gilbert B. Weaver, "Tongues Shall Cease," *Grace Journal* 16 (Winter 1973):1.

Further evidence of the demonic character of mediumistic powers appears in their close association with the pagan ritual of primitive tribes the world over. . . .

What is tragic is that many people in so-called Christian lands, which have become honeycombed with occultism, frequently mistake such mediumistic abilities for genuine spiritual gifts.[19]

When biblical doctrine is given second place and experience is emphasized, when believers do not stop to check out thoroughly what God has already revealed in His Word, and when they seek an experience or a confirmation of their acceptance with God, then they open themselves to counterfeit gifts, which the deceiver is waiting to give to the naive. This author has tested fifteen cases of tongues-speaking and found them all to be counterfeit, fourteen from demonic spirits and one from psychological pressure. The Bible warns us to test the spirits to see if they are from God (1 John 4:1-4). This is necessary when believers claim special gifts and a message from God, often putting their message on the level of an authoritative word from God. We cannot afford to be noncritical and gullible when it comes to such claims. In testing such, we are not grieving the Spirit but obeying what He has told us to do in His inspired Word.

We must say that there is danger in seeking gifts that may not be from God. Knowing that the counterfeiter is lurking to snare us, to distract and debilitate us, we must be on our guard. It may be that demons would invade those who let their guard down and are "open for whatever God has for them." We can never abandon the rational faculties and the reasoned approach to the Bible lest we defect from the truth and open ourselves to demons.

There is in 1 Corinthians 12:1-4 (treated in chap. 7) the suggestion that a believer spoke in an unlearned foreign language and cursed the Lord Jesus under the influence of an evil spirit. It seems that the control of the voice must be from within the person. We may say, then, extending the evidence theologically, that it is not impossible for a Christian seeking special gifts to become invaded by evil, counterfeiting spirits. There is no

---

19. Unger, *What Demons Can Do to Saints,* p. 162.

certainty that this will happen in every case, but the danger is such that Christians need to exercise all caution.

SENSIBLE DEDUCTION

Conrad Murrell, who has had a rather extensive ministry in counseling the demon oppressed, suggests, "It would seem not only scriptural but completely reasonable that those out of whom we are to cast demons are either already God's children or those who become God's children in the process of deliverance. This has been my experience."[20]

He finds the scriptural grounds for his position in Mark 7:25-26 where a Syrophoenician woman asked Christ to cast a demon out of her daughter. Jesus said, "Let the children be satisfied first, for it is not good to take the children's bread and throw it to the dogs." Murrell explains: "Jesus called demonic deliverance bread for the children. It is only for the children."[21]

Murrell seems to miss the point that Jesus came to the Jewish people first. They were the covenant children of Abraham. This Gentile woman approached Him as "Son of David," a strictly Jewish term referring to Him as the king of Israel according to the Davidic Covenant (Matt. 15:22). Jesus told her, "I was sent only to the lost sheep of the house of Israel" (Matt. 15:24). She changed her approach to, "Lord, help me," as a Gentile should, and then she asked for the crumbs from the Jewish table to be given to her as a Gentile, whom the Jews called "dogs" (Matt. 15:27). Her humility, her teachableness, and her faith were rewarded by the removal of the demon from her daughter.

But are we to limit what Jesus called "bread" to the casting out of demons, or is it wider than that—the Messiah, His kingdom, the forgiveness of sins, and attendant blessings? It seems to be the wider concept. Such great blessings were designed first for the Jewish people and then extended to the Gentiles (John 1:11-13; Rom. 15:8-9).

"The children" in this case were not necessarily believers but "the lost sheep of the house of Israel." The implication is that these were lost and not saved. We cannot declare that relief

20. Conrad Murrell, *Practical Demonology* (Pineville, La.: Saber, n.d.), pp. 46-47.
21. Ibid., p. 47.

from demons is only for Christians; therefore believers have been and can be demonized.

We must again ask the question, Were those whom the Lord Jesus healed and relieved from demonization all unbelievers? This may seem unreasonable to some.

SPECIAL OCCULT INTEREST

It seems theologically correct to assume that God's warnings against all forms of idolatry and occult practice is not in vain. What men sow, they also reap. Those who desire the services of false gods or demons may indeed receive such services. God's warnings are stern, and they are given to prevent giving to false gods the glory that is due the true God alone (Ex. 20:2-5) and to prevent corruption and devastation for God's people. In connection with the second commandment, God sternly warns, "You shall not worship them or serve them; for I, the Lord your God, am a jealous God, visiting the iniquity of the fathers on the children, on the third and fourth generations of those who hate Me." God hates idolatry, and He labels occult practices—such as divination (fortune-telling), witchcraft, sorcery (magic), spell-casting, mediumship, or seeking to contact the dead—as destestable things of the pagans (Deut. 18:9-13). God's people are to avoid and detest such abominations. The New Testament also carries strict warnings. Paul warned the Corinthians about participating in idolatrous festivities in a passage we treated in chapter 7:

> I do not want you to become sharers *[koinōnous]* with demons. You cannot drink the cup of the Lord and the cup of demons; you cannot partake of the table of the Lord and the table of demons. Or do we provoke the Lord to jealousy? We are not stronger than He, are we? (1 Cor. 10:20b-22)

How are we to take these warnings? Is it not true that God gave men over to the type of idolatry they chose and to the degradation and bondage that it brings with it? Consider God's stringent action described in Romans 1:21-32, particularly the statements beginning with, "Therefore God gave them over . . ." Is it logical for us to allow that God would chastise through circumstances, illness, and even death but that He would never allow demonization as a form of punishment for the unsaved or discipline for the saved? Why exclude only this means of discipline? If one objects that this involves the loss of salvation or the transfer of ownership, he has misunderstood the meaning of demonization, which we treated in chapter 2 and described as the inhabiting of one or more demons who control to various degrees and in various ways those whom they inhabit.

It is not theologically unreasonable, in view of all the facts we have considered, to think that God might discipline idolatrous and occult practices with just what the seekers desire—special attention from demonic forces—and the tragic results of such clearly forbidden seeking then follows—demonic invasion.

SUMMARY

The theological arguments that support the possibility of the demonization of believers are not all equally strong. Arguments based on the possibility of the loss of salvation and on the overpowering strength of Satan do not have biblical base. They must be rejected. The remainder of the arguments carry more weight. Though there may be points of weakness in each, there may be some good basis for saying that demonization is possible as a form of God's chastisement for sin, for seeking special gifts, and for seeking occult knowledge and power. It is also somewhat reasonable to suspect that not all those delivered from demons in the Lord Jesus' ministry were unbelievers. However, a degree of uncertainty still forbids a definite conclusion that believers may be demonized.

CONCLUSION

From the survey and analysis for arguments pro and con, we conclude that we cannot say with reasonable certainty that either position is correct. Arguments that some regard as good or indisputable evidence just do not carry the issue. There are flaws, or holes, or reasonable questions about each of the arguments on either side.

Just as with the considerations from the biblical passages, we must recognize that we do not have all the evidence we should have or would like to have to come to a settled conclusion. This may upset some people, but it is better to admit to uncertainty than to take a position and be found wrong and misleading in the light of reality. Though God's Word gives us clear information for the necessities of truth (such as the nature of God, man, sin, salvation, moral decisions) and sufficient information for living and operating properly in this world (principles for interpersonal relationships, educational procedures, extended ministries, etc.), it does not answer all questions as specifically as we might desire. But the Bible does give us parameters to define and recognize believers, demonization, and the resources and remedies God supplies. In our next chapter, we shall consider what additional sources of information are available to us and how to handle that information.

9

Clinical Considerations

We are ready to consider the contribution of clinical evidence to our search for the answer to our principle question, Can Christians be demonized? In the second part of this book we have sought evidence from biblical and theological considerations. We have found that though there is a great deal of information to consider and though men adduce evidence of varying weight, yet we could not come to a definite conclusion. We now must seek what other valid evidence there might be that could aid us in our quest to answer this important and practical question.

When we seek what may be called "clinical evidence," we are really looking at information that may legitimately be gathered and evaluated from clients and counselors who have been involved in handling demonic oppression. This general approach to acquiring evidence is commonly used and accepted in areas of medicine, counseling, and human services. It deals with personal, practical, and scientific approaches to everyday issues. It seeks to deal with the facts so that they may be analyzed and used in beneficial procedures.

In this chapter we will consider the place of reason and experience, an analogy to clarify, and the type of evidence needed to determine whether Christians can be demonized. In the next chapter we shall consider case studies of demonized persons. We hope this will be accepted as a legitimate and practical procedure in our search.

THE PLACE OF REASON AND EXPERIENCE

When we consider the proper place of human reason and experience, we should avoid the extremes and recognize the biblical balance. One extreme considers reason and experience as the only reliable source of factual evidence and truth. Thoughtful evangelicals would not accept this position. The Bible says that man's resources do not begin to know the mind of God, but that revelation is required (1 Cor. 2:9-11). Others deny any place to reason and experience in determining spiritual truth. In their opinion, these are rendered totally unreliable by the Fall and sin of man. They forget that men are not totally illogical and that experience may help us to understand truth in the world, as does scientific investigation. They also use their eyes and ears and reason in the practical matters and choices of life.

A mediating though improper position holds that reason and experience should be accorded an equal place with the Scriptures in determining the truth of God, and that God gives experiences that should be heeded as normative truth. Actually human resources cannot begin to be placed on the same level as God's revealed truth. God's knowledge is infinite, absolute, and infallible. Man's knowledge is finite, relative, and fallible. They cannot even be placed on a continuum. (This does not imply contradiction in true knowledge.) Therefore, we cannot allow human reason or experience to determine ultimate truth about God or judge His revelation in the Bible. We must not base biblical doctrine on human experience.

There is a legitimate place for human reason and experience, however, and we must consider that before we proceed to clinical evidence.

THE VALIDITY OF HUMAN REASON AND EXPERIENCE

There is a biblical basis and a practical basis for the use of human reason and experience.

Biblical basis. Reason is a gift from God. It is part of the image of God created in Adam's person and passed on to every person procreated in the image of God. With it Adam heard and responded to God. With it Eve listened and succumbed to the temptations of Satan. God had expected of Adam a positive response to the reasonable duties and limitations given him.

Even after the Fall, God reasoned with him and expected him to understand and obey. Even to sinful Israel God said, "Come now, and let us reason together" (Isa. 1:18). The prophets and the apostles appeal to believers' reasoning and explain God's requirements. Gordon H. Clark made a case for "straight-line" logic as inherent in God and in man made in God's image.[1]

Experiences may be used by God to help us understand the truth He has revealed. The truth of God's salvation revealed in the gospel is experienced when applied to the individual upon his faith. It is a by-faith salvation designed to be apprehended and experienced by faith ("from faith to faith," Rom. 1:16-17). Paul expects us to "not be foolish, but understand what the will of the Lord is" (Eph. 5:17). The Holy Spirit will control the yielded and obedient believer so that his reason and experiences will increasingly come into conformity with the mind of God as revealed in the Bible (2 Cor. 3:18; Eph. 5:18). We are to present our bodies, mind included, to God to prove by experience *(dokimazein)* the will of God (Rom. 12:2). And there are many other evidences that God would have us to use our reason to extend biblical truth into our lives.

Practical basis. There are basic practical uses of reason and experience. First, they may be used as confirmation of truth. They do not create truth, but they may support by research and logical presentation the evidence of God's truth. We can do this by noticing the design in nature that evidences the biblical truth that God is the intelligent First Cause of the world (Rom. 1:19-20). We can rationally perceive and apply the promises of God and experience their fulfillment in our lives. We are exhorted by the psalmist, "O taste and see that the Lord is good" (Ps. 34:8). Jesus encouraged us to pray in accord with His revealed Word: "If you abide in Me, and My words abide in you, ask whatever you wish, and it shall be done for you" (John 15:7). We experience His faithfulness in answering prayer.

Second, reason and experience may be used as the expression of truth. When we have trusted Christ and are walking in the light of His truth, then we love other believers. The reality of God's love toward us may be operative in us as we love others

---

1. Gordon H. Clark, "God and Logic," *The Trinity Review* 16 (November/ December 1980), excerpted from *Language and Theology* (Phillipsburg, N.J.: Presbyterian and Reformed, 1979).

who are also born of God. "We love because He first loved us" (1 John 4:19; see also 5:1-2).

Third, our reason and experience may be used to test the truth of facts presented to us. Claims to truth must be tested by application of the truth of the Word of God to life situations, such as in the testing of false teachers (1 John 4:1-6). The parameters of the revealed Word are to check the parameters of experience as to their validity and conformity with revealed truth.

LIMITATIONS OF REASON AND EXPERIENCE

Though we have touched upon this above, we can summarize the shortcomings of these human resources.

Creaturely limitations. As mere creatures we have limited access to information around us. Our understanding of the Word of God is limited to our acquaintance and proper reasoning upon the meaning and application of the Bible. Our proper evaluation of the facts in the world, as in scientific investigation, is limited. Our assessment of factual information may be faulty or perhaps relatively accurate; but it is relative, not absolute. There is absolute truth found in God's revelation. There is also relative or factual truth found in God's world. Both must be interpreted properly. Our application of God's written truth and truth in the world may be limited by our lack of perception and ability.

Sinful limitation. Unfallen angels are the only sinless persons among created beings. All others are corrupted by sin. This depravity prevents our thinking, feeling, and willing properly. Only through regeneration and the filling of the Spirit can we begin to use our God-given faculties properly. The personal, sinful limitations still remain in some degree even with the believer who is walking in the Spirit. Walking in the Spirit (Gal. 5:16-17) does not guarantee perfection in all aspects of life. The Spirit is the infinitely wise and powerful God, but He has finite and imperfect instruments. Paul admitted that he had not come near such a thing, and he expected believers to continue to press on toward maturity in attitude and action (Phil. 3:13-16). Peter says, "Grow in the grace and knowledge of our Lord and Savior Jesus Christ" (2 Pet. 3:18). Growth implies imperfection. We can make practical mistakes and misjudgments, even as believers who are filled with the Spirit. Of course, when filled with the Spirit, the believer will not sin (Gal. 5:16-17). We are to work out differences with the mind of Christ as God works in us to will and accomplish His good pleasure (Phil. 2:12-13).

All of us have biases. Some are honest due to ignorance. This ignorance may be due to lack of information or lack of skills or tools (such as not knowing Hebrew and Greek to gain better insight into Scripture). Honest bias may be due to lack of experience as well. Not all teach or counsel equally well due to differences in opportunities and development.

But there are dishonest biases also. These may stem from prejudice and selfishness that lead to opinionated or precipitous judgments and actions. They may stem from fear to face the facts and from defense mechanisms. They may also stem from the pressure to conform to society and popular opinion or acceptance. Further, we are open to false influences from men and demons.

Summary. Reason and experience may be helpful tools to extend our understanding of the facts of the world around us and to apply the truth of revelation to life. However, they have serious limitations and must be checked by the Word of God and with the aid of godly counsel.

An Analogy to Clarify

When we consider tapping clinical evidence to help us in determining whether believers can be demonized, we are not facing a unique problem. Other questions may be solved by a combination of scriptural and clinical data. If we use biblical parameters and clinical parameters, in the place where they overlap or contribute to the same matter we can come to some possibly valid and practical conclusion. In other words, we can take the biblical description of a believer and the biblical understanding of the nature of disease, and we can take clinical information about a disease for comparison. If we find that a believer has such a disease, we have evidence for saying that believers can have that disease. When we are done, we do not have a biblical doctrine; but we have used biblical doctrine in application to an experiential investigation. With proper validation, our conclusion may be accepted as fact, even though it is not taught specifically in the Bible.

ANALOGY WITH CANCER

For the sake of understanding the process of dealing with both biblical and clinical parameters, we might pose the question, Can a Christian have cancer? Before jumping to conclusions, we must investigate the facts. How shall we go about solving this question? There are several steps in the process: first we must consider the biblical parameters, then the clinical parameters, and finally come to a reasoned conclusion in keeping with both sets of evidence.

Biblical evidence. At this point we will not belabor the consideration with all the biblical proof needed, since some of it is quite obvious. From the Bible we must define a Christian. This can be done quite well. We have sought a rather complete definition to aid us in our search by adducing the definition in chapter 3, "What Is a Believer?"

From the Bible also we must consider the concept of disease. In general, disease is a result of the entrance of sin into the human race. Now it is part of the natural course of life. Not all disease is a direct result of an individual's sin, but God has allowed disease as one of the results of sin and a means of carrying out the sentence of death to all who participate in Adam's sin (Rom. 5:12-14). It may also be used as a loving discipline for God's children (1 Cor. 11:30-32; 2 Cor. 12:7-10). Though Christ's redemption provides the immediate forgiveness and justification needed to stand right with God, yet some effects of sin, such as disease and the presence of the sin nature, continue to plague even Christians until the redemption of our bodies (Rom. 8:10, 18-23). Are Christians members of the human race that is plagued by disease and death? They certainly are!

It is conceivable and demonstrable that believers may experience sickness and death. This is evident from both the Bible and human experience. The question remains, Can Christians have cancer?

Clinical evidence. Our next step in solving the problem is to investigate actual experiential data to see if there is any genuine evidence that believers have ever had cancer. This requires identifying the presence of cancer and certifying that the person afflicted is a genuine Christian. How shall we proceed?

From clinical or experiential evidence, we must determine

the presence of cancer cells. The marks of cancer by this time are quite obvious by scientific means. There must be an investigation of the afflicted body part through a test called biopsy. A sample piece of tissue or of the blood must come under laboratory scrutiny by a technician who can recognize the presence of cancer cells. The characteristics of the cells are compared with those of cancer cells. A determination is made and may be verified by other means of testing and by other observers. A basically reliable conclusion may thus be reached.

From interview and observation, we can determine whether any of those afflicted are genuine Christians. We could go to cancer clinics to gather this information. We should look for evidence, biblically and practically, to see if any person afflicted by cancer is actually a Christian. This evidence should be verified by other means and by other observers.

If we apply the two above clinical tests along with the biblical guidelines we have established above, and if we find that a person who has cancer is also a Christian, we have the beginning of evidence that a Christian may have cancer. If we find several other fairly certain cases, we have a stronger case. Now if several independent researchers applying similar methods also come to the same findings, we have a very strong basis for moving to a valid, reasoned conclusion.

Reasoned conclusion. Having properly considered the biblical parameters that describe believers and diseases, and having properly investigated the scientific evidence for the presence of cancer, we may come to the valid conclusion that Christians can have cancer. Of course we know many cases where Christians have suffered from cancer. Some may have been healed and others not. But the above procedure describes the biblical and scientific basis on which we may validly conclude that Christians can have cancer.

When we have concluded, we do not have the freedom to say that the Bible teaches that Christians can have cancer. It is not a matter of biblical doctrine or revealed truth because the Bible does not clearly teach that. What we do have is truth in the real world that we have discovered by investigation of both biblical and clinical evidence. It is useful and practical truth. After all, not all truth that can be known is found in the Bible.

Practical response. Now suppose someone would declare that Christians cannot have cancer because the Bible does not say so. Not only would he be improperly implying that the Bible supports his position, but he would be arguing from silence, the lack of statement or direct evidence. Such an argument is logically very weak. But some will say that you would expect God to clarify such an important issue; and if He didn't say Christians could have cancer, we may deduce that they couldn't have cancer. This is weak. We could very easily argue the opposite: that if God didn't say a Christian couldn't have cancer, we might expect that he could.

And supposing someone would declare that Christians cannot have cancer, although the evidence is abundant that they can. If those afflicted with cancer believed such a "doctrine," they would have trouble with saying that they were Christians. This position would allow doubt and confusion in the hearts and minds of Christians, not only those suffering with the disease but also those who love and care for them.

We can see that if biblically and clinically it has been established that genuine believers may have cancer and some still preach that Christians cannot, they are fair to neither the biblical or clinical evidence; nor are they fair to those Christians suffering with cancer. In fact, they have added greatly to their distress. They may have played into demonic hands in that they accuse and judge the brethren. Such erroneous teaching is unconscienable! Such persons must sweep aside their prejudices and concern for their reputations. They must consider the facts as they are, admit their ignorance, confess their improper and false teaching, and turn to help the afflicted Christians with openness of mind and concern of heart.

APPLICATION TO DEMONIZATION OF BELIEVERS

The parallel between the issues of cancer and demonization may be obvious to some readers by this time, but a brief demonstration of the legitimacy is in order. We may just as surely use the same procedure to determine in practical fashion, not of theory but of reality in the facts as they are, whether a Christian can be demonized.

Biblical evidence. Again, we can determine from the Bible how we can detect a genuine Christian. Chapter 3 of this book may be a guide here. Pastors, Christian counselors, and Christian workers do this all the time as a proper part of discipleship and loving care. We also have the description of demonization from the Bible. Chapter 2 deals with this adequately. There are fairly sure traits of demon inhabitation that may be discerned.

Is the Christian a member of a race that is subject to demonic opposition? Of course! In fact, the Christian is a special target of satanic and demonic opposition. Chapter 4 dealt with such spiritual warfare. Is there any biblical statement or properly deduced theological evidence that would lead us to conclude that Christians cannot be demonized? The evidence is inadequate. But there are several indications that such might be possible. Chapters 6, 7, and 8 treated these matters.

So we have the biblical parameters that describe a Christian and a demonized person, and allow that a Christian is subject to demonic attack and direct influence.

Clinical evidence. If we find by application of the biblical parameters that certain persons are demonized, we could proceed to test by biblical parameters if the person is a genuine Christian. If we find that he is a Christian, then we have one possible case of a demonized Christian. This is only a beginning of evidence. Should several others be found, the evidence is strengthened. If other independent researchers using the same procedure should find similar information, the case is strengthened further. As the evidence builds, we could postulate a fairly certain conclusion.

Reasoned conclusion. Having researched the evidence in broad fashion by proper application of both biblical and clinical parameters, we may come to the valid conclusion that Christians can be demonized. When we say this, we cannot say that this is biblical doctrine or theological deduction from biblical evidence. We recognize the lack of conclusive evidence in the Bible on this issue and would not elevate the conclusion to the stature of biblical truth. But we have found the factual truth to be that Christians can be and have been demonized.

Practical response. Now suppose some would teach that the Bible declares that a Christian cannot be demonized. In such a case, he would be unfair not only to biblical evidence and to proper theological reasoning, but he would be misleading men by elevating his inadequate conclusions to the stature of biblical doctrine. He would need to lay aside his prejudices and pride, recognize his lack of information, and change his attitude and teaching on this matter.

Again, if some would teach that a genuine believer cannot be demonized, he may cause great psychological and spiritual harm to the Christian who is demonized. He helps the enemy to continue his accusations and condemnations. For if a person finds the marks of demonization in his experience, and if a Christian cannot be demonized, then he must conclude that he is not a genuine believer—and is indeed self-deceived and lost. He might then affirm his faith in Christ again. But if he continues to have some of the demonic symptoms that will not be removed through the normal means of application of biblical truth and spiritual walk, then he will become greatly confused, defeated, discouraged, distraught, depressed, and even suicidal.

However, if we recognize that a Christian may indeed have symptoms of demonization, then the distressed person may use the appropriate means of warfare to face the real enemy. Then the counselor or friend may understand and help the demonized person with the resources granted to us in Christ. The outcome of this approach could result in strengthening, delivering, and causing the growth of the believer in greater measure. He would also be able to share the biblical truth and experiential considerations that have helped him in order to help others in similar distress.

OBJECTIONS TO THE ANALOGY CONSIDERED

There are possible objections to the analogy drawn between the problems of Christians having cancer and Christians having inhabiting demons. These must be considered.

Elevation of experience. Some will object that such an approach raises experiential considerations to the same level as biblical truth. They claim they would rather stand on the clear presentation of Scripture.

First, we must answer that nothing can stand on the same level of authority as the Bible, the revealed Word of God inerrant in the originals and a sufficient guide to doctrine and practice. Experience is not equal in authority when it comes to determining absolute truth. However, just as science has found the truth of God's world in its research, so may genuinely evaluated and reliably documented experience find the truth in this matter. It is not a case of elevating experience to the same level as the Bible. We have previously treated this stand in detail.

Second, it would actually be recognizing the proper teaching of the Bible—that it does not, in fact, teach either that a believer can or cannot be demonized. Also, biblical authority is properly recognized in taking its teaching and parameters as the starting point of investigation. And when we are done, we are not claiming with equal authority as direct biblical teaching that experience teaches that Christians can be demonized. To claim that there is clear presentation in Scripture regarding this matter is both ignorant and unfair.

Merrill F. Unger appropriately comments:

> Experience, of course, is never to be the real test of spiritual truth. Revealed truth itself furnishes the basic and only valid criterion. Yet it follows that revealed truth is never at variance with genuine experience. When a clash occurs, the culprit is the interpretation of the truth or the alleged experience, *not* the truth itself.[2]

Inappropriateness of analogy. Some might say that to compare the occurrence of cancer in Christians with demonization in Christians is not a fair parallel. Cancer, they say, is common in the human race; we can deduce easily that Christians might be subject to its ravages.

We answer that demonization, as well as the lesser workings of Satan's hordes, is common in the human race. Biblical and historical evidence is abundant. The objectors cannot say that Christians can have cancer but that they cannot have demons if they have not reached both conclusions by the same means. This cannot be determined by deduction only. It must result from the inductive approach involving investigation of the facts, then the organization of the evidence, then the drawing of conclusions. The inductive approach agrees with theological and scientific procedures. Actually the analogy between the determining of cancer and demonization in Christians is quite appropriate.

Reliability of research. Can we trust those who, having supposedly used biblical and clinical parameters, have come to the conclusion that Christians can be demonized? Are there not

---

2. Merrill F. Unger, *What Demons Can Do to Saints* (Chicago: Moody, 1977), p. 86.

problems of validity of the findings and of the witnesses?

The problem of validity is not special to this field. Those who present research findings must be subject to scrutiny. This applies to those who hold the negative position as well as those who hold the positive. The proper procedure in determining and applying biblical and clinical parameters must be checked. The reliability of witnesses or researchers may be questioned on the basis of qualifications and proper research techniques. However, we cannot dismiss all presentations of research just because these limitations are present with all men. It is amazing how Christians accept without question "the assured findings of modern science" or the testimony of Christians regarding the Lord's interventions and supernatural occurrences, and yet will not accept what appears as genuine evidence from clinical observation by reliable and qualified persons that Christians can be demonized.

We might also point out that in view of the lack of definite biblical and theological conclusion that Christians cannot be demonized, those who hold to that view must present their own clinical evidence to substantiate their suppositions. Their task will be all the more difficult. For though they find many Christians who do not have demons, and though they may find that some symptoms were not demonically induced but rather were psychological or physical, they must search all parts of the world to determine that no Christian in all the world, present or past, has ever been demonized. Such a task is not only herculean, but impossible.

Conclusion. We conclude that the analogy between cancer and demonization as above presented is valid and that the procedure presented is a sound one to help us in our search for the answer as to whether Christians can be demonized.

Type of Clinical Research Needed

What kind of evidence should we seek from clinical research that would be reliable? We must consider the research from the standpoint of the evidence needed and evaluate the evidence obtained. We must also consider the reliability of the research procedure.[3]

---

3. For an extensive approach to a counselor's investigation, see Kurt Koch, *Christian Counseling and Occultism* (Grand Rapids: Kregel, 1965).

RESEARCH NEEDED

We should seek reliable data rather than spurious reports. This requires some systematic type of approach and objective methodology as much as possible. This is the type of procedure expected in the science laboratory or in the counseling clinic. Problems of observation and interpretation will be present, but there are safeguards that may be employed. We would hope to minimize the nondefinable factors or questionable controls that are present in so-called psychical research where the demonic factor is ignored, God's Word is not the authority, and proper controls are often not present. There is no comparison of the two approaches. Kurt Koch states, "Parapsychology is the science of occult phenomena."[4] Clifford Wilson and John Weldon give evidence for the lack of objectivity of parapsychological research.[5]

We must be careful not to label research into demonization a type of divination or spiritism. It is directly opposed to such a thing. It does not gullibly seek information from spirits of men or of superior creatures. It does not seek to advance personal wisdom or power. It does seek to determine whether believers have been invaded by demons and in doing so depends upon the risen Christ to clarify the matters needed to help the oppressed.

Evidence needed. What sort of evidence should we seek? We must start with the biblical description of the *symptoms* of demonization. We must note along with these symptoms the possible *causes* of demonic invasion and seek to verify the reality of invasion with a confrontational *test* of demonic presence. If all three types of evidence point to the reality of demonization, a case of demonization seems well established.

First, then, we should look for *symptoms* that indicate possible demonization. We must be cautious here not to identify all possible symptoms with demonization immediately. There may be physical and psychological causes for them. Usually there must be a rather complete survey of the symptoms available in any one case before making a tentative conclusion. However, there are certain symptoms in isolation or in combination that immediately cause suspicion of demonization.

4. Kurt Koch, *Satan's Devices* (Grand Rapids: Kregel, 1978), p. 154.
5. Clifford Wilson and John Weldon, *Occult Shock and Psychic Forces* (San Diego: Master), pp. 331-38.

We urge the review of the symptoms we have discussed in chapter 2. We might reiterate here that the Bible does not purport to give an extensive list of these symptoms, even in the many accounts; but there are sufficient to use as a basis for identifying demonization. They also serve, along with the understanding of the general work of demons, to indicate the extended lines along which demons might work and additional symptoms that might be expected to surface.

Some of those symptoms, both biblical and extended, which cause immediate suspicion of demonic invasion include such supernatural abilities as clairvoyance (or ESP), predictive abilities (including repeated and accurate deja vu experiences), magical powers (not illusionary), and supernatural strength. In addition, we must immediately suspect voices in the mind—of antichrist and blasphemous or destructive and murderous character—repeated apparitions and pressures upon mind or body that are somewhat relieved with prayer, and rather constant and unreasonable or unwarranted depression not associated with physical causes or relieved by medication.

If the symptoms reported by the client and observed by the counselor are sufficient to make us suspect demonization, we should proceed to the next step.

Second, we seek the *causes* of the symptoms. There should be investigation of the history of physical and psychological illnesses and treatment. Even if the symptoms are uncertain, there should still be an investigation of possible occult or demonic causes for them. There well may be a combination of the physical and/or psychological with demonic causes for the symptoms.[6]

Causes may be ancestral involvement, personal involvement, and transferred affliction from the treatment or domination of another involved in occult or demonic practices.

By *ancestral involvement* we refer to occult or demonic practices of the client's ancestors. This has been found to be one of the most common reasons for demonic affliction or demonization. This follows the principle enunciated in the second commandment forbidding idolatry:

6. Kurt Koch, *Occult Bondage and Deliverance* (Grand Rapids: Kregel, 1970), pp. 160-64, 184. This discussion is by Dr. Alfred Lechler, medical superintendent for thirty-five years at the largest mental hospital in Germany.

You shall not make for yourself an idol. . . . You shall not worship them or serve them; for I, the Lord your God, am a jealous God, visiting the iniquity of the fathers on the children, on the third and the fourth generations of those who hate Me. (Ex. 20:4-5)

It is quite clear that the worship of idols is fostered and compelled by demons (Ps. 106:36-38; 1 Cor. 10:20). It actually involves the worship of demons. Demons, therefore, assume the rule of a god over their devotees and may invade them. This is in keeping with the principle presented in Romans 1:21-28 that God recompenses sin with the evil it involves; that is, God gave idolaters over to their sin. Their sin was the worship of and submission to demons. They reaped what they sowed; they became dominated by demons. This domination may involve demonization, as attested in the past and current times. The second commandment shows that God considers idolatry to be hatred of the true and living God. He judges it in a fashion commensurate with its abominable character. Both the idolaters and their descendants to the third and fourth generations are judged for this heinous crime, and this judgment may include actual demonization. This, too, has been borne out in history and in clinical investigation.[7]

By *personal involvement* we mean that the troubled person has himself experimented or been seriously involved in occult or demonic practices. This giving of oneself over to such forbidden practices invites the influence or invasion by demons. Dabbling with such things as fortune-telling, magic, and spiritism or becoming involved in witchcraft, Satan worship, drugs, false religions, and cults opens the door for demonization. Men are to flee idolatry (1 Cor. 10:14-22).

By *transferral* we mean that an afflicted person has come under the domination of demons by the influence of someone already demonized. To submit to that person's authority in certain situations is to submit to demonic authority. The laying on of hands by a mediumistic healer or magical treatment for charming or transfer of powers may result in demonic invasion. The so-called gifts of tongues and healing may be transferred by occult means as a demon invades or is transferred from one

7. Koch, *Occult Bondage* p. 39. See also Merrill F. Unger, *Demons in the World Today* (Wheaton, Ill.: Tyndale, 1971), pp. 114-15, and Conrad Murrell, *Practical Demonology* (Pineville, La.: Saber, n.d.), pp. 50-51.

person to another. Supernatural abilities and euphoria may result, but so do deception, bondage, and mental disturbances. "One of the worst things that can happen . . ." says Koch, "is for a disciple of Christ to suddenly discover one day that he has these abilities, and then for him to assume that they are some form of charismatic power given to him by the Holy Spirit."[8]

If the background factors of possible causes attest to the likely invasion of wicked spirits, this is a further evidence of possible or actual demonization. Sometimes it is necessary to proceed to the next step for another confirmation.

There is a third means of investigating demonization, a *confrontational test.*[9] After investigating symptoms and causes, the researcher or counselor may need to confirm the diagnosis with a command to wicked spirits to manifest their presence within the client. With the client sufficiently prepared and with his consent, the researcher-counselor should ask that God would control the situation completely and make clear to counselor and client the presence of any demons that have invaded. The response may vary. Upon demanding in the name of the Lord Jesus that the demon, if present, respond, there may be physical or mental signals that another personality is present. If a demon is present, he may seek to hide to keep from being detected. With prayer and command, repeated attempts to uncover his presence may be successful. Sudden changes of composure, attitude, or voice are possible clues. Sometimes a voice in the mind or an unexpected thought in the mind may reveal a mind other than the counselee's. A string of challenging questions designed to determine the difference in attitude of the counselee and the supposed invading demon may indeed disclose a genuine identification of a hostile demon. There may actually come to manifestation the change of appearance in eyes and face and another person speaking through the voice of the client, a clear manifestation of a demonic presence.

If the third test turns out positive, indicating the presence of a demon, this is further confirmation, along with decisive symptoms and adequate causes, that the client has been demonized.

A fourth possible kind of information to confirm demonization is *decisive relief.* If a biblical stance is taken in the authority

---

8. Koch, *Occult Bondage,* pp. 39-40.
9. Mark I. Bubeck, *The Adversary* (Chicago: Moody, 1975), pp. 115-25.

of Christ, if prayer is specifically offered for relief and removal of the demon, and if specific command is addressed to the invading demonic forces, there may be obvious and somewhat lasting relief. Total removal may not be obtained at once, but there may be enough relief to determine that God has honored the approach taken and has had mercy on the afflicted. For instance, if the destructive and blasphemous voices or the mediumistic powers cease upon prayer and renunciation in the authority of Christ, then they cannot be construed as merely human in source. This is a further confirmation that the demonic was involved.

Evaluating the evidence. All possible means must be taken to sift and weigh the evidence obtained by the type of research suggested above. The sincerity and reliability of the client must be considered. The cohesiveness and consistency of symptoms, causes, and confrontational testing should be checked. The evaluation by other persons, preferably qualified in this line, may be considered. In some cases, there will be no doubt. In a few cases, the evidence will not be clear.

This whole procedure outlined above is not to give a complete outline on how to counsel the demonically oppressed. It is part of the process of research to help answer the question whether Christians can be demonized. The researcher may have questions about some individual cases. But if he has come to a positive conclusion in several cases that Christians he has counseled truly have had demons within, he has evidence that Christians can be demonized.

RELIABILITY OF RESEARCH

How should we determine whether the research into this question has been reliable? We must consider the reliability of the data and the reliability of the researchers.

Reliable data. The approach to obtaining the facts regarding possible demonization should be as objective as possible. The counselor should allow the counselee to express himself and aid him in doing so by listening with perception and observation. There should be support, warmth, and openness that contributes to a climate of acceptance and communication. This will aid the counselee to be free and honest. There should be the pledge of confidentiality. The counselor should seek to clarify the communication by asking questions and checking to see if he understands what the counselee is trying to say. Personal bias and preconceptions of the counselee's situation should not be allowed to lead to premature analyses, conclusions, or solutions. The data should be evaluated objectively as reasonable and within the guidelines that biblical and clinical parameters might suggest in similar situations. There should be an attempt to make the data base as broad as possible in each case.

The investigation should also attempt to make the frequency of the data (the number of observed cases) as sufficient as possible so that similar repeated observations may be obtained. Independent investigators should be involved to help research the question of demonization of believers. He should seek information regarding family and personal background factors that could cause demonization. He must conduct an objective test for the presence of wicked spirits rather than making a general conclusion.

Reliable counselor/researcher. The counselor must be a genuine believer with biblical and counseling skills. He need not be a professional, but he should have sufficient acquaintance with these areas that he may do an objective job of investigation. He must be unbiased and open to determining the truth. His reputation must be good, he must have demonstrated good character, and his methodology should be reliable. We must stress that he have a biblical orientation and must be acquainted with the type of background or experiential factors that could lead to demonization.

He must have a clear concept of occult practice and of the type of bondage it engenders. He must be able to recognize the difference between emotional/mental problems and those complicated by demonic influence. In testing he must be able to sustain an approach that is as objective as possible and yet presses hidden spirits to differentiate themselves from the human oppressed. There are means to successfully discover for the counselor and the counselee the presence and identity of the demon within the counselee. This may include a series of questions that seek to differentiate the attitude and characteristics of the two. Some skill is required at this point. He should not quickly admit or dismiss evidence or fail to seek evidence by the proper means. There are professional counselors who have no idea of how to test for the presence of demons. They have learned scientific and secularly oriented tests for analyzing a person's profile and problems, but they have not once considered how they might use biblical and clinical procedures to identify demonization. On the other hand, the researcher should not seek to find a demon in every situation. We have at one extreme those who seek a demon behind every bush and, at the other, those who cannot or will not even recognize a bush.

CONCLUSION

We have suggested and supported the thesis that reason and experience, though not the basis of biblical doctrine and not on the same level of truth as revealed Scripture, are God-given tools to apply biblical truth and to reseach data in the real world that God has arranged and allowed. They may be used to confirm and express truth and to test truth claims. Reason and experience must be used carefully and within the guidelines of Scripture, since they are creaturely and sinfully limited and open to bias, error, and deception.

However, reason and experience are used every day in meaningful life and research. They are part of the social and scientific processes that are genuinely accepted. Evidence from these sources needs to be considered when researching the question of demonization of Christians.

The analogy steming from the question, Can Christians have cancer? is genuine and useful. This can be solved by using biblical and clinical parameters so that a reliable conclusion may be obtained. When we are done with such research, we do not have biblical doctrine. But if demonized Christians were found by such means, we do have valid evidence, provided the research and the researchers are reliable.

In the next chapter, we shall consider just such evidence— case studies from reliable researchers and counselors.

10

Case Studies from Noted Counselors

As we consider the evidence of actual cases of demonization to determine if Christians can be invaded by demons, there are several introductory matters to consider.

PERSPECTIVES

We should not seek to understand the material presented in this chapter or the next without first having read chapter 9 to get the perspective presented regarding the place of experience. Chapters 5 through 8 present the approach to and the consideration of biblical and theological evidence. The perspectives of others must also be properly considered.

A PERSONAL CHANGE

It was the evidence presented by missionaries and then his own case studies that compelled Merrill F. Unger, a leading scholar in the area of demonology, to change his view regarding the possibility of demonization of believers. He had written in *Biblical Demonology*, published in 1952, that only unbelievers are exposed to demonization. But in *Demons in the World Today*, published in 1971, he confessed that his previous position "was inferred, since Scripture does not clearly settle the question."[1]

1. Merrill F. Unger, *Demons in the World Today* (Wheaton, Ill.: Tyndale, 1971), pp. 59-60.

Several have charged that Unger changed his teaching on the basis of experience, thus minimizing biblical doctrine. To be fair to Unger and the facts, we must credit Unger with the courage to confess his error in improper interpretation and improper induction. He did not deny or modify what Scripture clearly teaches. He admitted, as should we, that the Bible does not clearly teach that Christians cannot be demonized. Furthermore, he forcefully states, "Doctrine must always have precedence over experience. Nor can experience ever furnish a basis for biblical interpretation."[2]

He changed his position regarding what he erroneously thought the Bible taught because he was challenged by the facts of many cases presented to him. Where there is such incomplete biblical evidence and unsettled interpretation, then a biblical interpreter and objective observer ought to be ready to consider the facts presented in case studies.

> Yet, if consistent experiences clash with an interpretation, the only inference possible is that there is something wrong with either the experience itself or the interpretation of the Scripture which runs counter to it. Certainly the inspired Word of God never contradicts valid experience. The sincere truth-seeker must be prepared to revamp his interpretation to bring it into conformity with facts as they are.[3]

Again we must emphasize that this is appropriate where there is not enough biblical evidence to support a former position and where there is sufficient foundation in experience properly interpreted to warrant such a change of position.

PARALLEL CHANGES

We have illustrations of this in the interpretation of the biblical doctrine of creation. Formerly, Christian scholars often accepted the interpretation that the geological layers are evidence of millions of years of earth's history. This was then a guide to the understanding of the "days" in the creation account of Genesis 1 as nonliteral. However, recent discoveries and reinterpretation of scientific data have led many who formerly sought to

2. Ibid., p. 59.
3. Ibid.

harmonize evolution with the biblical account to alter their position. With the boldness required in an established scholarly community, they now hold that the layers do not represent vast geologic time periods but rather may be interpreted as the contiguous layers of silt laid down by the biblically recognized, universal Flood. This position, such scholars note, agrees with other widely based scientific data regarding a recent creation and allows the Bible to be interpreted in normal fashion.[4] Thus a person's understanding of what the Bible teaches or does not teach may be affected by his presuppositions and altered by further investigation of the facts, especially where his original interpretation of the Bible was not well grounded.

We might also point out that many formerly interpreted the Bible as saying that the earth was the geometric and physical center of the universe and that the sun revolved about the earth, as did all the heavenly bodies. Scientific observation of the facts and practical reason brought about a new understanding of biblical statements and corrected perspective.

It would not be fair to charge that in the two illustrations above men based doctrine upon experience rather than on the Bible itself. So it is not fair to Unger or others of similar persuasion to charge them with sacrificing biblical doctrine on the altar of experience. It might be fairer to say that the Bible became better understood when inadequately based presuppositions gave way to a more comprehensive and accurate view of both the facts as they are in the world of reality and in the Word of God.

PREJUDICIAL CONSTRICTIONS

Ensign and Howe comment on the effect of our inadequate presuppositions:

> All of us are too slow to realize how strongly our traditional teaching may prejudice us to new truth, yet it is something that happens to all of us. We assume too easily that we have been correctly taught and whatever we hold is true, orthodox, and final; therefore anything that contradicts "our truth" must be false. It is easy, then, to dismiss another view without examination. The first struggle in

---

4. For this position, see Henry M. Morris, *Scientific Creationism* (San Diego: Creation Life, 1974) and many other publications of Creation Life Press.

growing in grace and knowledge is to throw out our prejudgments and to honestly research the data that is being presented. . . .

Both Unger and Cottrell have declared that they have changed their minds because of the evidence just as we were forced to do.[5]

STATEMENTS OF EXPERIENCE

We have stated that the testimony of reliable counselors or researchers should be considered as evidence in the solution of the question of demonization of Christians. At this point we introduce such evidence for consideration.

MERRILL F. UNGER

The testimony of the reputed authority Merrill F. Unger stands on the side that genuine believers may be demonized. We have cited him above. He further gives several case studies that we shall later consider.

ENSIGN AND HOWE

Grayson Ensign, a former Bible college president and professor and a missionary to Jamaica, was pastor of Christ's Church, Cincinnati, when he collaborated in writing a book with Edward Howe, an engineer with graduate work at seminary and extensive counseling experience. Ensign and Howe make this weighty statement:

> We have empirical evidence that Christians have been invaded by evil spirits, for we have extensive notes on the more than one hundred fifty with whom we have worked in securing deliverance by the Lord Jesus Christ. Some audio tapes of actual deliverance sessions were made in which one can hear the evil spirits speaking through the mouths of Christian brothers and sisters. Merely listening to the tapes will rapidly convince most Christians that Christians can be invaded.
>
> Our testimony is grounded in literally hundreds of hours of deliverance work where we have experienced the most wonderful liberation of Christians from the control of evil spirits. This clinical and autoptical evidence has convinced us of the possibility of

---

5. Grayson H. Ensign and Edward Howe, *Bothered? Bewildered? Bewitched?* (Cincinnati: Recovery, 1984), p. 139.

some demonic control of *some* part of a Christian's body, mind, or will even though we began the work in a very skeptical mindset. We have been reared in a tradition that taught that demons could not invade or control people and certainly not Christians. Severe questioning and review of the whole matter of the deliverance work were continued for several months as we tested every conceivable theory of explanation for what was happening. The only explanation that was systematically consistent and in harmony with the Word of God was that our brothers and sisters had been invaded by evil spirits.[6]

These men had found that at some period in the lives of the demonized believers, often before they trusted Christ, they had given opportunity to evil spirits by acts of sin.[7] Unger agrees with this, holding that Christians can be demonized as a "carry-over from preconversion days" or can become demonized after conversion by blatant sin or involvement in occultism. He states that clinical evidence abounds to support this view.[8]

KURT KOCH

Kurt Koch, theologian, clinician, and author, refers to "many missionaries and experienced Christian workers" who support the concept that believers can be demon-inhabited.[9]

Koch testifies that he met a "missionary in Africa who had actually been possessed himself for a period of eighteen months. He, like many others, had previously believed it was impossible for Christians to be possessed. However, his own experience made him change his earlier theological outlook."[10] He further cites several personal interviews with V. Raymond Edman, late president and chancellor of Wheaton College (Wheaton, Illinois): "He told me of the many cases he had personally come across when he had been a missionary in South America, which had finally convinced him in his own mind that Christians could be possessed."[11] Koch is inclined to "take the

6. Ibid., pp. 135-36.
7. Ibid., p. 136.
8. Merrill F. Unger, *What Demons Can Do to Saints* (Chicago: Moody, 1977), p. 137.
9. Kurt Koch, *Occult Bondage and Deliverance* (Grand Rapids: Kregel, 1970), p. 67.
10. Ibid.
11. Ibid., pp. 67-68.

side of those who believe in the possibility of a Christian being possessed," though he realizes that some cases may be uncertain.[12] He cites three cases of what he considers to be Christians who were demonized.[13]

Unger also refers to Dr. Edman as writing him a letter to state his convictions on the matter when Unger in his book *Biblical Demonology* had expressed his theoretical position that Christians could not be demonized.[14]

MARION NELSON

Dr. Marion Nelson, psychiatrist and student of theology, declared that those who deny the possibility of demonization of a believer "must bear the burden of proving that it cannot happen, using Scripture properly interpreted and applied. This is difficult in the face of numerous reports of people who seem to be real Christians and who apparently suffer from demon possession."[15]

KENT PHILPOTT

Kent Philpott, pastor and counselor, states:

> It has been my experience that Christians have become demon-possessed through involvement with the occult or by harboring and entertaining sin or a desire for sin. In my ministry to Christians who have been demon-possessed I have noticed that it is common for the demon to hide in order to escape detection. But when the believer starts to grow and draw close to Jesus, the demon will become more active and noticeable. . . .[16]

MARK BUBECK

Mark I. Bubeck, pastor, popular author, and noted counselor of demonized persons, also holds that believers can be invaded by demons and to some degree controlled by them.[17] He cites cases of believers invaded, including the unmistakable case of

12. Ibid., pp. 68-69.
13. Ibid., pp. 69-71.
14. Unger, *What Demons Can Do to Saints*, p. 61.
15. Marion Nelson, *Why Christians Crack Up* (Chicago: Moody, 1960), p. 145.
16. Kent Philpott, *A Manual of Demonology and the Occult* (Grand Rapids: Zondervan, 1973), pp. 127-28.
17. Mark I. Bubeck, *The Adversary* (Chicago: Moody, 1975), pp. 87-88.

one of his own daughters.[18] I had the privilege of teaching a course on counseling the demonically oppressed with Dr. Bubeck on the graduate school level, and I must say that he is an educated, committed, and skilled pastor and counselor who stands firmly on the Word of God and seeks to help his clients in biblical and practical fashion.

THE AUTHOR

I have encountered from 1974 to 1987 at least 400 cases of those who were genuine Christians who were also demonized. I am not gullible or easily convinced. My background is in engineering, theology, and New Testament. For twenty-six years I have taught Bible and theology (including angelology) and counseled Christians and non-Christians. I would not claim infallible judgment, but I know the marks of a Christian and the marks of a demonized person. I might have been wrong in a case or so, but I cannot conceive that I would be wrong in more than 400 cases. I have conferred with others to diagnose several cases. I have referred many cases to others, such as pastors, psychologists, and psychiatrists, who confirmed my diagnoses. I will include some of my own case studies in the next chapter.

CONCLUSION

We conclude that the evidence of these testimonies is such that it cannot be ignored or discounted. The counselors and researchers seem qualified and reliable. Some testify to the fact that they had to be convinced against their previous opinion, wrestling with both biblical evidence and the facts of actual cases.

There have been cases in the experience of counselors that have turned out to be physical or psychological problems, not demonization. I know none of the authorities above who would not admit to the possibility of such or the combination of the human and the demonic. That makes their testimony all the more creditable.

The burden of proof lies with those who deny that Christians can be demonized. They must adduce clinical evidence that clearly eliminates any possibility in any case, past or present,

18. Ibid., pp. 90-91, 117-22.

that a believer can have a demon. In the very nature of the case, this is impossible. Further, we must note that those who deny that Christians can be demonized generally are those who have not had counseling experience with the demonized. Their stance is largely theoretical.

SPECIFIC EXAMPLES

Here we must turn to actual case studies of demonized persons to examine the evidence afforded. We will consider some cases presented by other counselors here and then some from the author's own counseling cases in the next chapter.

DICK HILLIS

Well-known author Hal Lindsey reports a reliable case:

> An example of a demon-possessed Christian was given me by Dick Hillis of Overseas Crusades. Dick is a man who knows the Scriptures, not just as a theologian, but as a warrior of the faith. A man of careful discernment, not given to sensationalism, he has spent most of his life on the mission field. Hillis told me of one incident which happened while he was in China, before the Communist takeover, when one of the elders of his church, who was unquestionably a believer, became so demon possessed that his personality changed. He became vile and profane in his language and extraordinarily strong. Some of the members of the church locked him up in a room and sent for Hillis.
>
> When Dick walked in the door, this man became violent and a strange voice shouted, "I know who you are."
>
> Hillis said, "And I know who you are," and began to speak to the demon.
>
> This was a case when a believer was actually possessed by a demon who spoke in another voice.[19]

KURT KOCH

A most experienced counselor of demonized persons, Kurt Koch says,

> Some years ago now, a minister brought a possessed woman to see me. During her attacks she would begin to curse and blas-

19. Hal Lindsey, *Satan Is Alive and Well on Planet Earth* (Grand Rapids: Zondervan, 1972), p. 160.

pheme terribly. However, when the attack had passed, she could start to pray very movingly and would feel completely at peace with God. It appeared, therefore, that during her actual attacks the devil was ruling her life, but that when they had passed the Holy Spirit took over control. An experience like this is very difficult to understand, but we cannot just simply brush it aside because it does not fit into our rigid doctrinal point of view. Yet it was obviously God's will that this kind of double life in the woman should cease.[20]

Koch also comments regarding Christians who are demonized:

It is a matter of experience that Christians who have lived in houses where either magic or spiritism have been practiced, are much more likely to fall prey to possession than other believers. Already on a number of occasions I have been called to visit such houses in order to meet the actual people involved.[21]

Another convincing example is reported by Koch:

A Bible student in the Philippines had been a Christian for about one year. As I prayed with him, a rough voice called out of him, "He belongs to us. His whole family has belonged to us for more than 300 years." "No," I retorted, "he belongs to the Lord Jesus to whom he's surrendered his life." The voices spoke again, "That's not true. His ancestors have subscribed themselves to us. He is ours by right." The conversation revealed that the ancestors of this unhappy student had not only practiced sorcery, but some of them had even subscribed themselves to the devil with their own blood. This was the reason why, in spite of his conversion, the student had become possessed.[22]

In a later book, Koch gives more detail of the same case.[23] One of the faculty members present addressed these voices: "In the name of the Lord Jesus, tell us why you have invaded Pat."

"Because he did not surrender his life completely," the voices responded.

"How many are you?" continued the interrogators.

"Fifty," came the reply.

20. Koch, *Occult Bondage*, pp. 69-70.
21. Ibid., p. 70.
22. Ibid., pp. 70-71.
23. Kurt Koch, *Demonism Past and Present* (Grand Rapids: Kregel, 1973), pp. 141-47.

A faculty member tested a voice that claimed to come from Manchuria by reciting a Russian verse he knew. The whole group witnessed a surprising thing. The voice began to speak in fluent Russian. Pat knew only English and his local Filipino dialect.

The fifty demons were from all over the world—Russia, Tibet, Egypt, Sumatra, Holland. This could explain the many languages they spoke. All fear the name and the coming of the Lord.

After a long battle, Pat was completely set free. Coming to his senses, he first cried and then began to praise the Lord.

I should insert at this point that one of the missionaries present on that occasion reported to me in person that he had witnessed the above event and that it was accurately reported. The demonized boy was a Christian, and Christ had delivered him from strong bondage.

W. L. McLEOD

A pastor in Saskatoon, Saskatchewan, W. L. McLeod has frequently counseled occult cases. He writes of a Christian worker:

> She related that while I was preaching she had felt some strange power rise up slowly inside her. She said, "I began to cut you in pieces and everything you said and stood for." Never before had she had an experience like this. She was greatly agitated as to why it should happen now. In talking with her I found she had had some involvement in the occult. She had allowed a friend of hers to display her occult powers in her presence. This had included the locking of doors without touching them. Out of curiosity she had also gone into a witchcraft shop. . . . She had a further involvement which she did not tell us about. This came out in a conversation with the unclean spirits who had invaded her life. I asked her if she would be willing to renounce the Devil and all his works, naming the areas of involvement. She was willing to do this. However, when we got to the place where I led her to say, "I now renounce the Devil and all his works," she was unable to do so. There was a struggle as she attempted to get the words out but couldn't. . . . Kneeling, we went to prayer. Immediately, the demon powers rose to the surface and took over. The girl fell on her hands and knees. When we commanded these evil powers to tell us their names she hissed out the word "Satan" about fifty times. We then began to give her some advice as to how to get rid of them. At once

she was blinded and deafened. They did not want her to hear the advice we were giving her. . . .

She told us that for awhile all she could see was Satan but that as we prayed she could suddenly see the blood of Christ. This was the stronger and the Satanic powers seemed to withdraw.[24]

McLeod reports that at a later session, the demons began to speak through her voice, saying that Satan was the king of this world and that McLeod was absolutely nothing. They threatened to bring more demons. They also threatened to kill the girl and became violent toward others in the room. The Christians read Scripture and commanded them to leave. The girl, who had been blanked out, regained hearing and sight. He continues:

We then told her to pray to Jesus Christ and ask Him to completely deliver her. She did so and we all simply prayed and believed God for her. Suddenly, all demonic activity ceased. The next morning I got a phone call from a very happy girl. She said simply, "I'm free, thank God!"[25]

McLeod comments on his change of viewpoint:

Many Christians feel very strongly that a Christian cannot be possessed by a demon. There seems to be a wide difference of opinion in this area. Prior to my experience, I would have found it somewhat difficult to entertain this opinion. However, I was forced to modify my position somewhat after some of these experiences, as well as after a closer look at the Word of God.[26]

MARK I. BUBECK

Pastor and counselor Mark I. Bubeck has a sterling reputation and is well qualified to analyze cases and help those who are demon oppressed. He has related to me that many believers have been troubled by inhabiting spirits. He writes of such a case. When he began such counseling, a man called him at 2:00 A.M. threatening to commit suicide. Bubeck asked the man if he would at least like to talk about his hurting that would drive him to ending his own life. Bubeck describes what followed:

24. W. L. McLeod, *Demonism Among Evangelicals and the Way to Victory* (Saskatoon, Sask.: Western Tract Mission, 1975) pp. 11-13.
25. Ibid., pp. 13-17.
26. Ibid., p. 17.

"That won't do any good," he said. "No one can help with my kind of problem. I've been to Dr. _____ (naming a well-known psychiatrist in our area) and Dr. _____ (naming another psychiatrist). I'm a born-again Christian. I've tried to overcome my problem. Oh! How I've tried, but it's no use. I've counseled with several different pastors and Christian counselors, but no one can help any with my problem."

"Would you like to share your problem with me?" I inquired.

"No, that won't help. I just want to know, if I take my life, will I still go to heaven? I'm not going to fight it anymore. I can't live with the guilt; and I hate it. I'm a professional man, and if my associates knew, I'd be discharged in disgrace. I've prayed and I've prayed, but that hasn't helped."

I responded by quoting some Scripture and with some words assuring him of God's understanding, willingness to forgive and to help us when we're sincerely reaching out. Then with prayerful and careful tone I asked, "Have you ever considered that this bondage might be demonic?"

There was silence for a few moments on the other end of the line. He later told me that when I asked that question it was as if a surge of rage ebbed and flowed in him, but deep inside his being the first spark of hope he'd had in many a year was born.

"But I'm a Christian," he protested. "It couldn't be demons, could it?"

Bubeck prayed, then asked him to call the next day. The man did, and they had some counseling sessions together. The problem had many symptoms of demon activity, so Bubeck referred him to a friend who was experienced in such cases. Bubeck continues,

Four wicked powers revealed their presence. One of them had a name which was the same as the man's problem. Another wicked power's name was suicide. These powers were commanded to leave and go to the pit, which they did. A marvelous deliverance from his problem resulted, and a whole new life opened to him, which he is now enjoying with his wife and family.[27]

GRAYSON H. ENSIGN AND EDWARD HOWE

Grayson H. Ensign and Edward Howe, a team of pastor and engineer, tell of a Christian man, Smitty, formerly involved in

27. Bubeck, pp. 90-92.

the occult but now walking with the Lord, who still was harassed by evil spirits. They sought to determine if there were grounds for invasion since their last counseling session. He had sinned definitely since that time. They probed to detect any inhabiting spirits. They tell the story:

> As we came together we saw remarkable changes in Smitty. He was able to confess Jesus Christ as Lord with joy and enthusiasm and to be very truthful about everything that he had done allowing demonic takeover, even his recent actions which he suspected had led to re-invasion.
>
> It was clear that the more Smitty confessed his total surrender to Christ as Lord and Savior the more evil spirits within were agitated and pushed toward manifestation. Noting this I prayed again and again for Christ Jesus to keep complete control until Smitty had confessed everything that could give him trouble in the future.
>
> Faster than seemed possible for a man to move Smitty shot out of the chair and bolted through the door before we could move. . . .

The group counseling Smitty prayed that Christ would bring him back. The authors continue:

> As we prayed the door slowly opened and Smitty came back into the room walking in a rather wooden way almost as one sleepwalking. He seated himself in the chair facing me with resignation, weariness, almost as one defeated, and folded his hands. But that didn't last long, for after prayers were given, and I began commanding the highest evil spirits into manifestation in Christ's name, they came with vehemence and viciousness. But as we worked against them in Christ's name, we all noticed a difference. . . . There was a weakening, even a note of fear under their tirades. All of us were convinced that we were dealing not only with defeated foes, but with foes that *knew* they were defeated, that they were going to be expelled!

The group worked for two hours, noticing that God was driving out those wicked spirits.

> The body grew quiet, the eyes opened, and Smitty was with us, exhausted but the happiest, most radiant Smitty we had ever seen. "I'm free!" he shouted. "They've all gone! I know it! It was like a

flock of birds just fleeing out of me. I'm empty. Oh, I am so light I feel I could float. Hallelujah." Testing for evil spirits in the name of Christ did not produce any manifestation or evidence of demons.

The authors met with Smitty about a month later to review and to probe for any residual demons.

There was a calmness and peace, a confidence and wholeness, a happy radiance that was inspiring to behold. A son of God had matured amazingly through this most agonizing, painful experience that any Christian can go through. The thrill of a Spirit-filled life was unmistakable in Smitty.

Now many months later we are thankful to report that Smitty has continued to show freedom in Christ and maturity that is a remarkable witness to others.[28]

AN EVANGELICAL PASTOR

A trustworthy evangelical pastor reported an interview with a bright and attractive young woman. She suffered from physical, mental, emotional, and spiritual problems, some of which seemed to be demonic. She recalled that demons bothered her as far back as she could remember. Her mother, father, both sets of grandparents, her aunt, and her cousin's husband and family all were involved in occult practices. The woman confessed personal involvement in the following occult areas: Ouija board, automatic writing, visiting fortune-tellers, levitation, horoscope reading, tarot cards, palm reading, seances, ESP, tea leaves, and spiritualist meetings. She claimed to have been discipled by a demon that inhabited her cousin. She had had many dreams of demonic sexual assault, feeling that demons were having sex with her. She indicated her mind was plagued with lustful thoughts.

The pastor related that the counselee feared that she would commit suicide, but she believed as a Christian that she was restrained. She had a strong inclination to regard herself as a terrible person who would drive away all those she loves. Jealousy, anger, unforgiveness, pride, and sensitivity were problems as well, she reported.

The pastor reported that sometimes recently she had come

28. Ensign and Howe, pp. 198-99.

to church in a trancelike state, not being able to pray or read the Bible. One evening she quietly took a visitor card and wrote on it that the devil had control of her. She told another lady that the preaching was all nonsense, and she was restrained from leaving.

Two pastors of the church prayed with her and commanded that the powers of darkness leave her and go where Jesus would send them. Later in a Sunday school class, the counselee seemed to be stirred up within and once felt physical pain when one pastor was teaching about the removal of demons.

The woman said she actually heard the demons laugh and chatter with one another in her mind. She commented on how she struggled with strong feelings of lust. She had been to a psychologist and a psychiatrist about her problems but had found no genuine help. She had no known mental or physical conditions that adequately explained her problems.

The pastor reported on the precounseling session:

> Realizing from the causes and symptoms that there was sufficient evidence to suspect the demonic, Ms. A. and I met together so I could disciple her.
>
> We spoke of her worth in Christ, the position that is hers in Christ, and the authority that she possesses through her union with Jesus Christ. She learned how to put on and use the full armor of God. She has become acquainted with warfare and doctrinal praying. She is learning how to use the name of Christ, the blood of Christ, and the mighty Word of God as the sword of the Spirit as her weapons.
>
> It was exciting for me to receive reports from her of new power in her Christian life and victory that she was experiencing in her troubled areas.
>
> However, there were times when she would relax herself and fall spiritually. . . .
>
> She has experienced a greater degree of victory through warfare teaching and principles.

The pastor then describes a counseling session in which there was confrontation of the enemy spirits:

> Ms. A. was still having problems, especially in the area of lust. She had very strong, almost overwhelming thoughts and desires in those areas.

In our first confrontation session, we contacted the demon of lust. It was done through the relaying of the thought method. She told me the thoughts she heard in response to my questions.

The counselee was not cooperative in that she would not let the demon speak freely through her. She herself said she felt that the demons wanted to do this but she refused to let them, fearing she would be giving them control.

There were other demons we were able to touch upon—suicide, despair, death-despair, and resentment.

I attempted to concentrate on the one called lust. I asked for moral ground that it had upon Ms. A. Confession and application of the Word was made; and then telling the demon he had no ground to stay, a command was issued for the demon to leave.

When I tested, I found that the demon had not left. I asked why. The answer came back that it was too deep and strong.

I was somewhat disappointed that we were not able to get this unclean spirit out of her, but we decided it will have to go eventually.

During our second confrontation session, we were able to call to manifestation this demon. This time, I was able to get its rank, that of throne, and bind his entire kingdom to him. Ms. A. had a time of confession, confessing all known sin and desire in this area. She wanted it to go. . . .

I used a cassette player with a hymn of praise for the background. I began to read passages of praise from Revelation. I commanded the demon of lust to listen to the Word of God and the praise music. Ms. A.'s facial expression changed and she fell to the carpet holding her lower abdomen as if in pain. I commanded the demons in the name of the Lord Jesus Christ to stop causing her physical pain. It seemed to stop immediately. I continued commanding, in the name of the Lord Jesus Christ, for the demons of lust to come out of her and go to the place where Jesus sends them. Her mouth opened and moved as the commands were being given, as if something was coming out of her.

She later told me that as the commands were being given she felt them coming out of her. . . .

She noted a real sense of relief after this occurred.

We tested to see if the demon remained by commanding it to come to manifestation in the name of the Lord Jesus a number of times without any response.

The pastor followed up on Ms. A. to determine how she was doing and what else needed to be treated in her life. He wrote:

Ms. A. now has a grasp of the Scriptures to the extent that she is able to do battle and win. She is excited about it. Yet, she realizes she still has a long way to go before she is completely free.

As for the demons that have left her, how this will affect her life still remains to be seen; since this is a very recent happening.

However, Ms. A. has taken to heart that Jesus is victor in her life and the powers of darkness cannot win.[29]

Conclusion

The case studies presented above and quoted in some length supply the type of evidence that speaks directly to the question, Can Christians be demonized? The evidence is weighty. The symptoms, causes, and tests of which we have read argue to the internal type of control that comes with inhabiting spirits. The control of bodily actions and voice by spirits, speaking in unlearned languages, the difference in reaction between the counselee and the demon, the fact that the invader referred to the invaded in the third person (he, she, etc.), and the relief produced through biblical counsel and confrontation of demons are evidence that a separate spirit-person was expressing himself through the human by operating the control center of the brain.

The counselors cited are qualified theologically and practically, most well known to the Christian public. They are reliable witnesses with experience in the area of diagnosing and counseling the demonized.

It would be difficult to dismiss this type of evidence and witness or even to argue against it effectively. Alternate theories might be suggested to explain some of the phenomena. However, most of those arguments stem from those who deny any demonization at all, not to mention the demonization of Christians. Even those who recognize the reality of demonization often seek to explain away the evidence on the grounds of secularly learned and practiced psychology. Further, the objector cannot stand at a distance instead of on the scene to discount the evidence. Again, it is those who have little or no experience in this area who are the most vocal objectors.

---

29. From a pastor's report on file with me, submitted as a case study in a master's level course on counseling the demonically oppressed.

We must allow the distinct probability that biblically guided investigation and counsel has shown in experience that some Christians have been demonized. The evidence is heavily weighted toward that conclusion.

11

Case Studies from the Author

The examples in this chapter come from my own counseling of the demonized. The reader should read chapter 9 of this book to understand the legitimate place of documented experience. It does not determine doctrine, but it does help to ascertain the facts.

I would clarify that I never pursued such cases. They came to me. I estimate that from 1975 to 1987 I have encountered at least four hundred genuine believers who were actually inhabited by demons. Only two of the many I counseled were not believers in Christ. Due to my select clientele—those who were already Christians and were experiencing unusual difficulty that seemed not to be explained or relieved by other types of counsel or treatment—I found that most of them were accurate in their suspicions that they were being demonically harassed. Less than ten were not demonic but psychological. Many had a combination of psychological and demonic problems. This may be common, since demons work with men's minds and bodies.

I did not prejudge the cases. I sought to analyze the symptoms from their complaints and by observation. I searched the background factors that might have contributed to demonic involvement—such things as ancestral, personal, and transferred influences. If then there was warrant, I asked for permission to conduct a confrontation to test for the presence of wicked spirits who might have invaded. I sought to follow what has been presented in chapter 9 of this book as the proper procedure in the investigation. Keeping in mind the welfare of the individual and the responsibility I had to God and His Word, I sought to minister intelligently and considerately to the counselee and to deal authoritatively with the demons.

God has been faithful. I have learned much of His goodness and power and of His willingness to deliver those who call upon Him and seek to order their lives in accord with His revealed truth. I have seen the authority and power of the risen Lord Jesus Christ as He cut down the enemy, stripped them of their operative powers, and forced them to leave those they were inhabiting as squatters. I have seen the results in the lives of those freed in the process. Many of these have been a shining testimony to the grace and power of Christ as they have walked in new freedom and holiness of life to honor their Deliverer. They testify to the fact that Christ came to set the captives free from sin and from the snare of Satan.

The following cases come from my records of interviews, from tape recordings of the sessions, or from letters my counselees have freely sent to me. All identities are kept confidential, and names have been changed to ensure this.*

CASE 1: CONFUSED NURSE

Alice is a registered nurse and a Bible college graduate. She came to me complaining of harassment of her thoughts. We found that she had a poor relationship with her parents, who maintained a critical attitude toward her. Her need for acceptance had led her at one time to a charismatic group that practiced speaking in tongues. They laid hands on her that she might receive the gift, and she had a "tongues experience." She had taken that as a sign of God's acceptance and practiced it sometimes in public meetings and sometimes in private, thinking it gave her meaning and relief.

She had definitely trusted Christ as her Savior and was seeking to live for Him. She had recently come to a new appreciation of what it meant to be "in Christ" as she studied the Word of God. As we considered her background, her family, and personal experience, we found real reason to suspect that the harassment and molestation she had been experiencing may have been demonic in origin. We sought to ground her in the Word

---

*Notes, letters, and tapes cited in this chapter are on file with the author.

and deal with her attitudes regarding her self-worth, her position in Christ, and matters of proper interpersonal relationships,
including forgiving those who had hurt her or rejected her. She
confessed her sins and her wrong attitudes and rejected the
tongues if they were not of God. We had previously studied the
Scripture passages that treat spiritual gifts and tongues to clarify
the place of tongues in the early church as evidence to the Jews
that Jesus had replaced Moses and that His gospel was the truth.
I told her that I doubted that there were any genuine tongues
from God today in the New Testament sense. So she asked God
to show her the truth about her own tongues experience.

We asked God to govern the counseling situation and to
show us what was really going on in her mind and life. She gave
me permission to confront any wicked spirit present within her.
I then commanded that if there were any tongues spirit present
he would come to the fore and answer me as I claimed the
authority of the crucified, risen Savior. A tongues spirit did finally manifest itself in sullen fashion. It resisted me but did confess
that it had come in through the laying on of hands. It took the
occasion to come in to give her what she desired and to lead her
astray. After several counseling sessions, the demon confessed
that Christ was its victor, that Alice was his victor in Christ, and
that she had authority in Christ to ask him to leave for the pit.
After some arguing and resistance, he left as we submitted to
God, resisted the demon by the Word and by prayer, and commanded him to leave God's temple. Alice had rejected his false
acceptance and the false sign of acceptance, the tongues, and
acknowledged her full acceptance by Christ apart from tongues
or any works of human effort.

Alice afterward started growing markedly in her Christian
life. The harassments ceased. Then, some months later, other
harassments showed up. She came for counseling again. She
wanted me to see if there were other demonic forces present. I
tested again and found one of the rank of throne to be at the top
of the evil forces within her. This one informed me through her
voice—again in sullen fashion that indicated a personality completely different from hers—that he was the top ranking spirit.
"Tongues" had been only of the rank of principality. He claimed
he was stronger and would not leave. He said that he had sold
her on the line that Christians have no rights. She was supposed
to take all the criticism and maligning that her parents and

others had given to her, for she was no good.

We again applied the Word of God to show that God was truly a holy Person but was also an accepting Father. It was He who had created her in His image and built in inestimable worth that could never change. We showed how Christ's sacrifice did not create her worth but rather proved her worth, though she had no merit before God. She was to stand in her created worth and in her imputed righteousness and resist the evil one who would put her down by accusing thoughts in her mind, arranging circumstances in which she would feel rejected, and using others in her family and circle of legalistic church friends to criticize and depress her. She also had her responsibility to confess allowing these lies to govern her mind. She confessed also that she had sought false means to establish her worth—pride and rebellion. Her suicidal thoughts were also confessed and rejected.

She commanded the leading throne, Non-acceptance, to respond to our commands and to leave her. He, too, confessed that Christ was his victor, that Alice was in Christ and his victor. But he protested through her voice, "How can Christ expose me and eject me? I was here first!" True, he had come into her body early in life through the demonic involvement of her ancestors, but he had been upstaged by her redemption in the blood of Christ. We insisted that he leave. He delayed.

I asked for the moral ground on which he thought he could resist. He stated, "Her confusion hinders her freedom. She doesn't know how to handle her anger toward her parents while seeking to respect them. She resents their favoritism toward her sister." I talked to Alice about respecting her parents but acknowledging her anger and expressing it properly. She was afraid of hurting her parents. She was afraid of expressing herself, since she did not want to face rejection by others. She hated herself for being afraid and acting in such a manner. We pointed out the true nature of the Father. He was not to be created in her earthly father's image. He could be trusted to accept and not reject her.

I set her upon a Bible study that would reshape her thinking about God the Father. I encouraged her to praise God, pray against her enemies, and seek to communicate with those who had hurt her. She was to apologize for her wrong behavior and to express her hurt at their treatment of her. She has come a long way toward complete freedom in Christ. She has also been counseling with a Christian psychologist who has helped her a great deal.

There is not a doubt in my mind that Alice is a genuine believer and that a great deal of her problems were due to demons that had invaded her at an early age and then arranged for others to enter to further complicate her condition. She recognized that also and has stood in the Lord and the power of His might with the armor of God. She continues to grow in grace and in the strength of Christ.

In one counseling session with Alice, I asked the demon called Non-acceptance if he had used the concept that Christians cannot be inhabited by demons. He replied, "Oh, yes! We use it all the time. It is one of the best tools we have ever promoted." Now although we do not accept the testimony of demons as the truth of God, there are times when they are forced to tell the truth as they did when confessing that Jesus was the Son of God. The demon's statement is only confirmation of what we had discovered before. His forced admission was significant.

CASE 2: PSYCHIC BURT

Burt had disappointed his father, who wanted him to be a he-man. But Burt's slight frame and artistic personality did not suit his father and were the cause of ridicule by his childhood chums. Burt grew up with a rejection syndrome. He sought ways to make himself acceptable. As a young man he was introduced to tarot cards (face cards that spell out character and destiny). He became very adept at readings for people. They began to seek him for advice. He was glad for the acceptance and continued to develop his skills, not realizing that he was being duped by demons who supplied secret information in exchange for further control over him and those who sought his services. Soon Burt could read character, identify personal facts about his clients, and forecast their future without the use of the cards. He was an effective "psychic." He came under bondage to the desire to be a woman.

Through some disappointing experiences and a sense of great restriction, he followed the advice of friends and burned the tarot cards. But the compulsive desire to be a woman did not end. He experimented with psychedelic drugs, marijuana, cocaine, and peyote. Then he found a Bible and read that God was a spirit. He felt drawn to seek the truth in the Bible. He began reading the New Testament, even though he was Jewish. He stated in a letter explaining his experiences, "I began to feel God drawing me to Himself and away from those people and desires I had cherished and worshiped. On February 14, 1974, by God's grace I became a Christian."

His life was changed. Some Christians prayed over him that he might be relieved of the spirits that were associated with the tarot cards and against the spirit forces that had been associated with maternal domination. He relates:

I felt much freer, especially in my relation to my mother, after these prayers. In 1974, I also began to attend Catholic Charismatic prayer meetings and one evening a minister prayed for a large group, including me, to receive the gift of tongues. At that time I began speaking in two different tongues; but because the church I went to had no tongues speaking, I seldom used this gift.

Several times compulsive thinking led me to fantasizing about desiring to be a woman. I felt this desire was ever close to me waiting for a moment to express itself. Even after God brought me the gift of a wonderful Christian wife, the desire stayed close by.

In January, 1976, I began classes at the Moody Bible Institute. Several nights before my examination in theology (we were studying the doctrine of salvation) I felt horribly oppressed, and for several nights I received little sleep. Right after this I came to visit my teacher, Dr. Dickason, and after talking with me, he asked me to come back for a second session. During the second interview, he challenged the spirits within me to reveal themselves; and to my surprise, one responded by speaking in a feminine voice saying that she was sent by Apollyon; and another responded in a voice in tongues that Dr. Dickason commanded to stop speaking and to leave me. I felt much relieved and freer after this interview, but I was not at all convinced that every spirit within me had been revealed.

I have felt since then that spirits have come upon me, but God has given me grace through discernment to command them out. My only explanation for this is that there must have been areas of my life that have not fully been under God's control; and as long as I have kept these areas to myself, I have remained open to be troubled by spirits in these areas. Believing, however, that God intends that all things work together for good, I have thanked God for showing me my weaknesses and praised Him for establishing me in Messiah Jesus so that those areas outside His control might be brought before His throne of grace. . . .

So thankful I am to my Lord and Savior Jesus Christ who is the victor over Satan and his renegade army; for when I call upon Messiah's name, He is ever faithful to answer. In my defenseless and weak condition, He continues to uphold me by His grace and strength.

There is no doubt that Burt is a genuine believer. His understanding of the Word, his devotion to Christ, and his successful stand against the enemy are possible only through the power of the Lord Jesus operative in His life. I have heard from him since he wrote the above testimony, and he is continuing on with the Lord with his supportive wife.

Case 3: A Confusing Tongue for Carla

Carla came to Bible college a confused nonbeliever. During her first year, she came to understand the gospel and trusted Christ. There was a change in her life. Then she began to experience mental and sexual harassment from some unseen force when lying in her bed at night. This would often wake her and overpower her. She almost surrendered to this dominating force.

She was troubled and came to see me at the suggestion of a close friend. We found that there was a pact with the devil in her background. We broke that pact through the authority of Christ, who had purchased her and had defeated the devil. During confrontation, which she requested, a spirit called Pride surfaced. He confessed that Christ was his victor, just as the Bible says. He also confessed that Carla was his victor in Christ. He said he would obey and leave when the Lord Jesus and Carla agreed. But there was delay and resistance in a stubborn silence.

I instructed her in biblical truth that applied to her situation, using the sayings of Scripture as the sword of the Spirit. She began to grow by leaps and bounds. Her fellowship with the Lord was obviously affecting her whole life and all her relationships so that many noticed her progress. But she still had some harassment. She came back several times for encouragement and instruction.

In another confrontation session, I again commanded the

spirit Pride to answer me and tell me why he had not left. I commanded him to tell me the ground of his staying. Her jaws tightened and the muscles tensed. As she leaned forward as if to fall from the chair, I stayed her by a gentle hand on the shoulder. There was a startling reaction. Her body drew back as if in pain. I remembered her telling me of the laying on of hands by elders of a charismatic Lutheran church. I immediately suspected a tongues spirit was over Pride and was pressuring him to silence and not to leave. The following is a summary from a tape of the session:

"Proud spirit, Pride, is a tongues spirit over you?"
There was nod of the head.
"What shall I call him? Tongues?"
Another nod of the head.
"What is his rank?" I asked.
"Principality," the answer came back through Carla's lips. The demon was using her voice with an obviously different personality and attitude. She had been walking with the Lord and enjoying His fellowship. This resisting and devious spirit was not the expression of Carla's mind.

I commanded, "Tongues spirit, look at me. Are you the leader inside? Drop the jaw, open the mouth, use the tongue, speak to me. 'Every knee shall bow, and every tongue. . . .' "
There was a raising of a clenched fist against me.
"No, you don't do that," I said. "Put the hand down. 'Every knee shall bow and every tongue confess that Jesus is Lord to the glory of God the Father.' Tongues spirit, you confess. The Scripture says, 'Test the spirits whether they be of God.' And we know you're not of God, because you don't honor Jesus Christ, and you resist the servant of God. You have no power. Just relax her hands."

The clenched fists relaxed. "Put them on her lap and leave them there."
The demon obeyed.
I continued, "Tongues spirit, are you the one who came in at that church?"
"Yes," came the forced, clear answer.
"How did you ever get to be such a ranking spirit? Were you a principality for God once? And then you perverted and became a principality for Satan. Am I right? Confess it out loud!"

"Yes, you're right," he conceded with obvious irritation.

"You have really failed, haven't you? Satan used his communication device to speak to a lot of angels. You use a communication device to deceive people, don't you? You came in to give Carla what she wanted, didn't you?"

"Yes," came the weakling answer.

"What was that which she wanted back then? Tell me!"

A pause. Then the spirit stated, "She wanted a real spiritual experience with God."

"How did she seek it?" I asked.

Another pause. "Through the baptism of the Holy Spirit."

"Who laid hands on her?"

"Men of the church."

"What did they promise her through the laying on of hands? What did they tell her she would have?"

"That she'd have a fulfilled life with the Lord," he said.

"What was to be the evidence of this?"

Came the answer, "The speaking in tongues."

"Is that when you—?"

"But they didn't tell her that," came the interruption.

"They didn't tell her that," I clarified. "But you came in."

"Yes," he conceded.

"Why did you come in?"

"It was an opportunity for me."

I further inquired, "What were you going to do with her life, then?"

"Lead her to the point where she did give herself over to Satan."

"And you almost accomplished that, didn't you?" I responded. "But she has renounced all that; right?"

"Yes," came the dejected reply.

"What ground do you hold in her?"

"None." The reply was weaker.

"Is that the truth before the true and living God?"

"Yes."

"She has used her tongue to magnify Christ. She rejoices in the hearing of the Word, doesn't she? Whose side is she on?" I demanded. [Pause] "Answer me, whose side is she on?"

Then came a response in a form that surprised me: "My enemy!"

"And who is your enemy?"

"Jesus Christ!" The voice was filled with restrained contempt.

"And what is He to her?" I pursued.

With concession he confessed, "Her Savior."

"And what is she to Him?"

"His child," came the further resigned confession.

"On that basis I command you to leave her body and to take all your wicked spirits with you. But first I want you to confess that Jesus Christ is your victor. Right now!"

After a pause came the forced answer, "Jesus Christ is my victor."

"Carla is—" I sought to pursue the usual sequence.

The spirit broke in. "You're my victor, and Carla is my victor." He had heard the sequence in the confrontation of the power Pride. He volunteered the answer that I was his victor also.

"I will leave her body," I urged him to say.

He resisted.

"I will leave her body," I insisted he say.

"I will leave her body," he conceded.

"I will go now; I am undone. I give up. Tell her that!"

"I am undone and I give up. I will leave her body now," he repeated after me in resigned fashion. "I will take all my wicked hosts with me," he also repeated.

"Come, wicked angels; come, demons; come with me. Tell them that!"

There came a fearful sigh and then, "Come, demons; come with me."

"I'm leaving. Come, Pride; come, all principalities and powers. Tell them all," I urged.

"Pride and all principalities and powers, come with me. We are leaving this body now."

"Invite the holy angels to take you away," I commanded. And I prayed that God would send His holy angels to escort them under armed guard to the pit. (I doubt that any judge would allow the condemned criminal to walk out freely!)

There was a whimper from the demon.

"Holy angels, come and take us away right now."

Then I commanded, "All right, get out in the name of the Lord Jesus. Go to where Jesus sends you. Leave her body right now. Lord Jesus, send them out," I prayed.

It was the very next session that they all seemed to leave. For over a five-year period, Carla continued to recognize and rejoice in her freedom, but more important in the fellowship of the Lord Jesus Christ, her Deliverer. I have not heard from her since she wrote me a glowing testimony of what Christ had done and was doing in her life. She was freely enjoying the Lord, as far as I could tell.

Here is a graphic case of the recognition of a different spirit personality within the body of a believer, speaking, resisting, confessing crucial facts, and then leaving under duress as we applied the authority graciously granted us in the Lord Jesus. How could we not recognize the power of Christ overcoming the power of wicked spirits that were clearly manifesting themselves within a genuine believer?

CASE 4: TORMENTED PRINCESS DOTTIE

Dottie had been a Christian for a few years. She was a student in a theology class for college graduates. She had her B.S. in nursing and had special interest in psychology. There was a very difficult personal and family background. Confusion and inability to study biblical truth without distraction bothered her rather constantly. She did well in her classes, but not as well as she felt she could. Something caused her to almost blank out on exams. She felt defeated and frustrated. She was also fearful and distrustful, protective of herself, though thoroughly honest. She really had a heart for people and wanted to serve Christ. Her friends recognized many of her admirable qualities. She came to share with me some of her deep concerns. She wondered if some of her problems could be traced to demonic opposition.

We found from her symptoms and background factors that her suspicions had some basis. We talked about the procedure of confrontation, and she gave me permission to address any wicked spirits that might be present. We asked the Lord to dismiss any that might be externally present and to send protecting angels to attend our session. We soon found that defiant and devious spirits were present inside her body. Some had come in at birth and some thereafter. Her ancestors had long been involved in occult and demonic activity. That is the reason they felt they could enter her, and they were stubborn in their claims.

She was relieved in one sense to diagnose the problem more

accurately. She had had previous counseling that did not seem to help much. She wondered if she were "going crazy." I assured her that she was quite sane and that she could handle the battle if she continued on with the Lord and took her stance in warfare as the Bible describes. However, the enemies inside were not about to give up without a battle. She persisted in her submission to God and in opposition to the demons and found greater relief as time went on. Yet the battle continued.

During one counseling session I asked her to share her testimony as to why she knew she was a Christian. When she began her story, there were convulsive reactions and cries of hurt. She compared them to muscle reactions to electrical shock similar to the reactions of a person's chest to the electrical prods used in seeking to restart a nonfunctioning heart. There was obvious demonic opposition to her speaking about Christ's saving her. I asked why that was happening. She winced again and said, "They know you're taping this." I commanded the spirits to stop, and there was a good measure of relief. She was able to continue with her testimony.

She had gone to church because she had deep longings and problems unsolved. She had a background in psychology and heard that the preacher, a well-known evangelical, was going to speak on a Christian perspective on psychological problems. She wanted to hear how this "Christian bunch" handled this. As the preacher spoke, she saw that the message made sense. At the invitation, even though there was fear of responding, she went forward. This was not like her because she wouldn't talk to a counselor unless she knew the person's certification. When the woman counselor asked, "Why did you come forward?" she responded, "God is here. I mean Jesus is here." The counselor produced the booklet *The Four Spiritual Laws*. Immediately upon seeing the first pages, Dottie shouted, "This is it!" She listened to the presentation of the gospel and prayed to receive Christ. There was a change of outlook and even improvement of sight.

As Dottie finished her testimony and explained her progress and understanding of God's Word and of spiritual warfare, she was doing it freely without difficult attack, although her body was shaking all the time. Suddenly they punched her again. But she continued:

One of my sincerest wishes is that, by the grace of God, the Christian community could have a realistic viewpoint. The demons love keeping up the barrier between psychology and pastoral counseling; because the longer they keep that up, the better the chance they have of keeping up their deception. . . . Psychologists have been trained in even Christian institutions and have been trained well. But the biggest factors that they cannot understand are the theological issues and particularly the issue of angelology and how it relates to psychology; for it is an area that is untapped, so to speak.

She knew that some looked to parapsychological research, but she felt that was "hogwash" because she had been greatly involved in it with its resultant bondage. She said that since we had been counseling and dealing with demonic opposition and major demons had left, particularly one throne, she had noticeable relief, and her symptoms and attacks "were nowhere as severe or as chronic as they once were."

Suddenly, in the midst of the session as we spoke of their exposure, they broke in:

"They don't like you because you tell too much, and you talk too much, and too many people are getting convinced!"

"Too many are getting convinced of what?" I responded.

"We have been at war with you for too doggone long, and we are sick of it!"

"Who is 'we'?" I demanded.

"What do you mean, 'we'? You know who I am." Anger flared.

"What is your name?"

"Oh, come on!" Disgust filled the demon's voice.

"What is your name?" I insisted.

"You know my name. You named me. You named me last time I was here. You named me. You named me. So give me my name back!"

"No, you tell me your name," I persisted.

"Oh, shut up!" came the not-too-polite reply.

"You're not Dottie, are you?" I sought clarification.

"I didn't say I was."

"What is your name?"

"I will not tell you! I don't care!" came the sing-song taunting reply. "You've only got a few more minutes, and I will wait it out."

I began to pray to the Lord that we might use the time wisely and that the Lord would put the pressure on him and not allow him to take evasive action.

There was a fearful squealing. "Oh, no! No, no, no, no, no! Jesus, get away, get away, get away!" The squealing voice repeated rapidly.

"The Lord Jesus will not get away. He's inside of Dottie." I prayed, "Lord, Jesus, You're inside of Dottie; show Yourself to them in Your power, and cause them to stop this tormenting." Then I turned to the demon. "Now I want your name, leading ranking spirit. You're a throne; is that correct?"

"You know my rank; you know my name. Why do you ask me this over and over and over again? You know, you know, you know! You know too much!"

"Then why are you afraid of telling me again?" I asked.

"Maybe you have forgotten," came the parry. "And if you have forgotten, the game begins all over again."

"Oh, hardly," I countered. "I could just name you all over again."

"Oh, no!"

"Oh, yes!"

"No, you did that last time. You took everything away last time."

"Then why are you hanging around?"

"I didn't say you got rid of me. I said you took everything away. There's a difference, you know."

Then I called him by the functional name he had previously given me: "Confusion—is that your name?" I wanted to see if I was talking to the same spirit as last time or whether he had sent a lesser one to stand in the way.

"Sure! You named me!" he replied. Actually I had named him "Leading Defeated Throne," but his previous name was Confusion.

"Did you confess last time that Jesus Christ was your victor?"

"Sure!" he spurted in clipped fashion.

"And that Dottie was your victor in Christ?"

"Sure!" he admitted again.

"Did you tell her that you would obey and leave?"

"Sure!"

"When Jesus and Dottie agreed?"

"They haven't agreed yet!"

"How do you know? Because you are not gone?"

"I'm interfering."

I prayed that the Lord would stop his interfering and allow Dottie to be free. I praised Him that He is not a God of confusion but of order, and that He had given Dottie a mind not of fear but of love, and of power, and of a sound mind.

"Confusion, is Dottie God's child?"

"She's always been."

"No, not always. When did she come to know the Lord?"

"September 5, 1982, 7:30 P.M." The detail surprised me.

"Oh, you remember the day of your defeat!" I prodded.

"She makes me sick!"

I commanded the spirit to stop kicking my chair. "You are under my authority," I commanded as I reminded him of my position in Christ and His delegated authority.

"I know I'm under your authority. Rub it in! Come on!"

"You are under the authority of Jesus Christ. You are to respect Him and His servants! Now I want you to confess that you will leave today."

"We can play games again."

"This is no time to play games. You will have to face reality."

"I don't want to face reality. Fantasy is more fun."

I reminded him that he could not live in fantasy. "That's where confusion comes in, right?"

"Sure!"

"What do you deny Dottie?"

"Everything I can get my hands on."

"Including her personal dignity?" I zeroed in on her problem.

"Oh, shut up, shut up, shut up!"

I reminded him that she knew she was made in the image of God and was important to Him.

"Yes, but I put mud on it!"

"Not so. The image has been restored. Ephesians 4:24 says that she has been recreated in righteousness and true holiness according to the image of God who created her. She is clean through the Word that Christ has spoken to her."

"No! I'm in her body. That can't be!"

"You're in her body? When did you first come in?"

"When she was made," he replied.

"When she was born. You are ancestral."

"Oh, I've controlled her whole family for a long time. We were broken off for a while; but when her parents got married, we were reunited."

"Well, ancestral curses and spells have been broken by the authority of Jesus Christ."

"I know you broke them. That's why we're having such a hard time."

"And my sister has rejected any influence from her ancestors along this line," I added to declare her position and stance.

"I know. That's why we want her—Never mind!"

"You want her what?"

He responded, "We were going to get her parents and brother to get her to come around. She's being a renegade. She ignores her family; she ignores her race."

"No, she goes to her family. Her family tries to put her down. She's tried time and time again to relate to her family. She's glad she's black. She's glad she is female. And you have been interfering with her ability to appreciate all that. Those things are beautiful because God made them. Isn't that right, wicked spirit?"

"Yes, that's right. Yes, yes, yes. What do you want?"

"I want you to tell her that all this is your lie."

"What's a lie?" he stalled.

"That she is not accepted. That she doesn't have to face the fact that she is black and that she is feminine."

"She's a traitor. She deserted the false light."

"Yes, she did," I gladly affirmed. "She has turned to the true light. Jesus is the way, the truth, and the life."

"Oh, shut up!" he protested.

"Jesus is the light of the world, and he that follows Him shall not walk in darkness but will have the light of life. He has given her life, and you couldn't stop Him. Did you try to stop her from becoming a Christian?"

"We've not only tried that, but we want to get her back. We're not giving up!"

"Well," I said, "she has been inhabited by the Spirit of God, reborn by the Spirit."

"Ha, ha, ha! Prove that, prove that, prove that!"

"You hate her, don't you?" I pressed him.

"Why, sure!"

"Because she's in Christ, isn't she?"

His answer was cleverly devised. He knew the usual response of those that say a believer cannot be inhabited: " 'How can two walk together except they be agreed?' We agree, we agree; that's why I'm here."

"Who agrees?" I inquired.

"We do."

"Does Dottie agree with you that you should be there?"

"No!" came the cry.

"Does she hate you?"

"She and Jesus both!"

"Yes, because she's in Jesus, isn't she?"

"He's here too!"

"Yes, that's why you hesitate to look and—"

"I can't look at Him. He makes me sick!"

"Then He is inside of Dottie, right?"

"Sure! But most people don't think that! They think she's sinning. They think she's a liar. They think that she's not a Christian."

I asked, "Because there is a wicked spirit inside?"

"Yes, and how can a wicked spirit live in a temple of God? Ha, ha! They can't figure it out. They can't figure it out! But we know, we know, we know," he squealed in fiendish delight. "That's what confuses them. We're going to keep them confused!"

"No, God is anxious to make it clear," I reminded him.

"Oh, no, no! Why, why, why, why?"

"Now you go down. I want to talk to Dottie."

I addressed Dottie, "Were they giving you any question about whether you were saved? Whether you were a Christian or not?"

Dottie then spoke in an obviously different attitude and tone of voice: "No. But people I know have attacked me about that. And that's why I quit developing a friendship with one person in the last month."

"Yes, it cuts you off because it's a divisive type of thing."

She clarified. "They say I haven't submitted to Christ as my Lord and Savior completely and totally. And they didn't say it directly, but they got on this doctrine of lordship salvation. And I nicely told them, 'Well, you know, you take the Scripture and you look at that, and you are kind of putting a little more on it. You need to read Acts 15 all over again and see what it says. All it says is grace; it doesn't say obedience.' "

"Not to mention John and Romans, right?" I added.

I asked her, "By so much you have been put down and cut off, right?" She answered that she actually had to separate herself from them on this matter because she realized their doctrine.

She had to do this because they were putting pressure on her. They were saying that she couldn't be a Christian and have a demon. She commented that they were like Job's friends, accusing her that she was suffering because she deserved it, because there was sin in her life, because she had hidden disobedience. She commented: "For a long time I thought that myself. Well, I have been reading through the book of Job again, and I can see that Job's dismay is similar in a lot of ways to mine, because my whole life as a Christian has been spotless, blameless, and above reproach. As I learn something, and I know I'm supposed to do something, I do it. I don't question it."

And I could testify to that, for I had seen her apply the Word, obey the Lord, and stand against the evil ones. Her progress in the Lord was quite apparent. She just had not been freed as yet from inhabiting demons; but she was honoring Christ and walking in victory over them, putting them to shame ever since we had first talked over a year before. Several leading demons had left.

As she mentioned that, another physical attack came because, as she explained, they hate being reminded of their defeats. We reminded them of their defeat by the blood of the cross. They raised her hands to her ears, as if to block out the sound of the Scriptures that spoke of their defeat by Christ.

"We will close her ears off."

"Well, she knows all this. You open your ears! Christ made all things. He's your Creator, isn't He? Isn't He?"

"We rebelled Him," came the ungrammatical reply.

"He created you is the issue." I steered him back to the point.

"Sure."

"And then you rebelled against Him."

"That's right!"

"Who is your leader?"

"Oh, Lucifer," he answered as if in pain.

"And you followed him."

"He was our leader. What do you do? Well, you follow a leader."

"No, you chose to follow him. He wasn't your leader in unrighteousness. He was your leader in righteousness to begin with. He was one who praised God. He was the guardian cherub, right?"

"We didn't want to praise God anymore, and we left Him," came the rebel's answer.

"Weren't you satisfied from what you had in creation? You were created beautiful, weren't you?"

"We wanted to get more, more, more, more! This is not enough. This is not enough! We want more, more, more!"

"What did you get?" I retorted.

"We didn't get it yet. We still trying to get more."

I pressed him again, "Where are you going to end up?"

"Oh, you always—We'll burn!"

"Where?" I continued to attack.

"Fire, fire, fire, fire, fire!"

"Are you one of Satan's angels?"

"I was, but I'm not," he admitted.

"And now you are one of his demons," I checked. "And now you are going to have to leave Dottie."

"I know," he admitted.

"Throne called Confusion, I command you to leave by the authority of Christ."

"I'll kill her first," he repeated three times. "You can't stop me from killing her!"

"Yes, I can. I forbid you to do it!"

"How?" He tried to delay.

"Jesus forbids you."

"You can't do that!" he protested.

"Jesus did it!"

"I'll make her—"

I put a musical tape recording on her knee to symbolize her kneeling to Christ and said to Confusion, "You're kneeling in her body to the Lord Jesus."

"Don't touch me with that . . . tape! I hate that song!"

The title of the song was "Daughter of Heaven." "You should hate that song. She is the daughter of heaven, and Jesus is the life of her."

"She was *our* princess!" There was evidently some human sacrifice by her ancestors that dedicated all the children to Satan.

I protested, "She has been delivered from the kingdom of darkness into the kingdom of God's dear Son."

"She was ours! She was our temple!"

"You failed to keep her from trusting Christ."

"Yeah, Jesus desecrated her."

I interrupted the process with, "Dottie, come back to talk with me. Do you think Jesus has desecrated your body?"

Dottie's own personality immediately responded, showing that she was in charge. "Not hardly." She laughed. "Oh, hallelujah."

"Are you glad the Lord lives within you?" I asked her.

"Amen!" she affirmed.

"Amen!" I gladly supported her.

Dottie sought to command Confusion to leave, but she stated that she was getting choked. I bound them from choking her. She continued with some resistance to command Confusion to confess Jesus Christ is victor and to leave her body.

"It is mine and Jesus Christ's, and we agree and you go!" she emphatically declared.

They sought to wrench her body. I told them to listen to Christ and prayed to Christ. They had to go. We found out afterward that Confusion did leave with his underlings. Dottie had wrestled in the power of the Lord to a great victory and freedom by His grace.

I have told this story in quite a bit of detail because it so pointedly exhibits the reality of a demonic personality inside a believer. The demon exhibited all the knowledge and attitudes that the Bible pictures belonging to a demon. Dottie demonstrated so many characteristics of a Christian. The two were definitely at odds in the moral realm. One hated Christ; the other loved Christ. One had Lucifer as his leader; the other, Jesus Christ as her Lord and Savior. One hated me and opposed me; the other respected me and cooperated with me in the warfare.

The demon sought to confuse the issue but had to confess that Dottie was a Christian and his victor in Christ. That confession—that a person is "in Christ"—is the beginning of the removal of the demon from a believer, for then he must obey and leave when Jesus and the believer agree. That's what happened here.

The results with Dottie were noticeable. She was no longer confused in many areas of her life. She was able to think clearly about herself and her relationships, and she was able to take her tests without confusion and to raise her grades in a Christian graduate school. She continues to walk with the Lord, but without so much distraction. Some spirits still remain at this writing, but we sense that they soon will all be sent to where Jesus sends them, the pit.

CASE 5: HARASSED PASTOR

A Chicago area pastor, a graduate of an evangelical seminary, encountered a case of demonization with a believer who came to his church. She said she had a spiritual problem because of her previous involvement in Satan worship. When he prayed for her, she either trembled or went unconscious. A demonized husband had problems. The pastor contacted me to help.

The pastor shared with me, after the session with the couple, how his own father had many subtle symptoms, such as depression and an inability to understand the gospel. He wrote me for my files regarding the case:

> I went to see Dr. Dickason with my Dad. It was evident that there were spirits that had been inhabiting my father in a quiet manner for years. Since my father's problem was an ancestral one (result ing from my grandmother's involvement in the occult), I had questions how I might be affected. The night after we visited Dr. Dickason, I felt definite harassment from the enemy. God used that experience to confirm that I too had some problems along this line. As we began to pray for discernment regarding our children, one night after being punished, our daughter told my wife she wanted to cut off her head and jump out the window. My wife and I thought that this sounded extreme for a small girl, so that evening we spent time in the Word and prayed that God would dismiss any spirits from her. When we went to bed we checked in on our daughter and found her asleep at the foot of the bed. When we attempted to put her under the covers, she said she moved to the foot of her bed because she had vomited on her pillow. She had not shown any signs of previously being ill. At that time we re-called a time when spirits were dismissed from a girl and they caused her to vomit. My wife and I saw this as an indication that

God honored our prayers and released her from the harassment of evil spirits. Until now, even in outbursts of sadness, she has not verbalized any self-destructive tendencies.

I have seen personal growth and strengthening in my ministry since I realized that "our struggle is not against flesh and blood, but against rulers, against the authorities, against the power of this dark world and against the spiritual forces of evil in the heavenly realms." I thank God for using His servants to uncover the world of darkness.

Here is a genuine believer, a pastor, who found that the ancestral spirits, according to the second commandment, had taken advantage of occult practices to enter the line of a family including himself. He recognized it and dealt with it successfully.

CASE 6: TRANSFERRED TROUBLE FOR A PASTOR

An evangelical pastor in Colorado came suddenly under attack as he was wakened every morning at 3:00 o'clock for many weeks. We checked out his background and circumstances. Though there were suspicious things in his background, we were not convinced that demons were in his life. We found that the visitations started exactly six months after he and his wife had decided after much prayer to turn down a call to a church in the South. The "visitor" impressed him with the fact that he had missed the will of God and that his ministry would now be disapproved.

Knowing that God did not work in such condemnatory fashion, I probed for the presence of wicked spirits. But I found none. I was surprised, since this had all the earmarks of demonic attack. The Lord led me, I believe, to ask his wife if I might test her condition. I had learned that mental illness and depression had plagued her family. She agreed to allow me. Upon demanding in Christ's name that any spirits present identify themselves, there was a definite response that startled the wife. It was clear and definitely another person, not she, that answered.

The demon confessed he came through her ancestral line and that she had not really given him any opportunity to express himself, although he sought to depress her. But he admitted under examination that he had left her body every morning at

3:00 o'clock to harass her pastor husband. He did this to discourage him, keep him from effective service, and force him out of the ministry. We prayed for the wife and for the pastor, binding demons never to do that again. We left confident we had found the cause. The pastor wrote me that God had given the victory. The harassment had stopped completely, and they were rejoicing in the Lord.

Here is another case of a genuine believer, a pastor's wife, being inhabited by a wicked spirit.

CASES 7 AND 8: TWO DEFEATED MISSIONARIES

Two missionary ladies, effective in their widely separated fields, suddenly were nearly incapacitated and led into deceitful and destructive ways. Professional counselors who sought to help them could go only so far. One case was of longer duration than the other. Both counselors sought my advice and brought their clients from some distance. They were concerned for them as their sisters in Christ who were about to be disqualified from Christian service. Before the eyes of the counselors and friends, each of the ladies, in separate sessions, was demonstrated to have inhabiting demons. Since our counseling is in Chicago, these ladies returned to their respective counselors for more help. The last report on both of them is that they came to recognize their problem, dealt with it effectively in the power of Christ, and that wicked spirits had lost their hold in these lives.

A counselor of one of the ladies told me that he had never thought Christians could be demonized. But this man with good professional credentials and a record of helping Christian folk in four different organizations had to change his mind due to actual cases he encountered. Since that time, he has begun to see more cases where the demonic was a distinct probability. His eyes have been opened, and he has sensitivity to such things.

We praise God for the restoration of these two dear Christian missionaries who had been demonized.

CONCLUSION REGARDING CLINICAL EVIDENCE

From the above cases reported by other reliable counselors and by the author, it may be seen that genuine believers in

Christ have been inhabited by demons. Many other cases may also be presented. My written files and tapes record detection, confession, and dismissal of wicked spirits from Christians. By this we are not seeking to establish any credit or reputation for ourselves. We are seeking to establish the record that proper clinical evidence abounds that believers in Christ may be inhabited by demons. We do this to alert Christians and counselors that we might recognize the tactics of the enemy. Recognizing this, we will be better able to help those in dire distress—those discouraged, defeated, depressed, and even suicidal. We must not stay ignorant of his methods.

We have used biblical parameters for the recognition of Christians and of demonization. In clinical investigation, we have found substantial and convincing evidence that demons may inhabit believers under certain circumstances. We must hasten to repeat that demons cannot initially invade a Christian if he is walking with the Lord. However, where the background in the family, in personal experience, or in transferral from an occultly connected person opens the door for invasion, there well may be demonic presence behind the problems that some Christians experience.

Some may yet object that we have not taken into account other possibilities, such as deeper psychological problems or multiple personalities. We answer that the symptoms and interviews display such characteristics and behavior that cannot be explained by psychological pathology. The onslaught is often sudden with no seeming cause or history of psychological or physical pathology. There is the consistent opposition to Christ and Scripture by every personality present except the normally present human, the Christian. There are sudden changes in personality corresponding to the person addressed. There is the confession that they indeed are wicked spirits who serve Satan and that they are different persons from the humans they inhabit. They admit to being spirit beings in league with Satan and bound for the same lake of fire as Satan. They admit they have different destinies from the Christian, who is going to be with Christ. They fear the name of Christ and oppose the servants of Christ. They obey and leave upon detection and after being commanded to leave in the name of the Lord Jesus. As a result, Christians are relieved, some permanently, and more freely go on to serve the Lord, rejoicing in Him.

We have heard on several occasions, some of which are reported in the above cases, that demons promote the concept that believers cannot be inhabited by demons. That way they can keep on being more effective under cover. They fear that their cover will "be blown." We hope that these case studies may contribute to that defeat and to the effective helping of God's children who should not have to endure demonic harassment or the inadequate counsel of those counselors, even Christian counselors, who dismiss the spirit world or demonization as a factor in the lives of Christians.

Further, in several cases, those who are professionals with skill in discerning psychological problems have concurred that the clients suffered from a combination of psychological and demonic problems. They recognized the demonization.

I have on file the testimony of Christian psychiatrists and psychologists who have conferred with me on these matters. They also recognize and appreciate this dimension of counsel and therapy.

One psychiatrist wrote:

> Mrs. _____ was referred to me for treatment by Dr. Fred Dickason. On diagnostic evaluation and in exploring her history of difficulties, the vital role Dr. Dickason has played in helping her with his counseling has been apparent. Mrs. _____ is suffering from a chronic difficult psychiatric illness. She is a Christian and has the strengths of great faith and good intelligence. She has very real family and social problems in addition to her illness. . . .
>
> It is extremely important for Mrs. _____'s continued health and well-being that she continue to see Dr. Fred Dickason in counseling. His prayers, guidance and counseling have proven their merit in that she has not been hospitalized once while seeing him over the past four years. Prior to that time, she had multiple mental hospitalizations.

This same psychiatrist cooperated with me with other clients and referred to me on several occasions those she considered having demonic problems.

An outstanding testimony to the demonization of Christians came to me from a well-respected psychiatrist who had been firmly convinced otherwise. He phoned me regarding a girl I suggested be referred to him. He forcefully told me that I was out of my field and did not know what I was talking about. I asked him for his theological credentials. He fumbled. I asked him how I could help with the client. He said, "Just keep away from her. I don't want you feeding her with this demon business." I said I didn't agree with his rejection of this factor but that I would respect his wishes for the good of the girl. He asked me what I thought it meant that she would dream or envision lying naked upon an altar. I suggested that such is common in satanic worship. It may mean that she somehow was involved in such a thing. "Nonsense!" he declared. "It means sexual molestation." I questioned if it had to mean one without the other.

After many months of therapy, and after using relaxant drugs that were designed to unlock the suppressed memory, the doctor found that there had been sexual molestation by her family. This I had suspected. She was not progressing as the doctor wished. I had heard from her once during this time. She was confused regarding the part of demons. I told her that I would pray for her, but I did not counsel along that line. I urged her to cooperate with her psychiatrist. I also continued to pray for her and her doctor.

I was surprised one day when the girl and her psychiatrist came to my office in Chicago. They were beaming. She looked wonderful. The doctor asked her, "Do you want to tell him, or should I?" She said she had been greatly helped and deferred to the psychiatrist. He related how in therapy he had come against a block with her and could go no further.

Then he confessed, "I never thought I would be on the same side as you. But we had to confront demons in her and deal with their influence in her life." She had been much relieved. I thanked him for his good news and care for my student friend. We hugged one another as brothers in Christ. Our difference in this matter was over. We both felt good about it.

The young lady said to me, "You saved my life. I was about to commit suicide, but you listened to me and counseled me."

How wonderful the grace and power of God to rescue His child from such a tragic situation! He delivered her from the power of demons who invaded her body when she was dedicated to Satan and used in sexual fashion. She has continued on with the Lord. The doctor said she was to be completely released from clinical care within a few days. She was not allowed to return home but was directed by the psychiatrist to another home.

CONCLUSION

These case studies taken from my personal written and taped records demonstrate that genuine believers can and indeed were inhabited by demons. Those demons manifested themselves and were recognized as persons distinct from the believer. They were not so-called multiple personalities. Instead, they identified themselves as spirit beings under Satan and as enemies of Christ defeated by His blood. Most of the demons had invaded before the person had received Christ. Many of them came in as the result of ancestral sins. They could not prevent the person from receiving Christ, but they stayed on hoping to distract, defeat, and destroy the believer. Under pressure of the authority of Christ, they confessed Christ as their victor and the believer as their victor in Christ. Upon confrontation with Scripture and in the Savior's authority, there was significant relief and, in most cases, removal of the wicked spirits from the Christian. For this we can thank God.

Again, clinical evidence found by qualified counselors has helped us answer in the affirmative the question, Can genuine believers in Christ be inhabited by demons?

PART 3

Related Issues

12

The Dynamics of Demonization

We have found from a survey of biblical information that demonization is basically a demon-caused passivity or the control of a demon over a person that manifests itself in various ways and to various degrees. This definition has been treated in detail in chapter 2. We must briefly and simply treat the issues of how demonization operates. Total analysis of the dynamics seems impossible, since the matters involved are so complicated and research has been limited. However, we may describe certain practical observations from biblical and clinical data.

We will first consider the dynamics of demonization in general and then treat the special case of the dynamics within a believer.

GENERAL DESCRIPTION

We must consider the causes, the method, and the effects of demonic control.

CAUSES OF DEMONIZATION

What brings about demonization in a person is often complex and sometimes unclear, but certain common causes seem clear.

Personal involvement. Unger suggests that the person's own attitudes or activities provide the major cause for demonization. He writes:

In the great majority of cases possession is doubtless to be traced to yielding voluntarily to temptation and to sin, initially weakening the human will, so that it is rendered susceptible to complete or partial eclipse and subjugation by the possessing spirit.[1]

Ensign and Howe add this observation:

> The usual cause of demonic control over some area (and usually it is only a part of a person's life that is controlled) of personality, will, or body stems from that person's involvement in satanic-occult activities *before* he became a Christian.[2]

Personal involvements that lead to this include the areas of divination, magic, spiritism, or combinations of these. Divination embraces such things as the Ouija board, tarot cards, astrology, fortune-telling, palm reading, rod and pendulum, water witching, psychometry, predictive dreams or visions, and crystal ball.

By magic we are not referring to sleight of hand, or illusion. Occult magic includes demonic forces that actually produce detectable phenomena. Divination taps secret knowledge, whereas magic taps secret power. Included in magic are such things as healing and inflicting of hurt, love and hate magic, curses, fertility charms, persecution and defense spells, banning and loosing, and good and ill fortune ceremonies (such as Indian "pow wow"). The Bible recognizes magic and attributes it to Satan and his demons. They intervene upon the request of mediumistic men to accomplish their purposes and to further entangle those involved in their deception and bondage. Consider Pharaoh's magicians who opposed Moses (Ex. 7-11) and Antichrist who deceives men preceding Christ's return (Matt. 24:24; 2 Thess. 2:9; Rev. 13:11-15). All magic of supernatural origin is antichrist and is demonic in origin, even that done superstitiously in the name of Christ (Matt. 7:21-23).

Spiritism involves the attempt to contact spirits of the dead or supernatural spirits. Many desire personal peace, comfort, or advantage. Some seek special revelation for this life and the life

1. Merrill F. Unger, *Biblical Demonology* (Wheaton, Ill.: Scripture Press, 1957), p. 95.
2. Grayson H. Ensign and Edward Howe, *Bothered? Bewildered? Bewitched?* (Cincinnati: Recovery, 1984), pp. 150-51.

hereafter. Spiritism results in pride, deception, and bondage to demonic powers. Demons impersonate the dead and can, through their supernatural knowledge and contacts, actually "recall" privately known matters. Consulting with mediums who practiced this was strictly forbidden by God (Lev. 19:31; Deut. 18:10-12). Severe penalties, even death, were leveled against guilty parties (Lev. 20:6, 27). King Saul died for this sin and the sin of rebellion (1 Chron. 10:13-14). God condemns it elsewhere in the Old Testament (2 Kings 21:6; 23:24; 2 Chron. 33:6; Isa. 8:19; 47:9-14). Modern types of spiritism may be found in spiritistic groups such as the Theosophical Society and the I AM movement (now called the Church Universal Triumphant). Slumber parties may include such dangerous games as mirror mantic ("Mary Worth"), table tipping, and levitation (lifting bodies with light finger touch). All these invite the intervention and even possible invasion of demons. To think that Christians are automatically immune to such influences is naive. We are not immune to temptation, to sin, to worldliness, to deception, and a host of mental and physical illnesses. Why should we think that we are immune to demonic attack and invasion if we directly transgress the laws of God (1 Cor. 10:14-22)?

Ancestral involvement. Bondage, mediumistic abilities, and demonization are not transferred by genetic reproduction. Certain inherited and/or conditioned weaknesses may contribute toward one's seeking self-satisfaction through the occult, but the bondage is not inborn. However, if the parents back to the third or fourth generation were involved in the occult or had demonic abilities, then the children may be affected or even invaded as a legal judgment from God. Such is the effect of the warning in the second commandment. It is an unclean and wretched thing to worship dirty demons instead of the true and living God and His Son, Jesus Christ. God considers this a major evil (Jer. 2).

Worship of idols, ancestors, spirits, or gods of any sort other than God the Creator and Redeemer revealed in the Bible is essentially the worship of demons (Ps. 106:36-38; 1 Cor. 10:20).

The same principle of God's visiting the sins of the ancestors upon their descendents is found in Jeremiah 32:18, which says that God "repayest the iniquity of fathers into the bosom of their children after them." We read of this law applied to the descendants of Jeroboam. Because of the evil he had done, more than all who were before him, and because of his blatant idolatry,

God promised to cut off all of his males in Israel so as to make a clean sweep of filth (1 Kings 14:9-10). The same judgment came upon the house of Baasha, king of Israel, who led them to sin as did Jeroboam. God said, "I will consume Baasha and his house" (1 Kings 16:1-3). The principle is repeated for the house of Israel. Their judgment in removal from the land of promise was due to the sins of their forefathers and their own sins (Jer. 16:10-13). Nehemiah recognized the propriety of such judgment, for the people deserved it (Neh. 9:33-37).

Some mistakenly think that God has revoked this judgment connected with the second commandment. They quote Ezekiel 18:1-4 where God condemns the misuse of the proverb "The fathers eat the sour grapes, but the children's teeth are set on edge." God retorts, "As I live . . . you are surely not going to use this proverb in Israel anymore. Behold, all souls are Mine; the soul of the father as well as the soul of the son is Mine. The soul who sins will die." Note that God does not refer directly to the second commandment but to the proverb that the rebels in Israel used to cast the guilt for their judgment back on their ancestors. God is saying that they cannot ignore their own guilt and blame their fathers. They have enough of their own guilt to cause His judgment. Furthermore, we note that Ezekiel lived in the same period as Jeremiah, who spoke of God's removal of Israel on the basis of the second commandment.

Further evidence that this principle is in effect today comes from the Lord Jesus in Matthew 23:32-36. He warns the leaders of Israel who are rejecting Him: "Fill up then the measure of the guilt of your fathers." He says he is sending them messengers whom they will also reject,

> "that upon you may fall the guilt of all the rightous blood shed on earth, from the blood of righteous Abel to the blood of Zechariah, the son of Berechiah, whom you murdered between the temple and the altar. Truly I say to you, all these things shall come upon this generation."

Romans 1:21-32 describes the rebellion of the race and its descent into idolatry. In God's judgment for this, He gave them over to further sin and the penalty that results. This involved continuing the effects of God's judgment to the children of the idolatrous rebels. The visiting the sin of the fathers upon the third and fourth generations is presented by Paul as a continuing principle of God's judgment.

I have found this avenue of ancestral involvement to be *the chief cause of demonization*. Well over 95 percent of more than 400 persons I have contacted in my counseling ministry have been demonized because of their ancestors' involvement in occult and demonic activities. This may involve the above sins and immoral sins connected with idolatry.

Treatment received. Persons with occult or demonic powers may transfer their influence and cause the person treated to be invaded by demons. Laying on of hands, mystical contact by holding hands, hypnotism, or magic treatment received may be enough to do this. The so-called gift of tongues or the gift of healing may be transferred by occult means. Supernatural powers and personal joy may result, but there will be deception, bondage, and psychological and physical disturbance. Koch states that it is tragic when a Christian who has acquired mediumistic abilities through one of these means assumes that they are gifts of the Holy Spirit. Satan is the great counterfeiter (2 Cor. 11:13-15).[3]

METHOD OF DEMONIC CONTROL

As to how demons control a human, we can say some things with a degree of certainty, but total analysis is impossible. We are unable to deal with demonic manifestation in a totally controlled laboratory environment. However, we do know something of their operational methods from Scripture. There is additional information available from scientific findings about the mind and from clinical investigation of the demonized.

Capability of demons. We have found in the Bible that demons may affect the body and the mind as well as conditions external to a human. In demonization they affect speech, sight, and hearing. The matter of speaking through a human requires the control of a complex system of the brain, nerves, muscles, and organs. The mind controls all of these. We may view the mind as part of the spirit that God has placed within man. In biblical perspective, the mind is not an extension of the brain

---

3. Kurt Koch, *Occult Bondage and Deliverance* (Grand Rapids: Kregel, 1970), pp. 39-40.

(or body). The spirit of the Christian is said to depart the body and to be present with the Lord upon the dissolution of death (2 Cor. 5:8; Phil. 1:22-23). The mind functions without the body in the abnormal state of death, so that the person recognizes his identity, his difference from and relation to others, the sequence of time and history, and can trust God (Rev. 6:9-11).

While a man is alive, the relation of the mind to the brain is much like an operator to a computer, a storeholder to a storehouse, or a pianist to a piano. The mind selects the operations available from the brain—memory, reasoning and evaluative processes, control of the body, and control of speech. The mind makes the judgments and decisions and uses the brain to relay messages to carry out its determined actions. So the mind is the important entity in control of the human.

Control of humans. A related and informative study on the relation of the mind and brain is presented by Arthur C. Custance. He treats the mind/brain problem[4] and refers to recent experimentation that distinguishes the mind from the brain.[5] He states, "The evidence seems to indicate that 'will' initiates a preparatory signal in the brain which is then responsible for the desired movement."[6] He quotes John Eccles, who had experimented and written in this area of research:

> Eccles is quick to point out, however, that the outstanding problem which remains lies in the nature of the voluntary control mechanism which bridges "across the interface between the self-conscious mind on the one hand and the modules of the cerebral cortex on the other." The connection from there on in, from cortex to motor neurons, seems clear enough. All we can now say is that *experimental evidence of interactionism does indeed exist.*[7]

It follows that, since demons can control speech, cause great physical strength, and afflict various parts of the neurological system and body, they control humans by mind control. This may be done at two levels. (1) It seems that if they can affect electrical and chemical changes in the brain, they may bypass the mind, even operating parts of the body apart from, even

4. Arthur C. Custance, *The Mysterious Matter of the Mind* (Grand Rapids: Zondervan, 1980), pp. 17-24.
5. Ibid., pp. 61-86.
6. Ibid., p. 78.
7. Ibid.

against, the will of the human. (2) On the other hand, they may go so far as to control the mind through its cooperation, either by direct assault (similar to hypnosis) or by indirect means (such as conditioning and propagandizing, consciously or subliminally).

This approach helps us to understand how there can be an immediate change of personality manifest in demonized persons. At one moment the human mind controls; and at the next, the demonic mind controls.

A registered nurse in her thirties had sought help for her migraine headaches through the techniques of mind control in a group called Pathways. The process actually turned out to be Hindu-type meditation and positive mind-control technique.

At first she had some relief. Then came other problems, such as blanking out of memory, fear of having struck someone with her car during her blanking out of consciousness, and terrible guilt and anxiety. She also developed an unusual anger toward her second daughter, something she had not previously experienced. She came through friends to trust Christ as her Savior. She began growing quickly but still had some of her fears and unfounded guilt. Her nonrelieving and guilt-producing religion contributed to this also.

When she came to our interview, I deduced from all the evidence that demons could be at the root of the problem. With her permission, I addressed the leading ranking spirit. We found out that he had used the mind-control techniques of Pathways to control the nurse. He was causing the blanking out and the guilt. There was an obvious difference in personalities depending on who was addressed, the nurse or the demon. The nurse took her stand in Christ, confessed and renounced her involvement, dealt with other matters, and immediately had relief. Her anger toward her daughter disappeared. Her guilt was gone, and God gave her peace. Furthermore, she was able to drive her car without fear of blanking out. Demonic control of the mind had been relieved by their expulsion by the authority of Christ. She was now praising Him and continuing to grow in the Lord with understanding of His Word.[8]

In an interview with Alice, the first case cited in chapter 11, we had to distinguish for this registered nurse the difference

8. From tape of the counseling session.

between what was psychological and what was demonic in her thinking and behavior. At one point I queried the demon regarding his undercover mind control. He admitted to controlling the brain through electrical and chemical changes. "We have power in that," was his confession. Again we do not take such as scientific evidence, but his confirmation of controlling the mind through the brain must be considered.[9] Why would he give away such damaging information except he were under pressure from the Lord?

Eccles speaks of one's personal uniqueness. Self-consciousness cannot be simply a spin-off from the material brain in its development. He was constrained to hold to "a supernatural origin of his unique self-conscious mind or my unique selfhood or soul."[10] The mind is the determining factor in the operation of the brain, but the human mind may not be the only control possible. Demonic intervention may introduce another mind to control the brain, and the brain may condition the human mind.

"The brain is not, therefore, the physiological *cause* of the self, but as Victor Frankl put it, it does *condition* it. There is a great difference between causing and conditioning."[11]

Custance's analysis further clarifies the relation of mind and brain and helps us to understand how demons might affect the thoughts and actions of a human:

> The position which both Popper and Eccles take is one of interactionism, the mind governing and employing the brain as a necessary device for its own conscious purposes, but also being in turn influenced by the brain's efficiency, limitations, genetic endowment, and healthy or diseased condition. The brain is limited in its programming by the mind: the mind is limited in its program by the efficiency and capacity of the brain as a machine. There is an interaction but there is a separation between the two parties to the arrangement.[12]

Dr. Elizabeth Hillstrom, psychologist and professor, classes demonization as a type of altered state of consciousness. She points out that persons in such states frequently experience subjective disturbances in concentration, attention, memory,

9. From tape of the counseling session.
10. Cited in Custance, p. 84.
11. Ibid.
12. Ibid., p. 85.

and judgment. There is the blurring of real and unreal and of cause and effect. Commonly persons entering altered states feel that they are losing self-control and a grip on reality. They almost always *shift from the active to passive mode of thinking.* There may be sensory and perceptual disturbances such as hallucinations, illusions, or delusions. There may be changes in body image and a depersonalization in which there may seem to be *a division between mind and body.* Sometimes they may feel a *detachment* between the emotion they are experiencing and the behavior they are displaying. Normal critical thinking and evaluation may be set aside. Hillstrom names some categories of altered states of consciousness: sleep, hypnosis, psychotic states, drug states, demon possession states. Altered states may be produced by God's influence, such as in dreams or visions; *by demonization,* cases such as recorded in the Bible; or by a malfunctioning brain due to chemical imbalance or damage.[13]

Conclusion. From biblical data, from scientific analysis of the mind/brain relationship, and from evidence of counseling sessions, we may deduce that the method demons use in demonization is that of mind control. They are spirit beings with minds of their own and wills directed against God and men, especially those who love Christ. (They probably wrestle with good angels by mind-control attempts, since they have no bodies.) They may seek to affect the mind through the conditioning of the brain by electrical/chemical effects. They may affect the mind by some form of mental conditioning, such as propaganda. They may also use hypnotism to directly control the mind.

The use of drugs, alcohol, traumatic experience, or hypnosis may set up the conditioning of the brain and mind that could lead to passivity and lack of self-control that would allow demon invasion and control, given the critical moral circumstances. Involvement in gross sin or occult practices could create the dangerous circumstances.

RESULTS OF DEMONIC CONTROL

Control by demonization may produce varying results. We have seen the biblical record of the effects produced. The read-

13. From paper delivered at Moody Bible Institute graduate course, Counseling: Demon Oppression, January 1986.

er should review the symptoms noted in chapter 2. The same chapter presented the symptoms suggested by counselors of the demonized. We could treat the effects of demonization as either overt or covert.

Overt results. Obvious results vary from case to case, although there are similarities. Some of these are unusual physical strength, fits of rage, demonstration of different personalities, resistance to spiritual things, hatred of Christ, alteration of voice, speaking in unlearned languages, and occult powers. There may also be physical symptoms which may be difficult to distinguish from normally encountered pathology.

Occult-type powers showed up in a pastor's wife who was able to sense the need of others and to aid in sympathetic fashion to meet that need. Her parents seemed to have similar powers. Once she sensed that another pastor was working on his sermon and was wrestling with a third point in his treatment. She drove to his study and supplied him with exactly what he could use. It was just as she had sensed.

In relating this to me (for she had come to me for oppression she was experiencing), I informed her that I thought that could be a demonic stronghold in her life. She thought it was a gift from God. We studied the Bible on the matter of spiritual gifts and distinguished between permanent and temporary or evidential gifts. She seemed to understand and to agree.

Later, in a confrontation with demons and with her pastor-husband present, we found a leading throne called "The Majestic One." He had under him one that imitated miraculous gifts. I asked him what must she believe about miraculous gifts if she were to be free from his influence. He answered, "Just what you have showed her from the Bible."

"Then there are no miraculous gifts today?" I sought his confirmation.

"No," the demonic throne replied.

"But you confuse people about them, do you?"

"Yes, that I might bring them under control," he added.

This same woman also had symptoms of multiple sclerosis. We suspected that, since medical doctors were uncertain of the disease, there might be a demonic root to these symptoms. Demanding in the name of Christ who might be causing these effects, we found one named "Weakness," who admitted that he had caused the MS symptoms. After the Christian lady renounced her "special gifts" and asked the Lord to relieve her, her husband and I commanded the throne and his helpers to leave. They finally did. Since that time, she has experienced no special revelations or supernatural discernment; and the symptoms of multiple sclerosis completely disappeared.

This case illustrates the overt effect that demonization may produce in the life of a Christian who has had ancestral or personal background in occult practices. She had both physical and mental disturbances, but Christ relieved them by the removal of the demons who had caused them.[14]

Covert results. Some results are not easily noticed externally, but within the person there may be recognizable or subliminal activities of demons. We have mentioned some of these in chapter 2 as symptoms noted by counselors. Apart from any physically based problems, there may be continuous depression, self-depreciating thoughts, antagonism to or resistance to reading the Word of God, inability to pray, fears of going insane, fear that God has forsaken, and a pervading sense of isolation. The demonized person may recognize that thoughts are being forced upon his mind, such as violence to others, suicidal suggestions, commands from "God," threats from "God" or other entities. Some experience the presence of evil (especially at night and in the bedroom), see specters, feel pressure on the body, and experience choking sensations, sexual molestations, and blanking out of the mind on occasion. These are often the results of demonic activity within the person, though some may come from outside.

As I was counseling one lady who had previously rejected a false tongues spirit and was still bothered by one called Nonacceptance, there arose the strong urge to raise her hands and speak in tongues. She resisted the demon's repeated attempts to reestablish a ground for further control or reentry of a tongues spirit.[15]

A Christian counselor brought her client to me for evaluation of her problem. This lovely Christian woman since childhood had been troubled with perverted sexual thoughts. Her father was given to alcohol and repeatedly beat his wife and this daughter, though he did not treat his son in such fashion. The

14. From notes on counseling session.
15. From notes on counseling session.

client was unable to relate to her husband sexually, and he also beat her and their children. There was a conspiracy, it seemed, to continue a destructive methodology in this lady's life. We were able, by Christ's grace and power, to determine that there were wicked spirits within her who had entered from her father. Beatings and fears allowed others to enter her traumatized and weakened will. They did confess that Christ and the Christian woman were their victors, and there came some relief. The Christian counselor later reported that there was continued progress in Christian growth and psychological health.[16]

Almost every week someone calls me complaining of thoughts that occur to them repeatedly and even forcefully, thoughts which they hate. I encourage them to believe the truth of the Word of God and to reject those thoughts. I congratulate them on the fact that they hate the thoughts, for their hatred is the true expression of their own mind and heart.

We have the privilege of selecting our thoughts. No thought is really ours until we accept and use it. Any one or a number of things can present thoughts to our mind, but we don't have to treat them as truth. We have the moral privilege and responsibility from God to evaluate and then accept or reject them according to the standard of God's truth and our preference. I encourage those afflicted by repeated evil or destructive thoughts to first thank God for the privilege of being related to Him through Christ and for the possession of a new nature through which we may have fellowship with God and through which we may choose our thoughts. Then I urge them to reject those evil thoughts and tell any wicked spirits responsible for them to depart in the name of Christ. Many have found relief through this positive and biblical approach.

When relief is thus found, it may be assumed that demonic forces were involved. God does intervene to answer the prayers and to honor the command of a believer when he assumes his position of acceptance and authority in Christ and exercises his God-given rights in boldness. In such cases where the voices make sense (not nonsense as in the case of schizophrenia, a condition of chemical imbalance in the brain), are anti-Christ and depreciate the human, and continue despite the attempts of the human to resist them and think of other things, we should

16. From notes on counseling session.

not limit our diagnosis to human factors, but we should strongly suspect demonic forces and deal with the problem as such. If there is response or relief to any noticeable degree, we may deduce that we are on track and continue to pursue the demonic cause in proper fashion.

SPECIAL FACTORS WITH BELIEVERS

We should consider certain factors when we talk about the dynamics of demonization in the Christian. These involve his susceptibility, his two moral capacities (natures), and the demonic use of the flesh. Case studies may clarify some of these special factors.

SUSCEPTIBILITY

Strengths of the believer. Believers have certain strengths and certain weaknesses when it comes to defense against demonization. Our greatest strength is our position "in Christ." When we trust Christ we are immediately baptized (placed) into Christ (not water) by the Holy Spirit. This joins us to Christ so that we share in His righteous standing before God, and He grants us a position of authority over Satan and demons. When we stand in our position, depend upon the Spirit to live according to God's Word, and exercise the authority we have in Christ, then we can successfully defend ourselves against the incursions of the enemy. Even if a Christian has been previously invaded, he still has great resources from God to battle against the powers of evil. He does not have to be controlled or defeated. He can submit to God, resist the devil, and expect him to flee (James 4:7).

The believer also has enlightenment regarding the truth. He can know, provided he has studied the Bible, that genuine reality and life lie in the sphere of God's Son and God's Word. If he knows this, he will be on guard against false systems of thought that might lead him into error and open him to demonic influence and possible invasion. The Holy Spirit will raise a warning if the believer tests truth claims by the Word of God (1 John 4:1-4). Of course, if these are ignored, there is no automatic protection any more than if a believer ignores warning signs while driving on a strange road.

Community support and counsel are resources that the believer can tap. He does not need to walk and fight alone. He should use godly and experienced counsel. In this he should seek those of balanced biblical faith who understand the principles of spiritual warfare. He has the support of believers' prayers.

Weaknesses of the believer. Becoming a believer does not relieve one of human weaknesses, surroundings, and background factors. Many in the West have been schooled in humanistic tradition. Conversion does not erase this conditioning. A believer may discount the spirit world and consider that certain occult activities are but games and that demons attacking Christians directly is just superstition. Christianity, after all, rules out superstition. He fails to see the reality of the occult and the dangers of sin, and rules out spiritual warfare with the possibility of demonization.

The believer also has the same problem as unbelievers with the influence of ancestral background. If his parents or other ancestors have been involved in things occult or demonic, then he also may have been invaded at an early age. The same principle applies to his involvement in demonic activities before his conversion. Ensign and Howe comment on this point. From their experience in counseling they found that the usual cause of demonic control stems from the person's involvement in satanic-occult activities *before* he became a Christian. If he used predictive devices, witchcraft, or drugs; or if he was captivated by compulsive sins (fornication, stealing, lying, etc.) or by false religions; then demons may have used these sins of rebellion to invade through these opened doors.[17]

> Becoming a Christian will bring forgiveness of sin to the sinner through genuine faith, repentance, and baptism into Christ; *but* this often does not cancel the *specific* control over some area of this life if he has given the devil legal right earlier.[18]

As Joshua and Israel took land from their enemies, they had God's promise that they could have everywhere they placed the soles of their feet (Josh. 1:3). Yet they left pockets of resistance, bands of soldiers that held out despite the major victory. Certain areas of a believer's life may present just such parallel resist-

17. Ensign and Howe, pp. 151-52.
18. Ibid.

ance. There the enemies of God have a foothold. The believer must specifically eliminate pockets of ignorance, distrust, and rebellion. He must grow, and he must continue to conquer the enemy.

The believer's presumptions may put him in danger. He should not presume that since he has become a Christian he is exempt from Satan's attacks. He instead has become a special target of demons, since he has now joined their deadly enemy, the Lord Jesus (Eph. 6:10-12). Satan does not hate the unbeliever as much as he hates the believer. He is the accuser of the brethren, not of the unbelievers (Rev. 12:10). He opposes the building of the church of Christ, not the establishment of humanistic organizations (Matt. 16:18).

A believer may become open to spiritual realities and aware of the supernatural world. He may presume that all supernatural effects are from God. In his desire to grow spiritually he may seek supernatural signs and healings that are in reality the counterfeits of Satan and his hosts (2 Cor. 11:13-15). He may subject himself to occult or mediumistic ceremonies in the guise of Christian ministry. His noncritical and even loving attitude may prevent him from properly evaluating such activities. He may even be warned of grieving or blaspheming the Spirit by questioning whether such things are of God. This simply is not true, for the Word of the Spirit commands us to test the spirits to see if they are from God.

Unger comments regarding believers' susceptibility:

> Satan and demons have their most astonishing success in the religious realm. They are especially eager to deceive believers and lead them into gross error of doctrine and conduct. The modern Babel of cults within the confines of professing Christianity is a standing witness to the devil's high bid for believers.[19]

Regarding the misled and false teachers, Unger writes:

> And all too many of these have been influenced and invaded by spirits not from God in the religious realm—nice, goody-goody spirits whose one characteristic puts them in the demon class— they oppose the Word and will of God.[20]

19. Merrill F. Unger, *What Demons Can Do to Saints* (Chicago: Moody, 1977), p. 126.
20. Ibid.

His lament is true:

> No spectacle is more tragic to see than a believer despoiled doctrinally by Satan, blinded by error, and brought under the delusion and enslavement of demonic teaching. Not until an attempt is made to rescue such a person from his predicament does one realize the powerful sway the demonic holds over the religiously enslaved believer.[21]

We conclude that though the believer has a perfect position in Christ and his salvation is secure through the grace of God, yet he is specially open to demonic attacks as their peculiar target. He may be especially susceptible if he ignorantly presumes he is exempt from attack or that conversion eliminates all the enemy's influence in his life or excludes invasion. His openness and gullibility in the spiritual area often aids demons in their attempts to control him. Hence, he must be on guard.

THE TWO MORAL CAPACITIES

Though there may be some debate regarding the exact constitution of the two moral capacities within the believer, most agree that the believer has within him an entity that prods him to sin and another entity that desires to do the will of God. This is taught in Romans 7. Some call these "the old man" or "the old nature" and "the new man" or "the new nature." Actually, a person has but one human nature that includes body and spirit. But the term *nature* is used to define a capacity in the human spirit. With the old capacity, related to Adam and sin, the believer has the capacity to sin. With the new, related to Christ and righteousness, he has the capacity to do the will of God.

Paul presents these as opposing principles that reside within a believer. It seems quite clear that Paul is talking about a believer in Romans 7:14-25. There is a switch from the Greek aorist tense in 7:7-13, when he describes his presalvation experience of guilt through the law, to the present tense in 7:14-25, when he describes his present struggle caused by his two capacities. Paul takes the place of a morally astute believer who objectively analyzes the two potentials within himself. He loves righteousness but hates the sin that entraps him. This is something a

---

21. Ibid., pp. 126-27.

nonbeliever could not do. He speaks as a man born again. Regeneration by God has planted within him a new capacity to fellowship with God. But that old capacity to sin, inherited from Adam, still tenaciously presents all the old sinful desires to the mind. Note the treatment of the enemy of "the flesh" in chapter 4 on spiritual warfare.

It is this "old man" (Eph. 4:22) that presents demons with a moral toehold in the Christian. The believer's flesh is no more sanctified than the unbeliever's. The flesh has been legally judged by Christ's cross and our co-crucifixion with Him, but it still whirs about inside us seeking to engage our will. Our will is susceptible to such internal influence, and this provides demons with a tool within the Christian that they can use. The moral base of our personality has a new bent, but the old bent remains a blight to us and a "blessing" to demons. They love it and take advantage of that which is closely related to them in the realm of sin.

DEMONIC USE OF THE FLESH

If demons can invade a Christian, they have a natural resource to use, a territory of evil within through which they can influence and seek to control the Christian. If the believer is not aware of the danger posed by the flesh and by demons, he may ignore the signs of demonic incursion. Many Christians think that the evil they experience within cannot have any root other than their old nature. Thus they blame themselves for not being stronger Christians, and demons can accuse them by leveling the charge that they are not true believers or that they are so wicked that God will give up on them. In reality it might be that demons re working through their intellect, emotions, and will to affect the believer's intellect, emotions, and will. There may indeed be a mind-control battle as demons manipulate and propagandize the believer's mind directly or through the access they have to the brain as they reside within. The person of the demon seeks to control the person of the believer.

Figure 1 seeks to depict schematically the dynamic attempt of inhabiting demons to control the mind of the believer. They work through the old nature to inject their thoughts into the believer's thoughts. They manipulate the believer's emotions by their own emotions. They seek to impose their will upon the

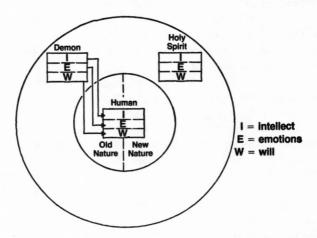

FIG. 1   An inhabiting demon seeks to control and dominate the human through manipulating his mind, working through the believer's old nature.

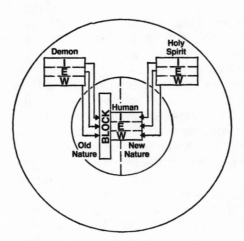

FIG. 2   The indwelling Holy Spirit seeks to control and cultivate the human through inclining and enabling his mind, working through the believer's new nature. The Spirit's control blocks the demon's use of the flesh.

believer to make him choose with them. The believer may indeed think their thoughts and feel their emotions, but he does not have to choose to *follow* what he thinks or feels. He is not an existentially controlled man. He is not a robot captive to his feelings and necessarily bound to express them. He may reject any thoughts, feelings, and choices that he determines to reject. He may turn his will to choose the truth and the will of God.

Believers who walk depending upon the indwelling Spirit of God are allowing Him to work through their new natures. The Spirit empowers them to obey the Word of God and serve Christ (fig. 2).

When believers follow the inclination of their old natures, then they remove themselves from the control of the Holy Spirit (Rom. 8:5-7; Gal. 5:13, 16-17). This opens them up to choosing the impulses from the sin nature (fig. 3). If demons reside within, they may use the occasion for inserting their own personal influences (fig. 4). When the believer yields to pride, to self-fulfillment in a nonbiblical manner, to sensual and sexual sins, to occult influences, to drugs, to false religious authorities, then he may be opening the door for demonic control in that area.

In certain counseling sessions, I have seen the anger and rage of the demon flare at me through the facial expressions of a Christian who loved me in the Lord. When the demon was expressing himself through the human's faculties, he mimicked the corresponding human expressions as he manipulated the brain and controlled the body. I have seen demons in fear and sorrow at their exposure and defeat express themselves through human tears. Often I would command them not to cry through the human's eyes, and the weeping stopped. The counselee would later report that he could feel what they were feeling and know something of what they were thinking but could at the same time distinguish himself from them. He was on the scene almost as an observer (but praying also) as the demon expressed himself under his command to speak to me and obey me. The believer could exercise his own will and resume control of his faculties whenever he wished to tell me of what was going on inside. This "inside information" aided me to be effective in the counseling procedure.

Some Christians are very confused as to the source of the problems that they have endured for years. Never once have

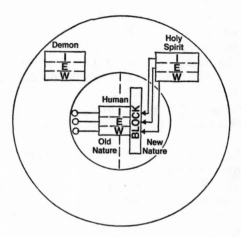

FIG. 3   The old nature does by itself condition and control the mind of the believer who does not yield to the Holy Spirit. Not all evil inclination comes from demons.

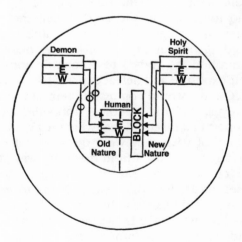

FIG. 4   If the believer does not walk in the Spirit but is controlled by his old nature, then demons may use the opportunity to force their own control upon the believer.

many of them thought that the problem might be demonic. They had been taught dogmatically that Christians could not be seriously affected by demons, let alone be "demon possessed." Such was unthinkable, since they had never seriously considered the weakness of biblical and theological arguments for such a position. Ensign and Howe comment on that confusion and the types of problems they have encountered:

> Many of the people we have worked with have admitted they had problems in various parts of their mental, moral, physical, and spiritual life; but they never identified that behavior with demonic control until they were actually tested by the Lord and His servants. Many think that these severe difficulties which they must fight against as Christians are just a part of their personality, inherited traits, or the way they happen to function. But compulsive and/ or irrational behavior which is immoral or which constantly defeats the witness and integrity of the children of God is almost always evidence of either demonic harassment (external) or demonic control (internal). Among such "normal" and accepted problems may be fear, rage, anger, pride, confusion of the mind, lust, sex, homosexuality, temper, lying, gluttony, depression, resentment, infirmity, sickness, inferiority complex, and others.[22]

CASE EXAMPLES

Case 1. A young, single man had problems in one of my evening school classes. As I was teaching about God's angels, a voice within him kept saying, "That's not true. You don't have to believe that." The man knew biblical truth and could recognize that I was teaching it. He was confused about the source of such thoughts. In an interview he disclosed his rejection by his father who wanted him to be a football player instead of an artist. He recalled that a man on a Christian retreat took a special but unusual liking to him. His reaction to the man was one of sexual attraction. He had never had this experience before. Thoughts in his mind were often of a homosexual nature. He experienced attraction and revulsion regarding this matter. He did not want to be homosexual. He thought he was inclined toward it because he was just constituted this way. A few sessions later we found, after some devious opposition from them, that demons

22. Ensign and Howe, p. 155.

had invaded him at an early age. The leader was a throne called "Control." This demon made him think that he was homosexual and kept manipulating his emotions to bring him into bondage. We had worked against lesser spirits at first; but when we identified this one and brought the finished work of Christ and His power against him, the young man felt great relief and had hope for the first time since he started having these problems. Demons had worked through his old nature to cause him to feel and then to think that he was inescapably homosexual.[23]

Case 2. Alice, who had self-image problems, counseled with me. We reported her case in chapter 11. This registered nurse had been invaded by a group of demons headed by a throne called Non-acceptance. He was brought to recognize that Christ had defeated him and that the nurse was his victor in Christ. This he confessed. She had taken her stand against him with good biblical and practical understanding. He challenged my authority and tried to make me dislike her. The nurse broke back in and laughed at his attempt. She liked me and was catching on to his technique. She gave me permision to continue speaking to the throne. The greater detail of the session is instructive here.

"My friend is getting stronger; you're getting weaker," I said to him. "And you have less and less influence over her mind."

"That's true," he answered, "but we use her feelings."

"That's true," I replied. "And she has feelings. How do you use her feelings?"

"Make them stronger."

"You have access to her brain," I stated.

"Uh-huh."

"Therefore you produce a synthetic feeling, and you remind her of her own feelings. She picks up on them, and she reinforces them. Is that right?"

"Right!"

"So the description of the psychological feeding the demonic and the demonic feeding the psychological is an accurate description."

"Yes," the throne admitted.

"You are mind-control creatures, and you work through the chemistry and electronics of the brain. Am I correct?"

23. From tape of the counseling session.

"Right! We have power in that," he emphasized.

"I bind you from using that power because that power is only allowed by God. You are an invader and a squatter; and you must leave this body because it is bought by the blood of Christ. It is dedicated to the Lord Jesus. She wants to serve Him, doesn't she?"

"Yeah," came the dejected answer.

"That frustrates you."

"Yeah. But if I can keep her confused, it keeps her side-tracked."

"How will you keep her confused?" I pressed.

"Bringing tongues to her mind. Bringing things to her mind to reject counsel."

"Whose counsel?"

"Her psychologist's, yours, and the other pastor, preaching."

"And you keep bringing incidents of bitterness to her mind, don't you?—rejection, because your name is Non-acceptance; and you play that game, don't you?"

"Yes."

"You are not accepted, are you?" I asked him.

"No."

"God has rejected you; Satan has forsaken you; and my sister has rejected you, hasn't she?"

"Yes."

So went the interview and confrontation.[24] I spent the time to develop this for the nurse and for her psychologist who doubted the reality of demonic invasion of her mind. The taped confrontation convinced the nurse that it wasn't just psychological problems that she was facing. They certainly were there, and the psychologist was helping her noticeably. But one of the root causes of her problem was the mind-control warfare that demons were continually pressing against her. They started by taking advantage of her emotions, which were rubbed raw by parents and others. There had been sexual molestation in the family. She was hurt, and the demons would not stop tormenting her emotions and thoughts.

Case 3. A strapping man with a well-developed body came to me full of fears and voices within. We found that when he was a child, his mother threatened him and struck him, often without

24. From tape of the counseling session.

warning. He grew up thinking he must be no good, a nobody, and that nobody cared for him. He compensated by building his body and joining a police strike force. He was proving his strength and power and that he did not have to be afraid. Yet he was.

My counselee gave me permission to determine if demons had invaded his body. I had strong suspicions from the personal and parental background. We found a demon throne called Fear. He confessed that he recalled to the man's mind the beatings and insecurities of his childhood. This was to make him doubt the love of God and prevent him from pursuing his desire of studying to become an evangelist. They made him feel that he did not exist, that there was no objective reality, and that there was no hope for him. These thoughts were repeatedly introduced each day. The man knew from the Bible that these inserted thoughts were not true, but he was wearing down under all the propaganda. At times he would rise above it by holding fast to the Word of God and resisting the enemy; at other times he was nearly overwhelmed by his emotions. We are still praying for him.[25]

CONCLUSION

These case studies, along with others on file, demonstrate that demons have worked in the minds of humans, Christians who had been invaded. Mind control and emotional manipulation came through the imposition of one set of personal faculties upon those of another. Each of the counselees had been invaded in early life due to the demonic involvement of ancestors, and further complications added to their bondage. Demons seem to arrange those situations and personal contacts, particularly with those under their influence, to further entangle their victims and reinforce their hold. The fleshly attitudes and actions of the demonized provided the basis for continued activity. When the Christian stood his or her ground, applied the truth of Scripture to the situation, and resisted the demons, the demons lost hold, and some left for the pit.

James commands Christians, "Submit therefore to God. Resist the devil and he will flee from you" (James 4:7). To do this

---

25. From notes of the counseling session.

we must properly recognize the Person of God and His claims. We must recognize the reality of demonic activity and their methods. We must act decisively against the enemy. Paul indicates that this spiritual warfare demands the application of the whole armor of God. That armor is a defense against various attempts, whether they be external or internal, to control the emotions, the thoughts, and the actions of the believer.

We must know the dynamics involved in demonization so that we might intelligently and determinedly war against the enemy in the strength and armor of Christ, the risen Lord.

13

Defense Against Demonization

There was little watchfulness and little warning that the Japanese were about to attack Pearl Harbor. Sunday was a beautiful day, and things seemed peaceful. War in the Pacific hardly seemed a potential reality. Then there were some scattered reports of sightings of unfamiliar aircraft; but those responsible did not seem to take the reports seriously, nor were those in command alert. The Japanese fleet was not recognized as anywhere near. An immediate attack was not a threat.

Then the enemy struck! With devastating accuracy and power the bombs fell—and so did the American fleet. Men and ships anchored in supposed safety suddenly experienced tragic and thorough defeat. They could not even respond. There was no capable defense and no possible counterattack. They were caught off guard—sleeping, even though some intelligence reports had given earlier warnings of possible Japanese moves. While the enemy lulled American leaders into false confidence, they were already on the way with their sneak attack.

As Christians, we must take warning. We have the intelligent revelation that we are indeed in spiritual warfare. We must not be caught sleeping as have so many. The enemy has his well-developed schemes, powerful resources, and great experience in battle. Satan goes about as a roaring lion seeking whom next to devour. We are to resist him steadfast in the faith (1 Pet. 5:8-9). Ignoring him will not make him retreat.

We must take a proper approach to warfare and have a proper perspective if we are to be successful in battle, especially in the area of demonization of believers. We have treated spiritual warfare in general in chapter 4. Now we must focus on combatting demonization of Christians.

PROPER APPROACH TO WARFARE

A proper approach to spiritual warfare involves, first, the recognition of its reality; second, reliance upon our position in Christ; and third, biblical and practical response in practice.

RECOGNITION OF ITS REALITY

Ignorance of demonization. Christians are often in spiritual conflict but unaware of its true nature. They seek to ignore it or put it from their minds, but it keeps coming back. Many living defeated or troubled lives never seriously consider that there might be demonic opposition. And the tragedy is that their spiritual helpers, pastors and counselors, never suspect it either. The enemy is having a heyday, a real slaughter among God's sheep; and the shepherds are sleeping or else do not recognize the wolf. They often call for the veterinarians instead of using the powerful staff that is in their hands, the staff of the Word of God and the authority granted them in Christ.

It is true that not every sin, problem, or disablement is to be blamed on a demon. We cannot blame on the devil the lusts of the flesh or all the aspects of the pull of the world. But when we have dealt with the normal causes of difficulty and do not find relief, we must suspect that Satan and demons may be at the root. Too often God's dear children are judged as being insincere or not really trusting Christ. They are often accused of deep hidden rebellion, at least lack of yieldedness to Christ as Lord of their lives. They do not have enough faith, they are told; and they go deeper into depression and despair. The possibility of demonization has never been a serious consideration.

Reality of demonization. We have noted the vast scriptural evidence of such a reality in the race. We have also found that the evidence from Scripture and theology does not deny the possibility of the demonization of Christians. Case studies from reliable counselors has produced good evidence of this reality. We cannot continue ignoring this potential struggle within believers.

Unger points out the possibility that demons sought to invade men in earliest biblical history. He points out that the grammatical difficulties of the Hebrew text of Genesis 4:7 are removed by taking the word *(robes)* translated "couching" as an Akkadian loan word, *rabisum,* meaning "demon." The translation then reads, "And if you do not well, sin is a *demon* at the door; and its (the demon's) desire is for you, but you must master it (the demon)."[1] It may be that a demon entered Cain in his rebellion against God and introduced the concept of the murder of his brother upon his rejection by God. Perhaps that is why Cain is described as "of the evil one, and slew his brother" (1 John 3:12).

The New Testament abounds with evidence of the reality of demonization, as we have seen in chapter 2. We cannot lightly dismiss such overwhelming evidence as represented by Christ Himself. W. M. Alexander strips Bible records of the supernatural and seeks to explain demonization in terms of "natural insanity" or "epileptic insanity." Present-day cases he explains as hypnotism or intoxication by hemp.[2] He ignores the testimony of Jesus and the apostles. He fails to account for the sane behavior, the changed condition, the witness of the crowd including His opponents that resulted from expulsion of the demons. He presents no facts to support his hypotheses that drugs and hypnotism were involved.

There tends to be a similar mentality among Christians today, even evangelicals. Many believe that such things cannot occur today. When they meet such things, they seek to explain them in terms of the natural as their humanistic training has conditioned them. This is not the day of the miraculous. Granted that miracles were part of the evidence presented by Christ and the apostles and that they are not a normal part of church experience today, but that does not rule out the continued presence of demons or current demonization.

The early church held to the reality of demons and demonization.[3] John Warwick Montgomery analyzes the report of a case of demonization in a letter written by Dr. Johannes Bugenhagen

1. Merrill F. Unger, *What Demons Can Do to Saints* (Chicago: Moody, 1977), p. 118.
2. William Menzies Alexander, *Demonic Possession in the New Testament* (1902; reprint, Grand Rapids: Baker, 1980), pp. 64-69, 98-101, 243.
3. John Warwick Montgomery, *Principalities and Powers* (Minneapolis: Bethany, 1973), pp. 177-80.

in November 1530.[4] There is overwhelming evidence that demonization occurs today in pagan and civilized cultures. Some of that evidence has been presented in chapters 10 through 12.

What must Christians do in light of all this evidence? Recognize the continued reality of demonization! We must also recognize the reality of the demonization of believers and respond to their urgent needs.

Unger sounds the warning against ignoring reality:

> To deny the possibility of demonic working in the lives of Christians is to fail to allow Scripture to speak in the full scope of its implications and to flatly ignore experience. To fail to grasp the full extent to which such sinister power may operate is perilous, for it denies to those who have been invaded by the enemy the understanding and help they so desperately need. Also, this teaching warns those uninvaded of the peril of invasion and of what will happen if they fail to reckon on what they are in Christ and backslide into gross and willful sin.[5]

RELIANCE UPON OUR POSITION

The Christian stands in a unique position to deal with all of this. He has been identified legally and morally with Christ. He participates in Christ's life and Christ's work. This affords the believer a powerful position from which to wage war against Satan and his armies.

Perfect acceptance. The believer in Christ has been granted a perfect standing before God. Upon trusting Christ, we are justified by the grace of God on the merits of the sacrifice of Christ (Rom. 3:24). By the blood of Christ God has been perfectly satisfied regarding the guilt of our sin (Rom. 3:25-26). God has placed to our credit the righteousness of the Son of God (2 Cor. 5:21). We have the same acceptance with God as does His Son (Eph. 1:4-7). God Himself could not improve our standing with Him, since He appointed the Son, is satisfied with His sacrifice, and has granted us a perfect position "in Christ."

This position grants us certainty of our relationship to God and provides the answer that shuts the mouth of the accuser of the brethren (1 John 2:1-2).

---

4. Ibid., pp. 180-87.
5. Unger, *What Demons Can Do to Saints,* p. 94.

Perfect access. As believers we also have complete and open access to the Father's throne of grace. With our great High Priest at the right hand of God we have reason for steadfast confidence and are urged to come boldly to the Father to receive mercy and grace in any time of need (Heb. 4:14-16). We ought not, then, to hesitate about casting all our concerns upon Him or to bring all our questions to Him for resolution. He is perfectly concerned about us. In this connection we are to be sober and watchful regarding the enemy and are to resist him firmly in the faith (1 Peter 5:7-9). We should pray for daily bread and for daily deliverance from the schemes of the evil one (Matt. 6:11-13).

This access allows us to pray for all that we need to stand firm against the enemy and his temptations. We may pray for our own needs and for the needs of others in their problems. God delights to answer our prayers along this line. I have seen immediate relief come to those oppressed who were relieved by God to continue their battle without debilitating distraction.

Perfect authority. When the Holy Spirit placed (baptized) us into Christ, He joined us to Christ in His death, resurrection, and ascension (Rom. 6:1-10; Eph. 2:5-6). To understand what that means in the matter of spiritual warfare, we must clearly see the position accorded by God to Christ.

In Ephesians 1:17-23, Paul prays, among other things, that we might be given insight by the Holy Spirit into the surpassing greatness of the power of God directed toward believers. This power is measured by the inscrutable power of God operating in Christ "when He raised Him from the dead, and seated Him at His right hand in the heavenly places, far above all rule and authority and power and dominion, and every name that is named, not only in this age, but also in the one to come. And He put all things in subjection under His feet, and gave Him as head over all things to the church." This pictures Christ's position as towering indescribably above all demonic forces. The terms used to describe these authorities are used elsewhere to identify demons (Rom. 8:38; Eph. 6:12; Col. 2:15).

Paul describes our union with Christ in Ephesians 2:5-6: God, "even when we were dead in our transgressions, made us alive together with Christ (by grace you have been saved), and raised us up with Him, and seated us with Him in the heavenly places, in Christ Jesus." So as Christ is far above all demonic authorities, so we in union with Him are also seated far above our enemies! We need to lay hold on the truth of our position of authority accorded us in Christ. The enemy trembles when we do. He will do everything he can to take our eyes off this powerful position granted by God's grace.

This helps us to understand more of the power behind Christ's great commission to disciple all nations: "All authority has been given to Me in heaven and on earth" (Matt. 28:19). There are no creatures, angels or men, who can successfully oppose this all-inclusive and all-determinative authority. It is with this authority that He commissioned us to do His work. He also said, "I will build My church; and the gates [place where the city authorities sat] of Hades [world of unseen spirits] shall not overpower it" (Matt. 16:18).

Understanding Christ's universal authority, His position in the heavenlies far above all demons, and our position as seated with Him, we may exercise under His direction the delegated authority He gave to us to carry on His work. This work includes making disciples. Making disciples involves freeing them from the power of darkness (Isa. 61:1; Acts 26:18; Col. 1:13).

The believer has complete authority in the will of God to oppose the powers of darkness. We must lay hold on this truth if we are to conquer in the name of Christ. When the believer utters, "In the name of the Lord Jesus," he is not using a magical or mystical formula; he is exercising His God-given authority by virtue of his union with Christ. This involves praying (John 16:23), preaching or teaching (Matt. 28:19-20), and opposing and commanding the enemy (Acts 16:18).

With such a position in Christ, we may confidently wage warfare to relieve the demonized. Christ has defeated Satan and all his host (Col. 2:15; Heb. 2:14-15). We are victors in Christ and can be more than conquerors even in the midst of battle (Rom. 8:35-37). We are operating in this warfare from the position of victors in Christ! We must never forget that.

RESPONSE IN PRACTICE

The grace of God that granted to us such a perfect position in Christ requires a fitting response. We must renew our dedication to Christ, reject false philosophies of life, and rely upon the armor of God.

Renewing allegiance to God. Whether in personal battle

against demonization or helping another in the battle, the believer must place himself under the authority of Christ. If he is to exercise authority from Christ in warfare, then he must be under the authority of Christ in life. Rebels cannot fight the great rebel; they are in a sense cooperating with the enemy. No one can serve two masters (Matt. 6:24).

God requests and requires full allegiance to Christ. Christ challenged His followers to such yieldedness (Matt. 16:24-26). We must choose whom we are to serve. We must hate (choose against allegiance to) all relationships of life that would hinder us from serving Christ, and we must love (choose for dedication to) Christ and His will (Luke 14:26-27). This means death to the selfish and self-directed life. It means living to Christ and the life He would cultivate for us (Gal. 2:20; 6:14). It means walking in the light of God's Word by depending upon the indwelling Holy Spirit and allowing Him to produce the fruitful character of Christ within us and to carry on the fruitful work of Christ through us (John 15:5-10, 16; Gal. 5:16, 22-23; Eph. 5:18).

Victory over the enemy, especially in confronting demonization, demands submission to the Captain of the Lord's Hosts. We must humble ourselves under the mighty hand of God, who cares for us. Then we will be able to resist the devil, and he will flee from us (James 4:7).

It is in this context that the request of God through Paul comes to us with even more meaning, "I urge you therefore, brethren, by the mercies of God, to present your bodies a living and holy sacrifice, acceptable to God, which is your spiritual service of worship" (Rom. 12:1).

Rejection of false world views. Paul continues: "And do not be conformed to this world, but be transformed by the renewing of your mind, that you may prove what the will of God is, that which is good and acceptable and perfect" (Rom. 12:2). This involves the rejection of false views of reality, of values, of methods to know and please God. We are not to be forced into the mold of this world's system or philosophy. All allegiance to creature-centered pleasure and profit must be broken. New attitudes toward God, life, ourselves, and others must replace old ones. We must seek to live according to the Word, to love God, and to love others as God would have us to do.

Practically, this involves renouncing before God the devil and all his works. Any involvements in things occult and demonic must be confessed and a stand taken against them. Specific confession and renunciation are tools that strip the enemy of his assumed rights that may have allowed his influence or invasion. We have seen the enemy wince and retreat under such treatment. As doors have been opened for demonic influence through specific actions or attitudes, so they must be closed in specific manner. God honors specific stands and specific prayers.

Paul writes in 2 Corinthians 10:4-5:

> For the weapons of our warfare are not of the flesh, but divinely powerful for the destruction of fortresses. We are destroying speculations and every lofty thing raised up against the knowledge of God, and we are taking every thought captive to the obedience of Christ.

By this Paul is saying that all philosophical or religious claims to truth are tested by the truth of God's revelation in the person of Christ and our relationship to Him in the grace of God. We are in Him who is true, and the whole world lies in the wicked one (1 John 5:19-20).

Demonized persons must renounce all false religious systems and practices, such as Hinduism, Buddhism, transcendental meditation, yoga, martial arts, Christian Science, Jehovah's Witnesses, and so on. Christians who have received mystical healings or special gifts by the laying on of hands may have actually participated in a typical occult transference. That also should be confessed and renounced. Participation in any New Age movement practices or in mind-control groups or secret societies must be judged also. Upon confession and stand against these things, God will break their hold over the life of the believer and remove demonic ground for harassment.

An excellent source of information giving perspective and insight into various types of occult practices is the book *Occult Shock and Psychic Forces*, by Clifford Wilson and John Weldon. They treat various expressions of Eastern mystical philosophy and religion, expressions of the "new medicine" (as in the New Age movement), and the influence of parapsychology.[6]

6. Clifford Wilson and John Weldon, *Occult Shock and Psychic Forces* (San Diego: Master, 1980).

Removal of false ways. To remove demon oppression, a believer must put away sinful practices and possessions. This principle of spiritual warfare has ample support from the Bible. Moses thoroughly destroyed the golden calf fashioned by Aaron and the people when he was away receiving the Law. He knew the dangers of allowing its influence in the camp of Israel (Ex. 32:20). Hezekiah, king of Judah, removed the high places, broke down the sacred pillars, cut down the idols, and even broke the brazen serpent Moses had made. All of these had become places or objects of idolatrous worship. Josiah, also a reforming king in Judah, caused extensive elimination of all that supported idolatry: the priests of Baal, the idols, the places of sacrifice, and the altars. He cleansed the land and then celebrated the Passover. God commended him for all this (2 Kings 23:4-25).

Even in the New Testament we find this practice. Simon the magician was warned to put away his heathen thinking and practice (Acts 8:18-24). Many who trusted Christ due to the preaching of Paul in Ephesus "kept coming, confessing and disclosing their practices. And many of those who practiced magic brought their books together and began burning them in the sight of all" (Acts 19:18-19). The cost of the magic books was about 137 man-year wages.

The necessity of removing all practices or objects associated with demon-inspired activities is quite clear from Scripture. We have found that it is necessary to free men from the bondage of demons today as well. A woman told me that she was being molested at night by unseen hands. She mentioned that she had over the head of her bed a gift from a man who had made sexual advances toward her at her work place. We dedicated the gift to destruction, and she removed it. The harassment ceased. A young, lady student, who was part of a Florida beach evangelism team, received a leather string bracelet from a man to whom she witnessed. He said it was a friendship bracelet. Sometime after he had tied it on her wrist, she began to have strange sensations and disorienting feelings. I suggested that this fit the pattern of a love charm and that there might be some demonic association. We prayed, I broke it off her wrist, and since that time the harassment has disappeared. God removed the demon influence.

Converted witches and satanists must destroy all paraphernalia, or lingering demon influence may keep them from spiritual growth and seek to drag them back into bondage. Magic charms, decorations of idolatrous nature, certain Indian dolls and paintings (especially sand paintings by medicine men), and books of magic practices and false religions should be destroyed along with other such things. It is naive and dangerous for churches to display a collection of idolatrous items, such as carved gods, religious masks, gemstone figures, war spears, etc. These have all been dedicated to heathen gods, and demons use them as centers of influence. If a person hesitates to destroy such things, they become a point of contention between the person's will and God's. God's will is quite clear: we must destroy such things.

Contacts and friendships with those still involved in demonic practices must be severed. The enemy does not give up easily and will use his human agents to continue their destructive influence in the lives of new converts. Often young persons who come to Christ cannot return to live in their own homes, since continued family idolatrous and demonic practices would have tragic effects on their spiritual lives, even their mental and physical well-being.

Reliance upon the armor of God. God has provided adequate defense and weaponry for the battle. We should not think that we can successfully stand against the enemy without it. Paul warns us, "Finally, be strong in the Lord, and in the strength of His might. Put on the full armor of God, that you may be able to stand firm against the schemes of the devil" (Eph. 6:10-11). Our first responsibility is to divest ourselves of trusting human strength and to allow God to strengthen us with His great power. Then Paul speaks of the full armor of God we may appropriate. Each item mentioned in Ephesians 6:10-18 has its proper and necessary function. There are six pieces.[7]

We have already put on the first three pieces mentioned. They are ours by virtue of our union with Christ. The expressions "having girded," "having put on," "having shod" all speak of action accomplished. We must recognize them and use them. This is supported by the change of Greek tense of the verbs in verses 16 through 18, indicating actions now to be taken.

7. For a practical treatment of the armor of God, see Mark I. Bubeck, *The Adversary* (Chicago: Moody, 1975) and *Overcoming the Adversary* (Chicago: Moody, 1984).

The first piece of armor is the belt of truth (v. 14). The belt tied up the soldier's clothes and held his weapons. The Christian soldier's belt is the truth system of God centered in Christ. We can be assured that God's truth revealed in Him and the Bible is the only system to trust. All other systems are false. We need not listen to demonic lies through the philosophies and religions of men or to any thought that Christ is not adequate or that we may be mistaken about Him. We must recognize this important mainstay of all the armor.

The second piece is the breastplate of righteousness. This leather or metal vest covered the thorax, protecting the vital organs. The righteousness provided us in Christ when we trusted Him is the protection against "the accuser of the brethren" (Rev. 12:10-11). Some take this to refer to the believer's practice of righteousness, but the meaning of the Old Testament sources for these expressions favors our positional righteousness that is the gift of God through justification (Isa. 54:14-17; 59:16-20). Our righteous living is far from perfect and is the object of Satan's attack. Only the righteousness of Christ can provide perfect protection against the thrusts of the enemy.

The third item provides for sure footing in the battle, the sandals of peace. This does not refer to spreading the gospel of peace, but to standing securely in the fact that we have peace with God as a legal standing in Christ. Justification results in that peace. It is not a feeling. It is a state of being fully accepted in Christ. God is not at war with us. He has not declared a truce that depends upon our fulfilling His conditions. He has declared peace—complete and lasting peace—established by the blood of Christ (Rom. 5:1, 9). We must not slip and become confused in the midst of battle, thinking that difficulties mean God's rejection or that inserted condemning thoughts come from God. He is for us; no one can successfully accuse us or stand against us.

It is extremely important that Christian soldiers keep these provisions up front in their thinking. This is especially so for those who experience the internal battle that results from demonization.

The next three items of armor must be picked up and used. They are available by the grace of God, but they are not ours automatically. Here enters the action of personal response—practices that we must follow.

We must first take up the shield of faith (v. 16). This was a door-sized shield that gave the soldier complete protection from flaming arrows. The Christian must lift up as a shield his confidence in God against all threats of the enemy. God is good, He is for us, He will never leave us or forsake us, He is sufficient, and His Word can be trusted! He will see us through despite the rigors of battle! We must not begin to accept, let alone embrace, the lies of the devil that would cause us to distrust God or to accuse Him of harshness or lack of mercy. If we find ourselves thinking that way, we have bought the enemy's propaganda, and we are about to receive serious wounds.

The helmet of salvation (v. 17) probably refers to what Paul elsewhere describes as "a helmet, the hope of salvation" (1 Thess. 5:8). In that context it speaks of the confidence that we will be delivered from the day of the wrath of God, the great Tribulation period. In Ephesians it speaks of the confidence that we will be delivered in the day of battle. Furthermore, we are on the winning side No one can withstand the power of Christ. Our job is to trust and obey the Captain of our salvation, who has broken the power of the enemy (Heb. 2:9-10, 14-15).

Then the Christian must take up his offensive weapon, "the sword of the Spirit, which is the word of God" (v. 17). This refers to the Spirit's inspired sayings *(rhema)* of Scripture that are appropriate to the occasion. Just as the Lord Jesus spoke words of Scripture to counter the temptations of the devil, so we may use scriptural statements that answer and attack demonic, lying assertions. Even if they tell the factual truth, it is always couched in their distorted lie system. We must know the Bible and walk according to its dictates to successfully wield this powerful sword. Ignorance of the Word of God causes the downfall of many a believer. Systematic study and memorization will enable us to use this great weapon successfully.

Repairing in prayer to God. Paul's command for the battle includes the effective and specific use of prayer: "With all prayer and petition pray at all times in the Spirit, and with this in view, be on the alert with all perseverance and petition for all the saints" (v. 18). Calling on God for protection, for wisdom, for the defeat of the enemy, for help for yourself and others, and for His will to be accomplished is necessary in this warfare. We must keep in contact with our Commander and Supplier, without whom we cannot survive, let alone be victorious.

In his book *The Adversary,* Bubeck quotes or writes prayers for us that are patterns of the type of prayer that is effective in spiritual warfare. Many have profited from them, often finding immediate change and relief.[8]

Usually Christians' prayers are anemic when it comes to opposing the enemies of God. They act as if there is no demonic opposition to face or overcome, no dire need of asking for strength in the battle, no point in calling on God to defeat the enemies of truth. We are just not used to warfare praying. We are embarrassed to seriously ask God to deal with wicked spirits. But the more pointed and specific our prayers, the more God sees our understanding and seriousness, and the more delighted He will be to answer them. God's people are slow to catch on even after being instructed and warned. We need to revamp our prayer lives to make them effective in battle.

Psalm 83 illustrates how believers may pray against the enemy. The principles presented for us to follow include (1) recognition of the enemy's schemes, (2) asking God to intervene, (3) calling for their destruction and dishonor, and (4) the exaltation of God through the victory. Psalm 28 is a call for help against the believer's enemies and an expression of confidence. Psalm 27 is a well-known song of trust in the midst of battle, dedication to the Lord, and a plea for deliverance. Other psalms present more principles of warfare praying.

We can pray that, if demonic forces are involved in a Christian's personal problems or relationships, they would be weakened and defeated in their attempts. If the demons are external, we can ask for their removal and that God would send angels to surround us. If the believer is inhabited, we can pray the following:

(1) that the demons may be cut off from all communication and help from other demons and Satan

(2) that the demons would be confused and weakened in their hold on the person

(3) that the person would be strengthened in his faith to understand his position in Christ and to trust and obey the Word above his feelings

(4) that the person may be able to distinguish between his

8. For warfare-style prayers, see Bubeck, *The Adversary,* throughout the book.

thoughts and feelings and the thoughts and feelings of demons
    (5) that the person might recognize the demonic presence
and not be confused, but seek the proper counsel and help
    (6) that God would protect and guide His child and set
angelic forces at work to break up every scheme of the enemy.

We have found the above requests to be extremely effective
when dealing with a demonized person or when such a condition is suspected. This will prepare the person for further help
and deliverance. The basis for such prayer is found in biblical
example, good warfare principles, and common sense.

Resisting with commands to the enemies. Many will pray and
quote Scripture, but few seem confident to command demonic
forces, even Satan, to obey and cease their harassment. The
Christian may command in the authority of Christ. He should
assume his position in Christ as far above all demonic forces
and exercise his God-given right to directly charge the enemy to
obedience. Demonized persons often are kept from taking this
bold stance because the demons dare not allow this to happen if
they are to survive. As James says, "The demons also believe,
and shudder" (James 2:19).

Some hesitate to issue proper commands because they confuse this with "blasphemous remarks." They point out that even
Michael the archangel did not bring a railing judgment against
Satan (Jude 9). The word means "a blasphemous remark." It is
compared to the reviling words of false teachers who attack
angelic majesties and reject all authority. We should not suppose
that the apostles did anything like that when they commanded
demons to leave men. They were following the example of the
Lord Jesus, and they were carrying out His work in His authority
when they cast out demons (Luke 10:17-20). Likewise the demons are subject to us by our authority in Christ. That authority
has been delegated to us by the Great Commission (Matt. 28:19-
20) and is to be exercised in making disciples and opposing the
enemy. Just as with Moses, God commands us to get up from our
knees and start moving ahead in the battle. We pray—and we
command.

Responding to godly counsel. Scripture speaks of the advantage of seeking wise counsel (Prov. 12:15; 13:10; 19:20). The
spiritual gifts of pastoring and encouragement may function in
this line. Actually all forms of good counsel may be heeded—

medical, psychological, and pastoral. Anything that improves the ability of a person to function psychologically, spiritually, and socially is of help in battle with demonic forces.

Pastoral counseling is most appropriate in spiritual warfare, since this should be the special concern of such counseling. God has given gifts to the Body of Christ, and their use is needed for the proper functioning of the parts and the whole. We need each other. We all need proper counsel. The demonized person especially needs counseling by those aware and able in spiritual warfare. There are several reasons for this. First, the person who suspects he is demonized should have his condition evaluated by a counselor with skill and experience in this area. There must be proper diagnosis as to whether he really is demonized or not. The diagnosis determines the approach taken to getting help. Second, a skilled counselor can help the counselee to clarify and examine symptoms and evidence. He would seek to help him distinguish between his own thoughts and demonic thoughts. Third, the pastoral counselor aids in gaining perspective and gives encouragement regarding the warfare. Finally, he may help the counselee in actual confrontation and dismissal of spirits.

PERSPECTIVE IN WARFARE

Christians and their counselors must keep in mind a biblical perspective and balanced approach in dealing with demonization.

MAJOR EMPHASIS

The major purpose in counseling and confrontation is not to expel the demons but to facilitate dependence upon God and personal development of the counselee. There are many people in the world without inhabiting spirits who are not rightly related to Christ. On the other hand, I have known many who were inhabited who were growing in fellowship with the Lord as they were battling demons. They were taking background as it was clarified and growing in their concept of God and their relationship to Him.

Counselors of the demonized must maintain the perspective given by Christ. When the seventy returned with joy reporting that even the demons were subject to them in Christ's name, the

Lord acknowledged that truth and spoke of the defeat of Satan. He reminded them that He had given them such authority. Then He said, "Nevertheless do not rejoice in this, that the spirits are subject to you, but rejoice that your names are recorded in heaven" (Luke 10:20). Our priority is to appreciate and foster our relationship to Christ established by His grace. Our authority and work should never minimize or cloud that priority.

We must ever keep before us that our first responsibility is to honor and glorify the Triune God. In the counseling of the demonized, this means encouraging them to praise and honor God in their thoughts and actions. Submitting to the Spirit of God, they are to honor God through obedience to the Scriptures and growth. This will keep first things first and will give them strength to wage warfare successfully.

We must also keep the balance between the divine and the human parts in this battle, as in every phase of Christian living. It is God's strength in which the believer stands, but it is the believer who must put on the armor of God and do the standing (Eph. 6:10-14). It is God who pours forth energy into believers to will and do His good pleasure, but it is believers who will and who act (Phil. 2:13). There is no place for either mere human effort or for passive reliance upon God. Believers must both trust and obey. Dr. Jay Adams addresses this subject with what seems good balance.[9]

Counselors have encountered some delay in the removal of demons from demonized believers. Why should this be? Is not the authority of Christ still the same as in biblical days? Doesn't the believer stand in the authority of Christ far above demons? Why not expect immediate relief upon confrontation and command of wicked spirits in the name of Christ?

There may be several good reasons for such delay. Even the Lord Jesus experienced a delay on one occasion. The demonized man of Luke 8 was not freed upon Christ's first command. Evidently Christ had repeatedly commanded the demons to leave. Such is the emphasis in the Greek imperfect tense used in Luke 8:29: "For He had been commanding *[parēggellen]* the unclean spirit to come out of the man." And the same imperfect tense is used of their action: "And they were entreating *[parēka-*

---

9. Jay Adams, *Matters of Concern to Christian Counselors* (Phillipsburg, N.J.: Presbyterian and Reformed, 1978), pp. 65-67.

loun] Him not to command them to depart into the abyss" (Luke 8:31). The Lord used demonic resistance and delay to demonstrate the reality of the demonic presence. There was the testimony of their fear and confession of Christ's identity and authority. He allowed the transferral of the demons to the swine. The subsequent rush and destruction of the herd of two thousand testified to Christ's great power. Immediate relief without the attendant evidence may not have been so great a witness to the reality and wretchedness of demonic power and to the authority and relief found in Christ.

Several counselors have noted that delay is rather normal today, since we are not working miracles to prove the deity of Christ and are not invested with miraculous gifts. Conrad Murrell writes:

> Conversion is instantaneous. Deliverance is usually a process. In conversion, the awful burden of sin is rolled away and the terrible wrath of God is displaced by His immeasurable, Eternal Love. . . . We are translated from the kingdom of darkness into the kingdom of light. . . . In deliverance we come to realize more fully the greatness of our salvation. We gain *experiential* freedom from these powers of darkness. Whereas conversion brings us into relation with God, deliverance acquaints us with more of the works of God. Conversion stamps us as God's property and deliverance disposes Satan's illegal claims on us. Conversion is more a crisis and deliverance is more of a dawning.[10]

Ensign and Howe agree. They point out that those who argue for immediate relief upon conversion or upon command in Christ's name do not deal adequately with the realities of Satan's power, which is allowed by God.

> This is not because the demonic spirits are greater than Christ but that they have a *legal* (God granted in His moral universe) right to hold on to the individual who earlier gave them that right through submitting to Satan or making an agreement (even tacitly) with him. The Christian may need to grow in the Lord and in surrendering all areas of his life to the control of the Holy Spirit. Then he may be aware of the control that some evil spirit does have in him

10. Conrad Murrell, *Practical Demonology* (Pineville, La: Saber, n.d.), pp. 99-100.

and he will at once seek to have it removed through the procedure of James 5:14 ff. through the full authority of his real Lord, Jesus Christ.[11]

Many have found that final freedom from inhabiting spirits usually comes when the person has fully submitted to God and resisted the devil (James 4:7). The demonized must deal with attitudes or habits that keep him from being all that the Lord has for him. This involves dedication to all that is good and true. It also involves the hatred of evil—in his life and in demons (Ps. 97:10; 139:19-23).

Unger gives his reasoning concerning why it takes some time to realize full deliverance from the presence of inhabiting demons:

> Many people ask why, in some instances, it takes so long to realize full deliverance. This woman, who is a veteran in this ministry, wrote me concerning this question. I can do no better than to quote from her letter: "I know the Lord *could* cast them all out at once. But I do not believe that is His will. These people *grow* in the Lord, as they take His victory day by day. They recognize the heinousness of sin, face the powers of the enemy, realize that they themselves cannot fight the battle. Through this they really learn to cry in faith to the Lord in their dire need. They learn the necessity of constantly abiding in Christ and living on His every word. By the time deliverance is complete, they are walking steadily in victory, fully desiring to serve the Lord faithfully.[12]

There are some specific reasons God may allow the continued presence of wicked spirits in the life of a believer. Some reasons suggested follow:

1. There may be areas of unyieldedness or sin that God would have the person recognize and judge. God does not bypass the human will in the growth process. Psalm 94:12-16 tells of God's child-training in the time of adversity and opposition from the enemy. (See also Ps. 81:11-14.)

2. There may be something for the counselee or the counselor to learn about the wretchedness of sin and demons and

11. Grayson H. Ensign and Edward Howe, *Bothered? Bewildered? Bewitched?* (Cincinnati: Recovery, 1984), pp. 145-46.
12. Unger, *What Demons Can Do to Saints,* p. 152.

about the goodness and power of Christ (Ps. 59:11; 119:50, 67, 71).

3. God may give opportunity to learn of how to recognize and deal with demonic forces in the lives of others who are confused and hurting (2 Cor. 1:3-4).

4. Christians may learn how to walk in dependence upon God in the midst of trying circumstances and in the face of demonic warfare (Ps. 119:59, 92).

5. God may put demons to shame in front of many witnesses, human and angelic, by the faith and obedience of Christians who walk in the Spirit (Pss. 21:7-13; 26:5-6; 35:22-26).

6. God may allow continued demonic presence for increasing the basis for judgment of wicked spirits who should have left and were under obligation to leave upon the first command. God established this principle in Genesis 15:16 when He permitted the full development of the iniquity of the Amorites in the Promised Land before He brought the Israelites back to defeat them and take the inheritance. The same concept is found in 1 Thessalonians 2:16.

7. God may through affliction show the need and proper place of Christian counsel and support in the Body of Christ.

THE "MIRACULOUS" ISSUE

Many do not understand the reason any delay should ever be encountered if Christians depend upon the power of Christ and command demons to depart in the name of Christ. It was so in biblical days, they say; so why should we not expect the same today?

Such a question fails to understand *the place of miracles* in the plan of God. The Bible does not present a continuous history of miracles but records periods of miracles performed by God directly or through God's servants. God used miracles at special times of need in His dealing with His people to introduce a new message and to give credentials to His prophets. There were three major periods of miracles as recorded in biblical history: (1) the deliverance and exodus of Israel, (2) the reformation under Elijah and Elisha, and (3) the redemption introduced through Christ and the apostles. In each case there was the opposition of unbelief and the need for certification of the messengers and their message. God used this method with the Jewish people, and they had been trained to look for the miraculous associated with the Messiah, "for indeed Jews ask for signs" (1 Cor. 1:22).

When Christ and the apostles preached the gospel involved in the New Covenant, the Jews sought confirmation that Jesus was the Messiah who replaced Moses. After all, Moses had been introduced with miracles, and the law had been in effect for about 1,500 years. It would take some striking proof for God's people to realize that God had made the law obsolete and had introduced a new era centered in Jesus of Nazareth (even though the replacement of the Old and the coming of the New Covenant had been announced in Jeremiah and Ezekiel in the Old Covenant era). So God sought to convince them through the miracles performed by the Lord Jesus and the apostles. Some were convinced and others were not (John 3:2; Matt. 11:20).

Casting out of demons took on a miraculous aspect when Christ cast them out immediately with a mere command (Matt. 8:16). The people were amazed. "What is this? A new teaching with authority! He commands even the unclean spirits, and they obey Him" (Mark 1:27). Upon His casting out of a demon, the people marveled and exclaimed, "Nothing like this was ever seen in Israel" (Matt. 9:32-33). Jesus Himself claimed that His casting out of demons was a miraculous sign that He was indeed the Messiah (Matt. 12:28-29).

Christ delegated this miraculous power to the apostles and to the seventy (Luke 9:1; 10:17). This special power was a confirmation to those who heard the apostles that they were genuine messengers of God and that Jesus was the Messiah who would save those who believed in Him (Heb. 2:3-4).

Two erroneous views are abroad today regarding the power required to cast out demons. The first is that believers have the same miraculous power as did the apostles and the seventy, either through union with Christ or through special miraculous gifts. This means that we must merely ask and command in the name of Jesus, and demons must immediately depart from the demonized. This cannot be demonstrated from Scripture. We do have authority delegated to represent Christ and to make disciples (Matt. 28:19-20), but we do not necessarily have the same miraculous powers required to introduce a new message and a new age. We have no new message. This age has been properly introduced. The era of miracles does not last forever.

There is biblical warrant to hold that firmly. Gifts of the apostolic office and miraculous types have been removed by God. The apostles were the foundation of the church; they are not found in the superstructure (Eph. 2:20). Paul's healing gift seems later nonoperative for Ephaphroditus and Trophimus (Phil. 2:27; 2 Tim. 4:20). The special gifts of prophetic revelation and a message of knowledge were to be rendered inoperative, and tongues were to cease at the completion of revelation and knowledge as found in the New Testament (1 Cor. 13:8-10). Further development of this concept may be found in reliable authors.[13]

The second erroneous view assumes that those casting out demons must hold that their ministry is miraculous and that other miraculous gifts also exist today. This is not necessarily so. Some counselors may hold to this, but there are a good many who do not. Our authority over demons does not require miraculous powers. It is ours by virtue of our position in Christ. There is a great deal of difference between continuing authority and temporary gifts. Authority is ours until the end of the age (Matt. 28:19-20), but miraculous gifts have ceased. The authority is ours because of the Great Commission; to assume that miraculous gifts continue is to introduce great confusion.

There is no question about God's power and freedom to do anything within the bounds of His character and pleasure, but He has limited Himself according to His wise purposes as revealed in His Word. He accomplished His purpose through miracles in the transition from the Old to the New Covenant, and we are no longer in a transitional age. The book of Acts records that transition. The emphasis upon the miraculous decreases as the record of the expansion and consolidation of the church continues in the New Testament. B. B. Warfield, in his book *Counterfeit Miracles*, demonstrates that the gifts of miracles and healing ceased by the middle of the second century.[14] The completed and living Scriptures testify to the gospel today.

Ensign and Howe say this "does not mean that God may not answer the prayers of His people in remarkable and extraordi-

---

13. John C. Whitcomb, "Does God Want Christians to Perform Miracles Today?" *Grace Journal* 12, no. 3 (Fall 1971):3-12. Also see Robert L. Thomas, *Understanding Spiritual Gifts* (Chicago: Moody, 1978) and Gilbert Weaver, "Tongues Shall Cease," *Grace Journal* 16, no. 1 (Winter 1973):12-24.
14. Benjamin B. Warfield, *Counterfeit Miracles* (1918; reprint, Carlisle, Pa.: Banner of Truth, 1972).

nary ways through His power through providence."[15] His power is still operating to meet the needs of His people in any circumstance, but that does not require the continuing of miraculous gifts. The Bible does not suggest that demons can be removed only by miraculous gifts. It does teach that it can be accomplished only through the supernatural working of God. That may be through providential means, such as the application of the Word of God through counseling, through prayer, and through direct confrontation. We must not place all supernatural events in the miraculous category. That is simplistic and naive and can lead to great confusion.

It is clear, even from the experience of Christ's disciples, that demons did not all leave immediately and that they could resist for some time the commands leveled in the name of Christ. Such was the case with the boy with seizures whom Jesus met upon coming down from the mount of transfiguration. The father complained to Jesus, "I brought him to Your disciples, and they could not cure him" (Matt. 17:16). This occurred after Jesus had granted them His authority to cast out demons (Matt. 10:1). Remember that even Jesus spoke to some demons over a period of time (Luke 8:29). Why should we think that today there might not be a delay between the command and the exit of demons?

Experienced evangelical counselors have found that delay is more likely than immediate expulsion. We have treated the possible reasons for such delay previously in this chapter.

MISPLACED EMPHASES

Besides misunderstanding the place of miracles, some also have *misplaced emphases*. Those of charismatic persuasion generally hold that no one can properly deal with the power of demons unless he has experienced the power of "the baptism of the Holy Spirit." This is the special qualification. There are two major objections to this position. First, such a view confuses the baptism by the Spirit with His filling. Spirit baptism grants us our position "in Christ," the position of acceptance before God and of authority to face the enemy (Rom. 6:1-10; 1 Cor. 12:13; Gal. 3:26-28). All believers have this as a gift from God at initial

---

15. Ensign and Howe, p. 140.

faith in Christ. It is done; it is not ever urged to be sought. On the other hand, the Spirit's filling empowers us to live godly lives and to serve Christ (Eph. 5:18-21). To confuse the two introduces doctrinal error and gives the enemy great opportunity. If Satan can convince a believer that he must seek the baptism of the Spirit and that the sign will be speaking in "tongues," then he may easily introduce a false experience and confirm it with a demonic tongue.

The second objection is that evangelicals who have never had or sought such an experience have dealt successfully with the demonized by exercising their authority in Christ and following the principles of the Word of God. In fact, those counselors who are biblically oriented, rather than experience-oriented, warn against seeking the special qualification of "the baptism of the Spirit." Along this line Unger warns, "The ever-expanding charismatic confusion in the Church today represents a clever halo-crowned stratagem of Satan to divide God's people and to bring them under a very subtle yet real type of occult bondage."[16]

To this Ensign and Howe agree:

> Too much of the inner healing from or among neo-pentecostal groups tends to be open to occult power and a subjectivism which is very unhealthy and proceeds from an inadequate scriptural context and control. The devil, the archdeceiver, is quick to counterfeit where possible the genuine product that the Spirit of God produces for the children of God; and we believe that one must proceed with great caution to avoid entanglement in undesirable and even dangerous activities when it comes to healing.[17]

Likewise Murrell warns:

> I would discourage your going to anyone closely aligned with any of the charismatic or Pentecostal movements. Although these people have been used to some degree in deliverance ministries, their theology and methods have serious failing. But the chief danger is this: Someone will want to lay hands on you and speak in tongues. I have dealt with dozens of demonized people who have gotten tongues demons in this manner.[18]

16. Unger, *What Demons Can Do to Saints,* p. 188.
17. Ensign and Howe, p. 114.
18. Murrell, p. 95.

Unger and Koch have significant studies on the doctrinal and practical aspects of confusing Spirit baptism with filling.[19]

Unger also warns against mistaking mediumistic gifts from demonic sources with genuine spiritual gifts from the Holy Spirit.[20] He points out three possible sources of mediumistic gifts: heredity, occult participation, and occult transference. He warns believers against contact with mediumistic practitioners.[21]

In my own counseling, I have found about fifteen cases of false tongues spirits who came in through the laying on of hands, a typical occult practice for transferring power. I have never found, nor do I expect to find, a case of genuine tongues. In my estimation they have passed from the scene, since they were given primarily for evidential purposes to introduce the gospel and the New Covenant era in Christ, especially among the Jews (1 Cor. 14:21-22). Present-day tongues phenomena are artificial, psychological, or demonic.[22]

Another misplaced emphasis involves regarding "deliverance" as a *full-time ministry.* Such a ministry is best done by those who are balanced in doctrine and practice. There is no special gift of casting out demons. This was so in the first century of the church, and it is so now. Then it was part of the gift of miracles or possibly healing. Now it is the application of the Word of God, prayer, and command by any who qualify by knowledge of the Word, faith, and some experience. There are some cases where a so-called "expert" is not available. In that case there must be help of the "first aid" type by anyone who can help. Certain troublesome cases may require the help of a counselor with expertise. None of the respected counselors I know or have read suggest "deliverance ministry" as a full-time occupation but rather warn against it. It would be too draining of energy and too narrowing in outlook and contact. A balanced Body-life ministry is much healthier.

What, then, is *the proper place of deliverance?* First, we must consider seeking the relief of the demonized a proper biblical

19. Merrill F. Unger, *New Testament Teaching on Tongues* (Grand Rapids: Kregel, 1971), pp. 162-64, and Kurt Koch, *Satan's Devices* (Grand Rapids: Kregel, 1978), pp. 206-10.
20. Unger, *What Demons Can Do to Saints,* pp. 155-71.
21. Ibid., pp. 158-60.
22. Donald E. Burdick, *Tongues: To Speak or Not to Speak* (Chicago: Moody, 1969).

aspect of ministry. The New Testament presents demons as real and continuing opponents. They, unlike certain spiritual gifts, are not temporary. They existed before creation as unfallen angels and now continue after their rebellion as creatures who never cease to exist (Luke 20:36). They will still be opposing God and believers until Christ returns (Matt. 25:41). Only when the Lord returns and casts them into the abyss for the thousand years of His kingdom will the world know any relief from demonization. Where there is continuing opposition, there is continuing biblical provision to meet the enemy successfully. The battle with demons is age long, the Great Commission with its delegated authority is age long, and the ministry of freeing the slaves from the enemy is also age long.

As mentioned above, the ministry of confronting and expelling of demons in Christ's name from the demonized should be exercised, but counselors should take caution against assuming it as a full-time ministry.

Conclusion

In this chapter, we have presented a proper approach to warfare with our recognition of its reality, reliance upon our victorious and authoritative position in Christ, and a proper response in practice. This practice includes rededication to the will of God, rejection of false views and practices, reliance upon the complete armor of God, use of warfare praying, the use of confrontation and command in Christ's name, and the help of proper counsel.

We also presented a proper perspective in warfare. Here we treated the major emphasis of honoring God through obedience and growth in grace. The development of personal fellowship is more important than the expulsion of demons from the demonized. We sought to clarify the issue of the miraculous in this ministry, cautioned against misplaced emphases in special gifts, and cautioned against making this a sole ministry. We concluded with the proper place of delivering the demonized from the powers of darkness.

It is our sincere hope that this approach has helped to clarify some of the theological and practical issues related to the question of the demonization of believers.

14

Deliverance from Demonization

The New Testament does not leave the demonized without hope. It presents a very positive deliverance from inhabiting demons through applying the authority of the Lord Jesus. Though there is no teaching of automatic relief of the oppressed upon his receiving Christ, the Bible does record descriptions of the removal of demons. There are specific terms describing their removal and the results. We may add to this the evidence found in clinical case studies. Such biblical and clinical evidence should be an encouragement to those afflicted and to those who are seeking to help them.

BIBLICAL TERMS OF DELIVERANCE

The New Testament presents the removal of demons from the demonized in terms of the actions and the agents involved.

ACTIONS OF DELIVERANCE

There are three major terms used to describe the actions involved in relieving humans of inhabiting spirits.

Healing. The general term for healing or restoration from diseases is applied to restoring of normalcy to the demonized. Luke the physician uses the Greek verb for curing or healing, *therapeuō*,[1] to describe what Jesus did for those who came to

1. William F. Arndt and F. Wilbur Gingrich, *Greek-English Lexicon of the New Testament* (Chicago: U. of Chicago, 1952), p. 359.

hear and to be healed of their diseases: "and those who were troubled *[enochloumenoi]* with unclean spirits were being cured" (Luke 6:18). He also speaks of "some women who had been healed of evil spirits and sicknesses." One of them was "Mary who was called Magdalene, from whom seven demons had gone out" (Luke 8:2). This term, then, describes the curing of the maladies suffered by the demonized and the removal of the demons who caused the maladies. We cannot construe the healing to be psychosomatic. It was due to the removal of demons by the authority of the Lord Jesus. The evidence He presented in these cases was the casting out of demons.

The healing from demons is also found in association with other healings. This is the case in Mark 1:34: "And He healed many who were ill with various diseases, and cast out many demons." Note here the differentiation between normal illnesses of various sorts and demonization; yet there is the general connection with His healing ministry. The same is found in Matthew 4:24: "And they brought to Him all who were ill, taken with various diseases and pains, demoniacs *[daimonizomenous]*, epileptics, paralytics; and He healed them." The general term for healing is used of all varieties of affliction. We see again the same general association in Christ's delegation of authority to the twelve disciples (Matt. 10:1).

Coming or going out. The Greek word *exerchomai,* meaning to "come out" or "go out," is used "of spirits that *come* or *go out* of persons."[2] This word is commonly used in the gospels and Acts to picture the relief afforded by the exercise of Christ's authority. Jesus met a man in a synagogue who had an unclean spirit. When the demon cried out in fear upon recognizing Him, Christ rebuked the demon, "Be quiet and come out of him!" Luke records that the demon "went out of him without doing him any harm" (Luke 4:35). Luke also tells of Jesus healing those who were sick with various diseases, and "demons also were coming out of many, crying out and saying, 'You are the Son of God'" (Luke 4:41).

When used of relief from demonization, this word pictures the inhabiting demons as coming from within the person and moving out to where Jesus sent them upon His command. The demons further described their departure as into the abyss

2. Ibid., pp. 273-74.

(Luke 8:31). They feared that Christ would send them to that place of confinement and torture. They had probably heard of those of their number who had been sent to the abyss before them. Luke uses this same word to describe the removal of the fortune-telling spirit from the slave-girl who annoyed Paul and his troupe when in Philippi. Paul said to the demon, "I command you in the name of Jesus Christ to come out of her!" Luke records, "And it came out at that very moment" (Acts 16:18).

How encouraging to know that Christ in mercy relieves the afflicted and in righteousness judges those who afflict His people (compare 2 Thess. 1:6-9). He also demonstrates His power in the face of heathen opposition to the gospel.

Casting out. The Greek word *exballō* is "used [especially] of the expulsion of demons who have taken possesson of a [person]."[3] This word emphasizes the authority of the person removing the demon. The ultimate authority is the Lord Jesus. He has all authority in heaven and on earth (Matt. 28:18). Others cast demons out through His delegated authority (Matt. 10:8; Luke 10:17).

There was "a dumb man, demon-possessed," brought to Jesus. After the demon was "cast out," the man could speak; and the crowd marveled. Even the Pharisees recognized that Christ cast out demons, but attributed His power to Satan (Matt. 9:32-34). In another tension-fraught situation, Jesus pushed His claims to messiahship with this word of action: "But if I cast out demons by the Spirit of God, then the kingdom of God has come upon you" (Matt. 12:28). Again we notice the emphasis upon the authority behind the casting out of the demon.

AGENTS OF DELIVERANCE

The Son of God. The gospels emphasize Christ as the source of authority in the casting out of demons. Though He took the form of a servant and did not exercise all His rightful divine authority on earth, there were times when the Father granted Him to use that authority delegated to Him as the God-man. So Christ exercised authority over demons while on earth to demonstrate His claims to be the Son of God, the Messiah, and to relieve those oppressed by the devil (Acts 10:38).

3. Ibid., pp. 236-37.

The people of His day were amazed that Christ spoke with such authority to the demons that they had to obey Him (Mark 1:27). He did not appeal to another authority as did the Jewish exorcists. It was He who spoke, and at His word the demons departed. Matthew 8:16 reflects the same observation: "He cast out the spirits with a word."

The Spirit of God. Evidently the Lord Jesus depended upon the empowering of the Holy Spirit to perform many of His miracles. Such seems to be case in His statement in Matthew 12:28 where He claims to be under the leadership and power of the Spirit of God in casting out demons. The authority of the Triune God stood behind the God-man as He performed the work to which He had been delegated by the Father. Jesus is not acting on His own authority but on the authority delegated to Him by the Father (John 6:38; 12:49). Jesus also said, "But if I cast out demons by the finger of God, then the kingdom of God has come upon you" (Luke 11:20). This is an obvious parallel with His statement in Matthew 12:28. "The finger of God" is a reference to the authority delegated to Him by God. The Jews would understand this in connection with the authority of God in the revelation of the law to the mediator of the law, Moses (Ex. 31:18). There also may be possible allusion to the agency of angels in carrying demons away to the abyss, just as there was the agency of angels involved in the inscribing of the law (Acts 7:52-53; Gal. 3:19).

The servants of Christ. Christ delegated His authority, received from the Father, to men appointed by Him. Others also cast out demons in Christ's name. There were those who were pretenders who presumed to cast out demons in Christ's name. They were not related to Christ, and their attempts were of the nature of magical ritual. To such persons demons do not respond. Such was the case of the sons of Sceva who failed to impress the demons but were the victims of their ferocious reaction (Acts 19:14-16). Neither did Jesus recognize the claims of those who asserted that they had cast out demons in His name but never knew Christ personally (Matt. 7:22-23).

However, it is clear that Christ's true servants exercised on occasion His authority to cast out demons. "And having summoned His twelve disciples, He gave them authority over unclean spirits, to cast them out" (Matt. 10:1). He had obviously granted such authority to the seventy, for they "returned with joy,

saying, 'Lord, even the demons are subject to us in Your name' "
(Luke 10:17). Christ recognized that truth and said, "Behold, I
have given you authority to tread upon serpents and scorpions,
and over all the power of the enemy" (Luke 10:19).

The Great Commission indicates that Christ delegated to His
disciples and to those who follow in their train that same authority over demons. The miraculous powers may be now with-
held by the purpose of God (see chap. 13), but the authority to
successfully oppose and cast out demons still remains throughout the age until Jesus comes (Matt. 28:18-20).

BIBLICAL RESULTS OF DELIVERANCE

What happens when demons are cast out? How does such
action affect the demonized and the witnesses of the deliverance?

EFFECTS UPON THE DEMONIZED

Removal of spirits. The first and most basic result of deliverance of the demonized is the removal of the wicked spirits that
were inhabiting the person. They were once inside the person;
now they are absent. This is the effect of the command of the
Lord Jesus and His servants in the New Testament. Jesus said,
"Begone!" and "they came out" (Matt. 8:32). Jesus said, "Be
quiet, and come out of him!" And "the unclean spirit cried out
with a loud voice, and came out of him" (Mark 1:25-26). Note
that the spirits were described as once inside and now outside.
This removes the possibility of control of the person from internal use of the mind and body. The Son sets men free from the
dominion of demons!

The removal was evidenced in various ways. In some cases
there were some immediate and obvious physical evidences.
There were *reactions by the demons* upon the command to
leave. The unclean spirit in the man in the synagogue gave
evidence of his presence through speaking in fear to the Lord
Jesus (Mark 1:24). He then gave evidence of his leaving the man
when he threw "him into convulsions" and "cried out with a
loud voice" (Mark 1:26). Luke says of the same case, "When the
demon had thrown him down in their midst, he went out of him
without doing him any harm" (Luke 4:35). When Jesus commanded a "deaf and dumb spirit" to come out of a young boy,

"after crying out and throwing him into terrible convulsions, it came out; and the boy became so much like a corpse that most of them said, 'He is dead!' " (Mark 9:25-26). In Acts 8:7, Luke records that there were signs, or attesting miracles *(sēmeia)*, "For in the case of many who had unclean spirits, they were coming out of them shouting with a loud voice." It seems obvious that these physical disturbances were allowed by Christ to witness to the reality of the removal of spirits who were distinct from and removed from the afflicted human.

The removal was also obvious by *physical cures effected.* The blind could see, and the dumb could speak (Matt. 9:32-33; 12:22). The woman with the back "bent double, and [who] could not straighten up at all" was freed by Christ so that "she was made erect again" (Luke 13:10-13).

A striking evidence of the removal of spirits from the demonized is found in *transference of demons,* as in the case of the maniac of the Gerasenes. Jesus permitted the spirits headed up by "Legion" to transfer into a herd of 2,000 swine nearby. The effect was very noticeable. "And the demons came out from the man and entered the swine; and the herd rushed down the steep bank into the lake, and were drowned" (Luke 8:32-33).

The removal of demons is also evidenced by the *loss of occult powers.* In Acts 16:16-18 Luke tells of "a certain slave-girl having a spirit of divination." When she persistently aggravated Paul and his group by unneeded and questionable promotion of their roles, Paul commanded the spirit in the name of Jesus Christ to come out of her. "And it came out at that very moment," resulting in her loss of fortune-telling powers. This was evident even to her masters who "saw that their hope of profit was gone," so that they seized Paul. The removal of demonic intelligence from the girl affected her occult ability in divination. This stands as a testimony to the fakery imposed by the schemes of demons and to the truth of the gospel and the power of Christ.

The New Testament record leaves no room for a purely humanistic or rationalized explanation of the phenomena associated with the casting out of demons. It directly attributes such to the actual removal of inhabiting wicked spirits through the authority of Christ.

Restoration of normal functions. The object of removing demons from the demonized is not just to overcome the enemy but to restore the human person to normal life and function. The removal of demons is but one step in that direction. There must be other means of rebuilding the person who was previously oppressed. But the New Testament records definite and encouraging restorations of the afflicted through deliverance from inhabiting demons.

As we have noted already, there are some *physical restorations* that result from deliverance. These include restoration of sight and speech (Matt. 9:32-33; 12:22; Mark 9:17-29), bone structure and connecting tissue (Luke 13:11-17), normal motor control (Luke 9:38-42), and normal social behavior as in the case of the wild man of the Gerasenes (Luke 8:35).

There are also *psychological and social restorations* resulting from deliverance. Consider the maniac just mentioned. After the Lord had removed the legion of demons from him, the people "found the man from whom the demons had gone out, sitting down at the feet of Jesus, clothed and in his right mind; and they became frightened" (Luke 8:35). The man had been wild and attacking those passing by, naked and in isolation, living in morbid surroundings in the tombs, and destructively powerful in breaking all chains. Now all this was reversed. He calmly sat at the feet of Jesus with others in peace, he was clothed and associated with other humans, he now attended to the words of life among the living, and he was in his right mind. What a transformation! Here was psychological and social healing stemming from deliverance from wicked spirits.

Redirection of life. Not only were those delivered freed from inhabiting spirits and restored to normal functioning, but they were set free to order their lives in godly fashion. The woman made erect now began "glorifying God" (Luke 13:13). There was praise from her mouth to God in the presence of all. The maniac of the Gerasenes upon his deliverance "was entreating Him that he might accompany Him" (Mark 5:18). He wanted to fellowship with Jesus and learn more of Him. However, Jesus directed him, "Go home to your people and report to them what great things the Lord has done for you, and how He had mercy on you" (Mark 5:19). The man obeyed the Lord Jesus: "And he went off and began to proclaim in Decapolis what great things Jesus had done for him; and everyone marveled" (5:20).

Luke 8:1-3 speaks of the itinerant ministry of Jesus and His supporting personnel. Some contributed of their private resources. Some also prepared the food for the group. There were among them "some women who had been healed of evil spirits and sicknesses," one of whom was Mary Magdalene "from whom seven demons had gone out." When Jesus delivered her from inhabiting spirits, she gave her life to serving the Lord Jesus by supporting His ministry.

When Christ sets the demonized free, they are no longer bound to follow the directions of their former life when they were under the influence of demonic propaganda and control. They are free to choose a new course of life and service—one that will honor their deliverer, the Lord Jesus. In this they will need the normal means of growth and Christian fellowship and support, but they may now choose to do what they were hindered from doing before.

EFFECTS UPON THE WITNESSES OF DELIVERANCE

When Christ or His ministers had effected freedom for the demonized, there were a variety of responses from those who witnessed the phenomena.

They were amazed. Of one occasion, Luke writes, "Amazement came upon them all," and the observers were discussing Christ's message, authority, and power (Luke 4:36). The deliverance had accomplished Christ's purpose; it had attested to His Person and mission. When the dumb man spoke, "the multitudes marveled, saying, 'Nothing like this was ever seen in Israel' " (Matt. 9:33). The uniqueness of Christ and His ministry was obvious through the accomplishment of this deliverance. When Christ freed the young boy of his demonic convulsions, the great multitude "were all amazed at the greatness of God" (Luke 9:43). The deliverance magnified God's majesty.

They were afraid. Not all took the demonstration of Christ's power with appreciation. Some were very fearful. When the people from the city came out to the country to observe the demonized maniac now cured, "they became frightened" (Mark 5:15). Luke more graphically states, "They were gripped with great fear"; that is, "they were seized with terror" *(phoboi megalōi suneichonto,* Luke 8:37).[4] So great was their fear that they

4. Ibid., pp. 796-97.

irrationally asked Christ, who had effected this great and gracious cure benefiting this man and all terrorized by him, to depart from them.

They were antagonistic. Not all appreciated the genuine relief Christ brought through casting out demons. Those opposed to His Person and ministry sought to use the occasions against Him. When the woman with the bent back was healed, the synagogue official became "indignant because Jesus had healed on the Sabbath." He turned to the multitude to order them to come on other days to be healed, not on the Sabbath (Luke 13:14). Christ immediately condemned such hypocrisy. He called for rationality and for compassion on this woman who had been bound by Satan for eighteen long years (13:15-16).

On at least two occasions, the Pharisees accused Christ of casting out demons by the ruler of the demons (Matt. 9:34; 12:24). They could not deny the obvious miracle of deliverance of the demonized persons, but they denied the source of Christ's power. They attributed to Satan the work of the Spirit in attesting to Christ's deity and messiahship. If they continued with this attitude, they would be in danger of blaspheming the Holy Spirit with resultant irreparable loss (Matt. 12:28-32).

It stands as a tribute to depraved man's resistance to the truth, even when quite evidently from God, that they regard that which is a great benefit to men and a credit to Christ as something to be feared and rejected. They are slapping the face of the only One who could help them. Antagonism to casting out of demons is irrational and morally perverted rebellion.

CLINICAL RESULTS OF DELIVERANCE

When we turn to the results of deliverance observed by modern counselors of the demonized, we notice some parallels with the results presented in the New Testament. Sometimes more specific results may be observed, since counselors are on the site and able to record more detail than was necessary to record in the New Testament.

These results confirm the reality of demonization of believers and confirm that relief is available through the application of biblical principles of spiritual warfare and removal of demonic invaders.

IMMEDIATE EXPERIENCES

Sometimes the delivered persons experience immediate realizations or sensations.

Weakness. Often after the rigorous battle involved in confrontation sessions with the enemy, the counselee will feel physically and emotionally drained. Such weakness should not be considered unusual. It often occurs after any strenuous emotional or physical encounter. But Murrell suggests that those who have been running on demon excitement for years may have their own emotions rather inactive. Now that the colorful and powerful is gone, they may be left with their own dull personalities.[5]

Freedom. Some have an immediate sense of lightness and freedom. One young lady from Pennsylvania left my office freed from a spirit of divination that had bound her for years. When she was a child, her grandmother had charmed away her illnesses. Her comment as she left was, "I feel so free, so clean. I feel like a different person."

Peace and love. New capacities to relate to God and others soon find expression. Ensign and Howe write:

> Usually in a day or two the counselee begins to appreciate the fact that he has really been set free of demonic control, and he begins to experience a great love of God and ability to obey God, while having the victory over the sins which formerly had enslaved him. All of them testify to a new peace and security in God that is very different from the harassment that they had been receiving before.[6]

LOSS OF OCCULT POWERS

Supernatural powers supplied by demonic residents and connections suddenly disappear with expulsion of the demons. A girl I counseled in Colorado was having depressions and suspected the tongue she was using was not of God. She confessed her nonbiblical seeking of tongues and renounced them. We confronted the tongues spirit and dismissed him in the name of the Lord Jesus. Her ability and even urge to speak in tongues immediately vanished. On behalf of her family she renounced

---

5. Conrad Murrell, *Practical Demonology* (Pineville, La.: Saber, n.d.), p. 100.
6. Grayson H. Ensign and Edward Howe, *Bothered? Bewildered? Bewitched?* (Cincinnati: Recovery, 1984), p. 185.

ancestral involvement in occult or demonic activities, and we prayed for members of her family. Within a very short time, her brother, who was not walking with the Lord, was suddenly led to stop along the road he was driving. He felt drawn back to the Lord, confessed his wandering, and rededicated his life to Christ.

A pastor's wife had ESP that disappeared upon her renunciation and the removal of a demon who called himself The Exalted One.

Koch tells of Henry Drummond, a friend and fellow worker of D. L. Moody, who before his conversion,

> had possessed some very strong mediumistic and suggestive powers. He thought that these ungodly endowments would disappear when he became a Christian, and yet to his astonishment, he found that his mediumistic abilities reappeared while he was working together with Moody. . . .
>
> He also noticed that he was able to bring the large audiences at Moody's meetings under his hypnotic influence. He recognized at once that these powers would only hinder the actual working of the Holy Spirit, and he therefore pleaded with the Lord to take them away from him. Drummond was completely delivered.[7]

We notice that this loss of occult powers upon dismissal of demons corresponds to what was found in the biblical record.

RELIEF FROM PERSISTENT PERSONAL PROBLEMS

Delivered believers often experience the remission of a wide variety of personal difficulties, especially those that were initiated or aggravated by wicked spirits.

Voices in the mind. Ensign and Howe describe the former condition of a woman they had counseled:

> This lady came to us with tremendous problems from hearing voices in her head that were urging her over and over, "Kill your baby, kill your baby, kill your baby." And other times it would be, "Kill your dog," or "Kill yourself." The constant bombardment of these voices had brought the woman to a consideration of suicide as an escape from the harassment. She previously had been hospi-

---

7. Kurt Koch, *Occult Bondage and Deliverance* (Grand Rapids: Kregel, 1970), p. 56.

talized in a psychiatric unit, and she was almost immobilized from carrying on any normal duties of a wife and mother. From time to time her arms would involuntarily begin to shake, and she seemed to have no control over them. She was tormented and terribly oppressed by Satan.

After a work of deliverance was provided by the Lord Jesus Christ, there was almost one hundred percent improvement. The physical shaking of her body and voices in the head were completely gone. Her physical appearance was one of radiance, happiness and serenity; and when she spoke in our assembly she thrilled the hearts of the people with her testimony of how God had completely transformed her life.[8]

Immobilization. After a counseling session, one of my students began to think about what demonization meant: to be demon-controlled, a demon-caused passivity. He wrote:

> For the first time I realized that this passivity was characteristic of my problem, depression. While I realize other factors can cause depression, I began to see that demonic influence was rocking my boat. I would dive into unexplained depression, then be unable to do anything. I was rendered passive, and they were in control. In this state I would feel helpless in regard to other temptation (i.e., lust and his partner, masturbation), and this only increased my problems. You encouraged me to fight, and this I decided to do. First, I had to face the fact that my depressions were demonic; then I determined I would be passive no longer. My school work was being destroyed by this attack, so I took my stand on God's side.
>
> Once I made the decison to fight, the cloud of depression left as God's grace shined through. Victory over other sins (lust and company) is also my experience now. Demonic power has been broken!

Others who have been delivered from demonization testify to freedom from immobilizing fears of hurting others, rejection, failure, change, and so on.

Mental and moral disturbances. Since demons use mind control and are unclean spirits, they promote mental and moral problems, as we have noted previously. In almost all cases that I have counseled, the demonized Christian hates the thoughts that come to his mind and wants to be rid of the moral problems

8. Ensign and Howe, p. 186.

and habits he battles. When the demons are removed, many of these problems are relieved.

Ensign and Howe tell of a man bothered with demonic problems of ancestral origin:

> A brother came to us with a great many difficulties and spiritual problems, among them lust, sexual perversion, pride, arrogance, depression, anxiety, and doubt. There were also problems with deception and lying, rebellion and rage, and physical infirmities. This brother received counseling over a two-year period and was set free from these evil spirits though deeper networks of evil spirits similar to these were uncovered over the period of time. By the grace of God the brother received strengthening of his spiritual character and his dedication to the Lord Jesus Christ. . . . After twenty-six sessions during which the Lord gave amazing deliverances, this brother is now exercising his freedom in the Lord to grow up into the servant of God that he wants to be.[9]

A clinical psychologist associated with a missions organization came to see me with a veteran missionary who since youth had been plagued with debilitating habits. She had problems with overeating, lustful thoughts, compulsive masturbation, and bedwetting. Her career as a missionary was in jeopardy. She could not relate properly to others, and her ministry on the field was about in shambles. She had to gain some relief over these or else the mission would be forced to require her resignation. She had been under professional counseling with very little success in overcoming these burdensome habits.

The psychologist heard some tapes of messages I had presented on spiritual warfare at a Christian school. She wondered if her client-friend could be demon oppressed. After sharing her concern with her client, they flew to Chicago. We determined that her problems were due in large part to demonic invasion. Ancestral and personal causes were involved. By the grace of God and the authority of Christ we were able to help her to a noticeable extent. Later I received a letter from the missionary in which she wrote:

> I am experiencing victory in all areas of the indulgences. The reducing diet is going well, and I have plans to stay here until I'm

9. Ibid., p. 187.

a normal weight. The sexual fantasy, all-consuming sexual desire and resultant masturbation are being replaced by a deep hunger to know the Lord ever more intimately. And, in fact, for the first time since I was a sophomore in college, I sense His presence continually. . . .

Always before, the fruits of the Spirit were only unattainable ideals. . . . Now the Lord has given me assurance that He is producing that fruit in my life. And I'm becoming so excited I'm not sure I can stand to keep silent. So I suspect the Lord is preparing me to share this testimony. . . .

The prayer language [form of "tongues"] is no longer a part of me. I converse with the Lord directly. The restlessness is gone. The agitation is gone.

This woman's clinical psychologist continued to work with her in follow-up and sought to deal with other personal matters. Of the sessions and results the psychologist wrote,

Although our time in Chicago was not for pleasure and I can even say it was a battle at times, the Lord has definitely used it to bring about growth in our lives and healing in Ginnie's [name changed] as well.

I would love to share all that God has done and is still doing in Ginnie's life since that visit with you.

Suicidal tendencies. Often demons introduce suicidal thoughts to lead a Christian to destroy himself and his testimony for Christ. Such constant raging in the mind can drive one to distraction and destruction. I have counseled many with this problem. After they dealt with crucial spiritual issues in their lives, faced the reality of demon invasion, and stood firmly in the power and armor of Christ, they were relieved of the torment.

One student with such a problem counseled with me. I referred her through school officials to a Christian psychiatrist. He diagnosed her as having a personality disorder and sent her back. Within two days she sought to hang herself in a health service room. The nurse on duty intervened to save her life and deal with the spirits, since she was aware of spiritual warfare principles. A fellow faculty member counseled the student and confronted wicked spirits. The girl was able to voice her renunciation of their thoughts and to confirm her love for Christ. The counselor stood in the authority of Christ and commanded the destructive spirits to leave. They did. The girl returned to normality. She now is engaged in a Christian ministry. She wrote me a note saying,

> I just wanted to let you know that I am growing in grace and praising the Lord. God has healed my mind and dealt with me so tenderly in drawing me closer to Himself. I can honestly say that I have grown a lot and I am walking in victory. I am free from any harassment from the evil one and am trusting God and living by the grace He gives me daily. I pray that I will be used mightily by God in the future, and that I will remain faithful to my calling. I want to live a life pleasing to the Lord as an example of His grace. I truly feel that my mind and body are trophies of His love, grace, and power. By His grace, I am what I am. Deliverance was just the beginning of the abundant life I am experiencing. Praise God. He works miracles!*

Physical problems. We have referred to some relief from physical problems in previous chapters. The pastor's wife who had symptoms of multiple sclerosis was completely healed of these fake onslaughts when the enemy was dismissed.

In Canada I met a woman who manifested signs of depression while in a church meeting. The pastor said she frequently had such problems. Though she wanted to live for Christ, she was mentally and physically harassed. Her physical harassment, we found through interview, was what some called "epilepsy." This affliction would roll her out of bed, throw her against the wall, and throw her down stairs. This was not what I had understood to be the symptoms of true epilepsy, a disturbance in the signals of the brain that causes seizures that vary from slight blanking of the mind to complete collapse of the body, depending upon the particular case. I thought the cause might be demonic due to the ancestral background and other symptoms the woman manifested. That was the case. We confronted the spirits, and one declared his name to be Epilepsy. He confessed to causing the seizures. After dealing with ancestral and personal issues, we commanded the demon to leave with his helpers. The next day the woman was in church smiling and thoroughly

---

*Letters cited in this chapter are on file with the author.

enjoying the ministry of the Word of God and worshiping Christ. Later we found out that her epileptic fits were gone.

The parents of an eight-year-old girl brought her to me. They were very concerned for her, since she had Tourette's Syndrome. This malady is evidenced by tics, vocal or physical repetitions such as grunts, hissing, swearing, blasphemy, and jerking of part of the body. Some noticed that the tics became worse when passing a church, attending a church function, or when trying to read the Bible and pray. She had been to reputable medical men. There seemed little solution. The parents thought it might possibly be demonic in origin. They had beautifully prepared the little girl for my pastoral approach to counseling the demonic. She was a precocious young lady. We explained to her what we were about to do and that the Lord Jesus would take care of her because He was so powerful and loved her so much. She and the parents renounced all ancestral background in the demonic, took their stand against the enemy, and prayed with me that "the Lord would tell any of the devil's helpers inside Becky [name changed] to leave and go to where Jesus sends them." I followed that with a direct command to any wicked spirits that they should leave. I pressed the authority of Jesus Christ and His claims upon her life, since she was a believer. We finished with some sense of accomplishment. Later I heard from the parents that things had greatly improved and that the tics had disappeared.

FREEDOM FOR SPIRITUAL GROWTH

The cases above testify to the new freedom granted by Christ through the removal of inhabiting demons. It is difficult for those never so afflicted to imagine the hindrances, restrictions, and bondage that demonization, even in its milder forms, brings. I have never experienced anything of what my counselees have suffered; but I can understand something more of the oppression that demons produce, since I have seen so much of it in their lives and witnessed the terrible battles in which they are embroiled.

One counselee wrote, "The awful depression, doubts, guilt, and self-loathing followed by a desire to die have ceased. There is no conflict in my soul, and joy is welling up from my inmost being." Another wrote:

Concerning deliverance, I came to Moody Bible Institute oppressed with fear: of cancer, of other serious physical illness, of death, or rather dying, of doing anything new, of writing papers. I was paralyzed by continuous inner accusations of worthlessness and of inadequacy, much of which was so deep within that I barely recognized its influence. I was so worried about what other people thought of me—and dependent on their approval to the point of bondage. But I left MBI free! Victorious in Christ, at peace and released from the powers of darkness. I am now aware [of] and daily reckoning [on] my position seated with Christ in the heavenlies. Full well do I know the significance of His shed blood to me and the power of His resurrection. Ah, but it's grand to face the future unafraid—knowing to my fingertips that He has marked out my way and is with me always—and that nothing, *no thing* can ever separate me from the love of Christ. . . . Oh, what a great God we know!

A trusted and approved counselor from Indiana passed on a letter to me in which a woman who had been horribly intimidated by ancestral demons for years wrote:

It's been about three weeks since you were here. I feel so very different. I seem to be able to pray a lot easier. I'm not frightened or confused. I don't hear voices or hear my name being called. I haven't had any nightmares. I feel a real peace and joy. I feel like I love every body. . . .
God's love and power are what have brought me to my present ideal state. Praise God! Praise God!

Ensign and Howe comment on the new freedom Christians have gained through the removal of evil spirits: "It has been a most rewarding work as we have seen the newness of life and freedom of Christians who were in severe bondage to Satan."[10]

RESTORATION OF PERSONAL SOUNDNESS

The way a person senses his own being or identity and how well he relates to others is important to his sense of well-being, of personal wholeness. Christians who had problems along this line have found new soundness of life through deliverance from the influence of inhabiting spirits.

Ensign and Howe speak to this issue:

10. Ibid., p. 179.

In spite of the hours and the many sessions it has taken to free individuals from demonic invaders, we rejoice in the powerful working of God against all evil spirits and for the grand liberation that has been given to these individuals. All of these in this broad classification have been helped tremendously in their spiritual stability, personality integration, and wholeness of life.[11]

Sense of personal worth. One of the first points I stress in counseling those with personal problems, especially those I suspect as demonized, is the matter of one's personal worth. This worth is built in by God because He made us in His image—persons, as He is personal, and capable of relating to Him and to other persons. Christ did not shed His blood and give His eternal life as a sacrifice for the sin of worthless creatures but for unworthy creatures—not for valueless persons but for meritless persons. Satan and his henchmen cannot stand this truth. They are achievement-oriented and works-based. That is why they promote all sorts of religions based on works-righteousness. That's why they attack the worth of persons made in the image of God. It is a way of attacking God. The wise counselor must accept the worth of all men, even unsaved men, since they are created in God's image—persons of great worth. Restoration of the sense of personal worth is one of the results I have found in seeing the demonized freed from the enslaving and degrading propaganda demons force on humans.

A "missionary kid" had been subject to demonic invasion in a culture of demonized persons when she exposed herself in a child's game of "doctor and patient." Her self-image had been under attack since childhood by various factors, but the demonic causes were forced along this line particularly. She was a very bright student who did well academically, but socially she was lacking self-confidence and the ability to relate to the opposite sex. Yet she had her deep problems. She wrote me: "My journal of October 6, goes like this: I really wish I knew and understood my real self. But I don't know who my real self is. I'm terribly confused at times—most of the time." She continued in her letter to speak of her contact with me, the discovery of inhabiting spirits, the evidence she witnessed, the confusion that followed, her temporary relief, and then renewed battle within. She felt she should give up. She wrote:

11. Ibid., p. 182.

My faith in God was small; my concept of His greatness and strength was very weak. Yet I really believed He would rid me of the evil. Continually I had to remind myself of my position in Christ. But continually doubts were thrown back into my face. I knew my sins were forgiven, but past sins were dragged across my mind like dirty wash. . . . For two months my life was a series of ups and downs. . . . I was often plagued with headaches, the inability to concentrate while reading assignments and sleepiness when reading my Bible or trying to memorize. These physical symptoms added to the emotional stress I was going through.

Finally, one day in December Dr. D. was given discernment to see the ground they held. It had to do with my self-image—it was really poor. There has always been competition of some sort with my older siblings, and I felt I always had to live up to their standards. In fact, I even felt I had to surpass them in order to prove to myself that I was as good or better. I always considered my weight a problem. In grade school I was the fattest one and that view of myself continued on through high school and college even though I was not fat. Now this was something I really had to deal with, and this one really hurt. It was the hardest thing for me to give up myself, but I did with God's help and Dr. D.'s encouragement. Once that foothold for Satan was gone, his evil spirits had to leave, and they did.

I knew there was still work ahead. My view of myself had to change; my whole mindset had to be turned around. And I knew it wouldn't happen overnight. But I felt a new kind of freedom in committing that to the Holy Spirit knowing he was waiting to help conform me to Christ's image. One more thing I might say is that there were at times psychological leftovers or reactions. . . . Today, I am ever more convinced of God's grace and mercy in my life. My experience with the powers of evil was a reality—though a confusing reality at times. I know a little of the power of Satan, but I know ever more and more the power and protection of Christ.

I notice a change in myself now; it's really kind of fun. No more headaches (except the normal kind), and my glasses are useless to me! My morning devotional sleepiness is gone. It's a joy to be able to accept and love others for who they are now that I have begun to accept myself the way I am. It's a challenge to pray specifically against the powers of Satan not only working against me but working against friends—Christians and non-Christians—and to see the power of God at work.

I recently heard from this young lady who used to be so limited in expression of her personality. This one who used to be uninterested in relating to men is now happily married. When I last saw her, she seemed very free and rejoicing in the Lord. Her self-esteem had improved with her better concept of God. This was made possible by the Lord's removing wicked spirits from their place of control within her.

Another student from a Christian leader's home had problems of confusion and identity. She felt she was a failure and wanted to die. She writes:

> I could not concentrate on anything. I could be talking with someone and totally forget what we were discussing. I couldn't hear or concentrate when the Bible was being read, or when someone was exhorting me. I was arguing with myself. I had two totally different opinions in my mind. I was so totally depressed. I was so frustrated and desperate. I thought I was going crazy.

Since her sister, who had counseled with me had many of the same symptoms, she came to me to see if she also had demonic problems. She had suicidal thoughts, premonitions, definite sensations of demons' presence, and lack of concentration much of the time. We tested and found inhabiting spirits that were of ancestral origin, just as with her sister. They talked, and she realized that there was a battle going on within—and not just with the sin nature. She continues in her letter:

> During our first session we also went over my sinful attitudes and practices of the past. I confessed those and renounced them. This was to make sure the demons had no grounds. You asked me three questions about God and His Word. I had trouble believing that God had a wonderful plan for my life. I confessed and renounced that. You tried to talk to the demons, but they would not speak. There was a sensation of their presence though. You gave assignments. I was to particularly read about God and His attributes of goodness, mercy, love, sovereignty, and power.
>
> During the second session the demons talked. It was not a thing of your hynotizing me. I was in total control the whole time. I was aware of everything that was going on, and I could speak any time I wanted to. I had two totally different emotions. I myself was at peace while there was also such a strong panicky fear. You called up the head demon to talk to you. My eyes would burn, and at times my vision would be cloudy. When you would ask them a question, I would have a thought in my mind, but it wasn't mine. I

was praying that the Lord would make them speak. It was hard to realize that those thoughts weren't mine. Their thoughts were rebellious, negative and against Scripture.

I gave her encouragement and Scripture that dealt directly with her areas of struggle. She said that wicked spirits would inject an awful thought, and she would tend to feel guilty rather than reject it. Her personal wholeness, however, showed marked improvement. She also writes:

> You have helped me in so many ways. The first is in my concept of God. You helped me see how good He is and how that He does have a great plan for my life. You have helped my self-concept. I was so afraid of failing. I know that my acceptance doesn't have anything to do with my failures. I have been meditating on my position in Christ. I also am learning to see failure through God's eyes rather than the world's. My fiance has helped me a lot here too.

Establishment of true identity. Demons will seek to substitute their identity for the human's, confusing the person's thoughts and emotions with theirs. I have often encountered a spirit that acted as an "alternate ego" and claimed to be the person but then talked about the human in the grammatical third person saying that he hated the human and would confuse and destroy him.

One such lady, an employee of a Christian institution, complained of a confusion and "darkness" that often settled over her. She was living for Christ and came from a good church background. There were difficulties in her marriage because of her poor self-concept. While talking with her, I asked permission to check for wicked spirits, for there were several symptoms indicating their presence. Immediately the Lord caused one to surface. He came up at the demand that Dark Ginger (name changed) should answer to the authority of Christ. The Lord dismissed that one upon our prayer and command, and Ginger was relieved of the "darkness" and confusion about her identity.

Another person, who was going through counseling that used the transactional analysis approach, had great difficulty in one session. The counselor had instructed her to imagine entering a dark room and approaching a person seated in the darkness. The person was to be someone she would like and who would like her. As she approached, she reacted in fear and withdrew. The face was horrible. It was her "other self." This person had also been counseling with me. She knew she had demonic problems. She had lost a "tongues" spirit already and was working on one called Non-acceptance. We found out in a confrontation session that a demon had caused that vision to appear to her. The demon claimed to be Dark Alice (name changed). The young lady rejected that one and did not submit to TA therapy again. She came to a better concept of her real identity through this and rejected attempts by spirits to divide her sense of wholeness of personality.

Ensign and Howe tell of a Christian woman who was "unable to distinguish between her real self as created by Almighty God and the pseudo-personalities that had for so long dominated her thinking." They write of an evil spirit

> who was able to deceive the sister into believing that it was impossible for her to be delivered and that "she thinks I am her." The signing of the Renunciation and Affirmation paper [a means these counselors use] also proved to be a powerful means for the Lord Jesus Christ to separate Satan from the sister's personality.[12]

Ability to make decisions. Demons often cause such confusion that decisions are very difficult; and a sense of frustration, failure, and guilt will often follow. They want to keep a Christian from being effective in his life and ministry. A pastor brought to me a physical therapist he had been counseling. Demonic inhabitation had been determined previously, for the pastor was skilled along this line of counseling. He sought further help, because the spirits were stubborn. The Lord enabled us to help the woman a great deal. In Christ's name, we retook some strongholds and dismissed several leading spirits. Her resultant freedom was expressed in her professional relationships. Whereas before she felt pressed to follow another's suggestion and guilty if she didn't (dependent as she was upon others' acceptance), now she was able to voice her own opinion freely

12. Ibid., pp. 190-91.

without hesitancy and without negative emotions. She could now make clear and rational decisions rather than those based on expediency and motivated by guilt and desire for acceptance.

She tells how she was able to relate positively to her parents in making a decision and expressing her opinion without fear and guilt: "Previously I would have been petrified to discuss it and probably not have brought it up, or I would have labored over it much before doing it. I was so astonished and excited." Her deliverance from these ruling demons had freed her to make rational and confident decisions. She is not the only one to find new rational and relational capacities after the removal of wicked spirits.

Improvement of marriage relationships. I have often counseled couples whose marriages were upset not only by the human factors involved but by demonic influence. Often one or both of them were demonized. Dealing with their personal spiritual lives, the considerations of communication, and the dynamics of demonic control has brought improvement in many cases. Demons will often use the weaknesses in one partner to aggravate the weaknesses in the other. Their design is to make both miserable and break up the marriage. They hate true love and attack Christian marriages. In this way they may carry out their desire for destruction of life and testimony.

A couple came to me with great concern for their marriage. The wife was unreasonably jealous. She admitted she had no reason but just could not help it. The distraught husband loved her greatly and had been faithful in all respects. After discovery of wicked spirits within the wife, she and her husband stood against them, confessing and renouncing sins of attitude and action. Soon she was free from Jealousy and his hosts. The marriage so improved that they were able to help another young Christian couple who were being harassed by demonization. Both related afterward that they were progressing well in their marriages, and their families were reaping the blessings.

GREATER RESPECT FOR CHRIST

Ensign and Howe speak concerning increased respect for Christ:

The deliverance ministry itself is of such a high spiritual order of trusting in the Lord Jesus and His finished work on Calvary that all persons involved gain a tremendous respect for Christ and a higher dependence upon Him. . . . No one has been hurt, to our knowledge, or hindered in his spiritual development.[13]

A woman freed by the help of a trusted counselor writes:

I am very thankful for God's protection and care in my difficult times. And whenever the voices made me doubt His existence I would see a sign of God's love and care through the Christian people around me.

The MK ("missionary kid") quoted above wrote out her testimony for me, and she ended her letter with these words:

To you who are reading this, I hope and pray that it may be an encouragement to you to continue on in faith knowing that the Lord is faithful to His promises. The Psalms are full of promises for deliverance from evil and the evil ones, and examples of His faithfulness are numberless. My experience is only one more.

GREATER AWARENESS AND HATRED FOR EVIL

Almost all of those I have counseled have become more properly and acutely aware of the tactics of the enemy. They have also learned to hate more both the enemy and the sin in their own lives. Recognizing the demons' hatred of Christ and of them, they have taken their stand with Christ against sin and Satan. This expresses the principle of Psalm 97:10: "Hate evil, you who love the Lord, who preserves the souls of His godly ones; He delivers them from the hand of the wicked."

Unger shares the letter of a retired military man who battled wicked spirits and who wrote of his reaction to the discovery and some victory over indwelling demons. He wrote,

Being a Christian, confident in Christ, and having direct knowledge of their presence and tactics, I am, of course, not about to give in to their threats or to accomodate their desire for my destruction. However, I am persuaded that many other human beings have.

13. Ibid., p. 186.

I thank God for the strength, hope and saving grace of our Lord and Savior! Had the others known, and believed as I do, perhaps they too could have endured and their lives been salvaged. . . .

I wonder how many other people are being harassed, tormented and misled by these same demonic spirits that invaded my life. In one respect I was fortunate. I eventually did discover my real enemy—through coming to know my real Friend—Jesus Christ the Saviour and Deliverer, who promises me victory over these powers of darkness.[14]

As in the illustration of the pastor on pages 208-9, satanic harrassment sometimes resurfaces in the form of attack on family members.

RETURN OF SOME ILLNESSES

With the removal of wicked spirits and their supernatural effects in a believer's life, there may be in some cases the *return* of maladies that were removed by demonic "healings." However, it is better to be free of wicked spirits than to continue with the magical cures they use to bargain for invasion.

Koch tells of such a situation. A mother had allowed her epileptic daughter to be charmed. The magical treatment resulted in the disappearance of epileptic symptoms. But they both stopped attending their church. The pastor inquired for the reason and soon discovered the magical healing. He also found that the "spirit healer" had given the girl an amulet to wear.

Asking them to show him the amulet, he opened it and found inside a piece of paper containing what amounted to be a contract with the devil. It said in effect that in exchange for her healing the devil would be able to have her soul. Both women were terribly frightened by this discovery. They repented immediately and burnt the amulet. Now what happened? The epilepsy returned. But after their confession and repentance the mother and daughter were once again able to pray, and they started to attend the church services once more. But although the illness had returned, it was not a case of the return of evil spirits, but rather just the opposite.

14. Merrill F. Unger, *What Demons Can Do to Saints* (Chicago: Moody, 1977), pp. 54, 56.

The reappearance of the illness was actually an indication that the occult ban had now been broken.[15]

Koch expressed concern that the pastor did not pray for God to genuinely heal the girl now that she was free.

BENEFITS TO THE COUNSELOR

Counselors of the demonized testify to the benefits they have received in being used by God to deliver them. I must say that the first time I was introduced to such a counseling situation, I was a bit uncomfortable. I had never witnessed such a thing; there was hesitation and some definite concern. However, I was quickly relieved when my fellow teacher handled the situation with calmness and confidence that the Lord had given him.

In my first cases I had some remaining concern, but the Lord soon conquered that and gave me boldness and wisdom to handle the cases He had sent my way. I never sought out such opportunities, but I never shied away from them when God brought them to me. Although I had known the Lord for years and was an experienced teacher of the truth with great confidence in His Word, yet my confidence in the Lord, in His Word, and in His willingness to intervene grew quickly and definitely. I saw His Word take effect in the lives of the oppressed and against the attitudes and desires of His enemies. I saw prayers specifically directed against demonic forces answered immediately in some cases; in other situations where He took time to work in the will of the counselees, I saw His intervention come soon. I saw demons cringe at the use of the authority granted us in Christ. They often would change from bravado and brash opposition to obedient confession that Christ was their victor, and they would obey us as His servants and victors in Him. I saw them plead not to be sent to the pit and seek to bargain with us, but victors need not bargain or compromise in obedience to their Lord.

In all this, we are reminded to rejoice, not in the fact that demons are subject to us, but that we are related to the Savior, the Lord Jesus, the King of kings and Lord of lords So we have

---

15. Koch, *Occult Bondage*, pp. 116-17.

sought to keep this perspective in serving the Lord and helping those who have fallen prey to the evil ones. We have gained new perspective on the biblical truth that God is good, loving, gracious, kind, longsuffering, compassionate, powerful, and sovereign, and that He intervenes to rescue His own from the clutches of darkness.

The psychologist who brought the veteran missionary to me (as told in the story above), wrote me after she witnessed the confrontation and deliverance from some of the demons inhabiting her client:

> I have given a great deal of thought to why God has permitted me/us to learn so much about "angels elect and evil" and have no pat answers to this question. However, this I do know, He never wastes anything and that He holds us responsible to use that which He gives to us to bring Him honor and to be a benefit to others. To that end I am committed.

A Christian counselor now working on an advanced degree was herself harassed by demonic forces. She writes:

> I so appreciate your ministry to me both in class and counseling. You have surely helped me see my Saviour more clearly. I'm grateful that God has opened my eyes to the working of the enemy. I'm grateful for your balanced, biblical approach to the spiritual battle.

A pastor asked me to help counsel a couple whose daughter was afflicted with what had been diagnosed as Tourette's Syndrome. This was the second child I had encountered with this malady. We met with the couple and their daughter in the presence of the pastor and one of the elders of the church. Afterward the pastor wrote, "Last Monday night was unique and considered to be a privilege for both Mel (name changed) and me. We both learned so much and commit [ourselves] to be good stewards of what we learned." This pastor has been used of God to help others as well.

Ensign and Howe testify to the benefits of participating in the ministry of freeing God's people from demonization:

> We have learned a great many things from the involvement in the ministry of deliverance, and almost all of these have been

beneficial and useful to us in becoming better shepherds and in watching over the flock of God. We have learned to entrust the work of deliverance to the guidance of Almighty God rather than our own efforts to gain discernment. The Lord has graciously led us into more effective prayers against the evil spirits which have resulted in a dramatic cut in the time needed for deliverance. . . .

Again, we have seen some changes in the Lord's working through us as we became more aware in understanding the procedure that the Lord would honor. . . . The determination and spiritual maturity of the client is of major importance in the speed and the thoroughness with which the evil spirits are exposed and expelled.

Another major change that has come about is that we no longer use physical restraints to keep the demonized person in the counseling room. . . .

Nothing has become more clear to us during these many hundreds of hours involved in spiritual counseling than the fact that the Lord God Almighty does *everything* in the deliverance work, and we human beings are but the instruments or mere voices of Him to use as He may choose. This is the only proper and safe position to occupy because it is true. . . . All glory, honor, and thanks must be given to the triune God for the deliverance and not to the individuals who have been used of God in the matter.[16]

When God's people take seriously the battle with wicked spirits in heavenly realms and face it in the power of Christ, they grow and are able also to help others. Experiencing God's encouragement in these circumstances enables us to encourage others to the glory of Christ (2 Cor. 1:3-4).

CONCLUSION

We have surveyed the biblical terms that describe the deliverance of Christians from demonization as well as the biblical record of the results. We have examples of the results of deliverance in modern counseling situations. There is a definite similarity of the principles and particulars involved in both the biblical and the clinical record. Clinical results include such benefits as immediate sense of freedom and well-being, a sense of peace and security, loss of occult powers, relief from persistent problems, freedom for spiritual growth, restoration of personal

16. Ensign and Howe, pp. 179-81.

soundness, greater respect for Christ, greater awareness of and hate for evil, return of some charmed illnesses, and confidence and skill for the counselors.

All this supplies additional testimony to the fact that we must recognize the reality of demonization among Christians and that we must seek sound biblical and clinical methods of relieving God's people from this awful and undeniable blight.

15

Propriety of Counseling

There is a proper place in caring for a person's welfare, whether Christian or non-Christian, to extend counseling help that treats the matter of demon oppression. Some may object to this type of counseling, but there are good biblical and practical supports for such. In fact, it is the God-given responsibility of the organized church, the Christian counselor, and lay members of the Body of Christ to recognize this need and to meet it in intelligent, biblical, and considerate fashion.

We must briefly treat the matter of counseling in this volume to round out the subject, but to handle the subject more fully requires another full-length book. The reader may receive quite a bit of insight into the counseling procedure through several books listed in the bibliography.[1]

SUPPORTS FOR COUNSEL

We find support for counseling the demonized and the removal of inhabiting wicked spirits on both a biblical and a practical basis.

---

1. Particularly helpful for counseling are books by Bubeck, Koch, Ensign and Howe, and Murrell The last four chapters in Dickason, *Angels, Elect and Evil* give helpful background and some specifics.

BIBLICAL BASIS

Several biblical considerations supply a strong basis for counseling in a deliverance ministry.

Expectation of Christ. The Great Commission given by our Lord Jesus in Matthew 28:18-20 makes three supportive contributions. They are all interrelated, and the support for such counseling and confrontation builds as all three factors are considered. First, the authority Christ claims includes not only the earthly realm, but the heavenly also. The heavenly realm includes God, angels, and demons. This is the authority with which Christ commissioned the disciples. They needed the assurance that our Lord could manage all opposition, even the demonic.

Second, the major responsibility of the Commission is found in the main verb "make disciples" *(matheteusate,* v. 19). Discipling persons involves teaching and applying the truth that Christ taught and left through the apostles and writers of the New Testament. When demonic opposition was encountered in the New Testament record, there were actions taken and written instruction given by the apostles for the church age. Part of being a good disciple of Christ is knowing how to battle the enemy. We have seen their tactics in previous chapters, and we know that they attack externally and internally. Gary Collins holds that pastoral counseling is part of the Great Commission. "As followers of Christ, we are duty bound to make disciples of all men and to help those who are weak."[2]

Third, the force of the Commission extends to the end of the age (v. 20) The end of the age is marked by the second coming of Christ (Matt. 24:3, 14, 30). The authority over demonic forces and the responsibility to disciple men is commensurate with the challenge of facing the opposition of satanic powers. We must deliver men from the kingdom of darkness and encourage them in the battle until Jesus Christ returns. The authority, the discipling, and facing the opposition continue today.

Example of Christ. Christ compassionately met men where they were and as they were. He did not dismiss the possibility of demonization. He did not recoil and withdraw in horror, nor did

---

2. Gary R. Collins, *Effective Counseling* (Carol Stream, Ill.: Creation House, 1972), p. 59.

He condemn those who were demonized. He met them in their needs with the deliverance that only He and His delegated authority could supply. He did not depend upon psychological suggestions, or follow conventional counseling procedures, or make referral to the medical practitioners of the day when He faced demonization. He met it head-on with His unique power and ministry of deliverance.

This is not to say that there is no place for more usual counseling and for referral to medical practitioners. But we must face demonization primarily with spiritual resources. This involves the application of the Word of God for spiritual and psychological health. It also involves confrontation of the powers of darkness in the authority of Christ. He expected His disciples to do as He did (Matt. 10:1; Luke 10:17-20).

Examples of the apostles. The gospels and the book of Acts record the disciples' actually extending the ministry of Christ in confronting and casting out demons. Should we merely note that this occurred and relegate battle with demonic opposition to that day? Or does not the same sort of battle with the same sort of demonic fiends continue today? We have demonstrated previously that it does continue. We cannot back down any more than did the original disciples. We do not need apostolic position or special miraculous gifts. God has not allowed for their continuance. But He has allowed for the continued existence and opposition of demons to His church. For this battle He has promised that the authorities of the unseen world will not prevail against us (Matt. 16:18).

Exhortation of the New Testament epistles. The epistles are repleat with instruction and exhortation regarding the warfare in which we are engaged. There is little warrant for thinking that the battle is all external. As we have noted in detail before, Ephesians informs us of our position in the heavenlies, far above all demonic levels of authority. It describes our battle as hand-to-hand wrestling. The armor of God provides for defense against mind-control techniques of demons. It warns not to give place to the devil. Paul also warns in 2 Corinthians against ignorance of Satan's tactics. James and Peter urge submission to God and resistance to the devil.

Besides reminders of this reality, Galatians and Romans also command us to bear one another's burdens. This involves personal interchange or counseling in one form or another. Certainly the area of spiritual warfare and deliverance from the oppression of Satan is not to be excluded from this.

Expression of Body life. The New Testament speaks of the church as the Body of Christ (1 Cor. 12:12-13; Eph. 1:22-23; 4:12-16). Members are to support and minister to each other in interdependent (not independent) fashion. For this Body-life ministry the Holy Spirit gives gifts to each believer (1 Cor. 12:7, 11; Eph. 4:7, 11). These spiritual gifts include such things as pastoring, teaching, exhorting, and administration. These are gifts that involve counseling for the Body members. The church had counselors long before the present field of counseling was ever developed. It is the duty of modern members of the Body of Christ to counsel one another in the principles and practices of the Christian life—and this includes spiritual warfare and deliverance.

Exigencies of humans. All around us we see persons who are afflicted by the torments of Satan. If we have a biblical world view and eyes open to see life as it really is, we can hardly overlook the possibility of demon influence and oppression in many forms. The practice of occult arts, witchcraft, satanism, the New Age movement, mind-control organizations, the influx of Eastern religions, psychic healers, diviners, masochism, child-beatings, incest, sexual exploitations of men and women and even children, the homosexual explosion, the pornographic industry, drugs and alcohol, religious persecution, international terrorism, lack of respect for human life, anarchy and rebellion, breakdown of biblical morals, unalleviated mental illness, jails filled beyond capacity, abortions occurring every twenty seconds—all these and more testify to the inroads that demons have made in promoting their godless and creature-centered philosophy of pride, madness, and destruction. To view these destructive factors as merely the ills of society and not see behind them the schemes of Satan is to be ignorant of the basic plot of evil unmasked in the Bible and to be blinded to the true dimensions of a universal conspiracy against God and humans made in His image, especially Christians.

If we have any insight into the cause for all this human tragedy, and we have biblical resources for dealing with it in any helpful measure—even one by one—then we must rise to the occasion to meet the needs of a tortured and dying world. But what of the Christian who is tormented? Galatians 6:10 commands us: "So then, while we have opportunity, let us do good to all men, and especially to those who are of the household of the faith." Of those who are tormented by wicked spirits, our first responsibility is to fellow believers.

_ *Expectation of love.* Christ's new commandment is to love one another as He has loved us. He gave Himself sacrificially for our good. He did not consider the cost of obeying God and delivering man from sin and Satan too great and back away. He did the will of God. He expects us to do the same. We are to love one another, to bear one another's burdens and so fulfill the law of Christ (Rom. 13:8-10; Gal. 6:2). We cannot ignore those burdened by the bondage of Satan, especially our brothers in Christ.

PRACTICAL BASIS

There are apparent practical reasons we should counsel the demonized and seek their deliverance from wicked spirits.

Plight of the oppressed. The historical record and the clinical accounts of Christians oppressed by inhabiting spirits call us to face this reality and the necessity of helping them. We cannot ignore it, explain it away, or defer to nonbiblical counsel. We must face the fact that God has called us to ministry to the brethren (and the unsaved) in biblical and practical fashion to gain relief for those who are crying for it. We must instruct and warn about demon opposition and oppression. There is no valid excuse for refusing to the needy what is rightfully theirs in Christ. We must take our rightful authority and meet the needs of those in dire circumstances. We are moved to share the gospel with the lost and to share food with the starving, but who is moved to relieve those demonically oppressed and dragged down the road to depression and destruction? Too many Christians have let too many Christians fall into the clutches of Satan without knowing how or having the courage to help the oppressed. Christ came, says Isaiah 61:1, "to bring good news to the afflicted; He has sent me to bind up the brokenhearted, to proclaim liberty to captives, and freedom to prisoners." We need to be about His business!

Parallels with other counsel. Counseling the demonized may not seem biblically proper to some, but there is just as much or more biblical support for this realm than for other types of counsel we accept without much question. The Bible encourages us to seek good counsel from qualified persons in making decisions in a variety of circumstances. Proverbs 11:14 states, "Where there is no guidance, the people fall, but in abundance of counselors there is victory." This applies to groups and to individuals. (See also Prov. 15:22; 24:6.) The Bible also warns against ungodly counsel (2 Chron. 10; Ps. 1:1).

We often seek financial, medical, and construction advice from non-Christians because they have expertise in their areas. We engage the services of counselors in psychological and psychiatric matters. Most professionals in this area have received thoroughly secular training, often from unbelievers. But many never raise a question regarding this kind of counsel, and they pay dearly for it—from the pocketbook and from their subsequent difficulties. Furthermore, we staff Christian clinics and schools with counselors who have never thoroughly oriented their counseling techniques or substance to biblical priorities and principles. That is not to say that we cannot obtain genuine help from secular or secularly trained counselors who are not anti-Christian. But how much more help might we obtain from equally skillful persons who have biblical orientation and practice it? Why should we not use gifted men whom God has placed in the church in pastoral or counseling services to help the demonized?

Failure of other counsel. Many of my counselees have related how they have been to secular and even Christian counselors who have not considered the possibility of demon oppression; or if they did, they dismissed it as not involved in this case and sought to explain the problems in purely natural psychological terms. Their secular humanistic training and orientation controlled their diagnosis and subsequent treatment of these cases. It seems that most persons complaining of demon harassment and voices are treated as having hallucinations. Often those depressed are given drugs or are hospitalized or both. There was no basic cure, though there may have been some relief caused by the change and rest.

Now there are cases where chemical imbalance in the brain and physical and psychological illnesses may be helped by proper medical treatment. But demons do not leave when a person is so treated. The person may obtain some relief by development of better mental attitudes. But there are some depressant drugs that cause a state of passivity in which the demons find advantage. In such a state they are freer to control, and the human is unable to resist them as he should. Treatment such as this does not help but adds to the confusion. Secular treatment of those actually demonized has resulted in their being constantly hospitalized and drugged, kept in a state of stupor, because the medical profession has not found an answer to their condition.

The general disarray of the field of psychoanalysis continues as does the attack upon Sigmund Freud, its father. Frederick Crews, a professor of English at the University of California (Berkeley), reviewed Adolf Grunbaum's book *The Foundations of Psychoanalysis*. Crews writes, "And with the publication of Adolf Grunbaum's monumental new book, people will now begin to comprehend that the entire Freudian tradition—not just a dubious hypothesis here or an ambiguous concept there—rests on indefensible grounds."

He further says, "Moreover, many of Freud's other major tenets were not derived from observation but extrapolated from his premise that repression is the mainspring of neurosis." Concerning the value of psychoanalysis, he writes, "[It] is by far the most costly and time-consuming of all psychotherapies, yet it has not been shown to be more curative than a single one of its hundred-plus rivals, even those that require only a few weeks of intervention." Crews comes to this critical conclusion: "Psychoanalysis now stands irremediably exposed as a speculative cult." He continues, "We can no longer suppose that he [Freud] discovered a cure for neurosis or unlocked the secrets of the subconscious. So far as one can tell, the only mind he laid bare for us was his own." He concludes, "And analysts themselves, insofar as they can bear to recognize that they have been caught up in a medical and intellectual charade, face the most awkward reappraisal of all."[3]

Christians who follow the latest trends, or even the "tried and proven methods," in psychological and psychiatric care may be venturing into the dark or trying to walk on water. Modern science and theory are always in the process of correcting and updating themselves. Professionals, embarrassed by the changes,

---

3. Frederick Crews, "The Future of an Illusion," *The New Republic*, 21 January 1985, pp. 28-33.

hesitate to admit they were wrong.

Koch speaks to the relation of pastoral and medical counsel:

> And yet it is extremely encouraging from time to time to meet a Christian psychiatrist whose spiritual eyes have been really opened. To this effect a Christian neurologist once said, "60% of the inmates of my psychiatric clinic are not so much suffering from mental illness as from occult subjection or even demonization." And an English psychiatrist declared once, "If I were able to obtain forgiveness for the sins of the patients in my clinic, I would be able to discharge half of them tomorrow." Statements of this nature imply that many more of our so-called mentally and emotionally ill patients are rather "ill" toward God than either the public or the medical profession care to recognize. Anyone who is prepared to go into the problem more deeply will soon realize that many "mental" and "emotional" illnesses require the services of an authoritative Christian counsellor rather than a rationalistic medical doctor.[4]

Koch balances the picture for us in this matter:

> Yet medical science must be given its rightful place, for it too, is of God. But at the same time we must not allow our right to spiritual and charismatic counselling (using proper spiritual gifts such as pastoring) to be taken away from us. Both have their rightful place. And it is often extremely beneficial for the two to work side by side in cases where the diagnosis is doubtful. In this way everyone should use that gift which he has received from God.[5]

Success of deliverance counseling. There is a good record of genuine and lasting help received from counseling that directly deals with the matter of demon oppression or demonization. The previous chapter recounts the cases of many who received partial or complete relief through confrontation and removal of wicked spirits. There are many more cases not reported in this brief and representative report. Numerous case studies and testimonies from my own file and those from other reliable counselors with theological and psychological credentials speak of

4. Kurt Koch, *Occult Bondage and Deliverance* (Grand Rapids: Kregel, 1970), p. 13.
5. Ibid.

the success of this type of counseling. Shall we deny such needed help to the Christian public because it does not fit nicely into the accepted academic and professional approach? If so, then on the same basis we would have to rule out much Christian doctrine and practice. There is a place for a proper biblical and practical approach to counseling the demonized.

OBJECTIONS TO COUNSEL

Objections or questions regarding counseling the demonized are often raised. Some are legitimate, and others need not be considered. Here we seek to answer briefly some of those that need an answer. These seem to fall into the categories that question the biblical sanction, relegate counseling to "recognized professionals," or hold that it is in some way dangerous to counsel the demonized and confront demons.

LACK OF BIBLICAL SANCTION

Many declare that the Bible does not support Christians' dealing directly with the demonic. We will seek to state and answer various assertions along this line.

No specific biblical teaching. The objection is lodged in this fashion: "If the Bible says nothing specific regarding Christians being inhabited by spirits, why spend time helping those supposedly inhabited?"

We answer by saying that no specific mention does not eliminate the possibility of the fact and need. We suggest rereading the summaries in chapters 5 through 10 where we treated this problem extensively. The illustration of what the Bible might teach about believers having cancer is particularly appropriate (chap. 9). We must face reality in light of biblical truth and clinical fact.

"But wouldn't you expect the Bible to say something specifically along this line if we are to counsel the demonized?" This is basically the weak argument from silence: the Bible says nothing about it; therefore, we should not be concerned about it. But this does not hold water. The Bible does not say anything about many things we know to be true (electrical devices, motor vehicles, space travel, psychological therapy). Are they therefore any the less useful or true? The fact that the Bible does not forbid counseling the demonized leaves it open to possibility.

"The Bible says so little about demons and demonization; so why teach and counsel along this line?" Actually the Bible says a great deal about demons and demonization. Those who level this objection do not know their Bible or recognize that the Bible has more to say about Satan and demons than it does about such things as the Trinity, the reproduction of the spiritual nature of man, or our resurrection bodies and the new heavens and new earth, our eternal dwelling place. I would recommend that those who hold this objection begin with reading my book *Angels, Elect and Evil*[6] in which there are 112 pages expressly relating to Satan and demons. Furthermore, we have seen that Christians have specific maladies that fit the category of demonization. We must treat them from a biblical viewpoint.

Battle with demons is external in the epistles. This objection may be stated, "In the epistles (taken as norm for the church age) the battle with the flesh is internal, but the battle with demons is external." This objection is presumptive. It cannot be finally demonstrated that this generalization is true. We have shown in chapters 6 through 8 that there is no final biblical or theological conclusion to this matter. It must be settled using a combination of biblical and clinical parameters (chap. 9).

This objection is also an oversimplification. Just as the battle with the world is both external and internal, it may be allowed that the war with demons may have both aspects also. There is some biblical warrant for suspecting this when we consider the evidence. Ephesians 6:10-18 speaks of a mind-control battle that demons wage against us. First Corinthians 12:1-3 speaks of a demonically controlled "tongue" in the assembly of believers. Second Corinthians 10:3-5 tells of opposition from a mind-control philosophy or religion that is obviously influenced by Satan and his agents (2 Cor. 11:1-3, 13-15). First John 4:1-4 warns against demonically deceived teachers in the assembly, who are to be tested lest Satan lead true Christians astray. How are we sure that all this is external to the believer? That it is all external is merely a proposal that is not capable of being proved. Clinical evidence testifies to the fact that Christians can be demonized.

No epistolary teaching on casting out demons. This objection may be stated, "Why is there no instruction regarding casting out demons in the epistles if we are to do such today?" Again

6. C. Fred Dickason, *Angels, Elect and Evil* (Chicago: Moody, 1975)

this is the weak argument from silence. However, there are some good answers. First, the record of Acts runs through the same period of time during which many of the epistles were written. Except for the prison and pastoral epistles, Paul's were written during this time. Even the prison epistles were written during the time of his first Roman imprisonment, recorded in Acts 28. During the time Paul wrote many of his letters, he was also dealing with demons and the demonized. The accounts of confronting demons in Philippi (Acts 16:16-18) and in Ephesus (Acts 19:8-12) occurred during Paul's personal and written ministry. Such procedures were not foreign to the believers of that day. Specialized instruction was not needed. Note also that there is very little specific instruction on methodology of teaching, preaching, administration, and general counseling—although there are principles that apply to these skills.

We also answer that the epistles often refer to demons opposing apostolic ministry and Christians in general. Second Corinthians, Colossians, Ephesians, 1 Timothy, 2 Timothy, 1 Peter, James, and even the book of Revelation speak of this.

Underlying this objection stands the assumption that demons do not operate in demonization as much today, that they change their tactics, or that their influence has faded away. Nothing in the New Testament supports such an assumption.

We might point out at this juncture that it is not absolutely necessary that a specific ministry be listed in the Bible in order to be in keeping with biblical principles. What shall we say for any specific mention of Sunday schools, midweek prayer meetings, parachurch organizations, mission boards, clubs for children and youth, seminaries, and so on? But there is specific mention of the casting out of demons in the New Testament; and there is no revocation or hint of its ceasing. As we reasoned before in chapter 13, there is biblical evidence that certain evidential spiritual gifts would cease; but we find no evidence that demons will cease existing or stop assaulting the Christian community or that we should cease opposing them in teaching, counseling, or casting them out.

LEFT TO THE PROFESSIONALS

Some say, "Emotional and mental problems should be left to the professional counselors, and spiritual ones should be treated by pastoral counselors. We know so little about this area that it is safer for all involved to send those who think they are troubled by demons to see a psychologist or psychiatrist. They have the training and the skills pastoral counselors lack."

Having stated the objection in general, let me seek to answer it in several particulars.

Improper bifurcation. We do disservice to the counselee and to the process of counseling if we rigidly divide the spiritual from the psychological. The human is a whole being. We recognize the disorders and the effects that body chemistry can have on the mind and those of the mind on the body. Spiritual maladjustment may also cause mental and physical disorders. Consider the case of David before he confessed his sin with Bathsheba: "When I kept silent about my sin, my body wasted away through my groaning all day long" (Ps. 32:3). God was chastening him. But when he confessed his sin, God forgave him, and David's confidence and joy returned (32:5-7). If the spiritual problems are caused by sin, demon oppression, or demonization, then the pastoral counselor is the one with proper orientation and resources to help the afflicted. If the problem is one of the usual personality disorders or is physical in nature, then the afflicted should seek psychological or medical help.

General unbelief or ignorance. There is no place in secular psychiatry or psychology for the demonic. It is considered nonexistent and the product of imbalanced if not fanatical thinking, a blight of religious imagination. Even most Christian counselors are trained under such presuppositions and are not ready to accept or deal with the whole field of the demonic, let alone the demonized. In the case of a genuinely demonized person, to send him to a secular psychiatrist or hospitalize him is comparable to sending a fine sports car with a fuel injection problem to a neighborhood teenager who loves to work with mechanical things.

I have counseled many who have had secular counsel and have come away not helped or worse off. As the demonized nurse mentioned earlier expressed:

> One of my sincerest wishes, by the grace of God, is that the Christian community would have a realistic viewpoint. They [the demons] love keeping up the barrier between psychology and

pastoral counseling; because the longer they keep that up, the better chance they have of keeping up their garbage.

At this point, I said to her, "Psychologists and psychiatrists are helpful when dealing with their area of expertise, but they will limit the matter of their solution to the area of their knowledge. Is that right? Is that what you are saying?"

She responded,

> What I am saying is that psychologists, and even at Christian institutions, have been trained well. But the biggest factor that they can't understand is theological issues and particularly the issue of angelology and how it relates to psychology; because that is an area that is untapped, so to speak.[7]

Another nurse who came to me for help spoke of her previous treatment by the medical profession. She was aware of the demonic factors in her life. She was cited in an earlier chapter as a demonized Christian. An excerpt from an interview follows[8]:

I asked, "By what factors are you aware of demonic influence in your life—that they have been involved?"

She answered, "I think I realize more that they are involved by what I don't feel now." (She had had two sessions with me in which we found inhabiting demons and asked the Lord to remove them. She had found some noticeable relief.) "Like I don't feel that spirit of violence. I don't feel as fearful as I used to feel. My self-image is improving. Now I'm aware what control they had over my life."

"How do you know that wasn't just psychological?"

"Well, because I went to a psychiatrist for so many years—three years at one period of my life and two years at another point, and they were unable to help me, even with shock therapy and medication."

I asked, "You've been through medication, and were you hospitalized as well?"

"Yes, I was hospitalized."

"You went through shock therapy how many times?"

"Seven. Seven electric shock treatments."

7. Tape of counseling session with the Christian nurse now in training for counseling.
8. Tape of counseling session.

"But your problem was not solved. You estimate, then, that your problem was not—and you are a registered nurse—"

"Yes, I am."

"You estimate that your problem was not totally psychological, though it might have been partly so?"

"I believe it is partly psychological, but now I feel it has a lot to do with demon spirits."

Here is evidence to support the fact that we cannot relegate all mental and emotional problems to professional psychologists and psychiatrists.

Lack of training and experience. I know of no school of psychiatry or psychology, even of Christian orientation, that gives serious place in the curriculum or training for counseling the demonically oppressed or demonized. I know of only one Christian postgraduate school that recognizes this possibility and has faced it to some degree. Why is this so? First, it is not considered a reality or, if recognized at all, a proper domain for their studies. Such education suggests no way to recognize the possibility, to diagnose with certainty, and to treat with any confidence or expertise a case of demonization. If they did, they would be the laughingstock of the professional community, just as evolutionists laugh at the creationists.

I have had several professionals refer cases they suspected to me for diagnosis and treatment. The counselees were then returned to their professional counselors for their expertise in the continuing personal adjustments. I have referred some of my counselees to trusted professional counselors with good success.

One of my counselees, a nurse with public health, wrote:

> Due to past hurts and painful experience I have had to seek out Christian psychological counseling, which incidentally Dr. Dickason recognized the need for and referred me to. My psychologist . . . has encouraged me to keep up my relationship with Dr. Dickason and has at times encouraged me to go see him for his help.
>
> There are so few around with his expertise and solid Bible background and so many who need the type of counseling he can provide.[9]

9. Letter on file.

A psychotherapist writes concerning "the need for counselors who are aware of the possibilities of demonic influence in emotional symptoms." She says:

> It has been my experience that counselors who are able to differentiate between the two and are able to work with clients in both areas can relieve and/or prevent emotional trauma that results when demonic influence is ignored.
>
> I have known Dr. Dickason for over ten years and have known people counseled by him. Because of his knowledge of the occult and his knowledge of counseling, he has been able to help people find relief from emotional and physical pain when medicine and psychotherapy could not.[10]

A Christian counselor of unwed mothers brought a dear young Christian woman to me. She writes that she saw this

> unwed mother delivered from seven demons who bound her from experiencing a victorious Christian life. As a counselor for these women, there was no doubt in my mind that she was a Christian. The young woman was daily in the Word, she was memorizing scripture, and yet she was controlled by a "force beyond her control" as she described it. . . .
>
> In the end times . . . there is a tremendous need for more men of God to understand and to be willing to help Christians to come to grip with this issue. As professional men and women, we do not hesitate to do a psychological or physical test, but we as Christians do hesitate to do a spiritual test with our clients and our people in our churches who consistently struggle in this area. As a professional counselor for six years in a Christian agency it burdens my heart to realize how we do not and cannot help people because we fail to deal with this issue of demonization. We are scared of it, and so we ignore it.[11]

The professional counselor's lack of training and experience disqualifies him from treating the demon oppressed and the demonized. If Christian professionals such as those who wrote the letters above and such as others quoted in previous chapters will study and find training in this area, then they may be used effectively to help those whom Satan has ensnared.

10. Letter on file.
11. Letter on file.

Only Christians are qualified. To refer a Christian who has demonic problems to a secular professional may further complicate his problem. The non-Christian professional has no authority to deal with demonic forces. Witness the fiasco of the sons of Sceva in Acts 19:13-16. These unsaved "exorcists" sought to cast out a demon, but the demon mocked them and attacked them. Furthermore, if the secularist denies that the person could have demonic problems, he will harm the person's progress and possibly do irreparable damage.

Christians have the authority that qualifies them to successfully face demonic forces. They alone participate in the victory Christ has won over Satan. They have the perspective, if properly biblically trained, to understand the dynamics of the situation and to help. There are Christians who are qualified professionally to do the job if they will be open to this area of counsel. There are pastoral counselors who have their particular professional training also. Many of these are good counselors. Why should we send those oppressed to unsaved or uninformed Christian professionals who are not qualified in this area of counseling?

Gary Collins speaks of the need of lay counselors who can help when the professionals cannot, or are not available. He refers to a report of the Joint Commission on Mental Health sent to Congress several years ago in which it was noted that we have far too few professional counselors to do all the counseling that needs to be done. He writes:

> In absence of professional personnel, the report concluded, "a host of persons untrained or partially trained in the mental health principles and practices" are working to help people with their problems. Church leaders are among this host. They are already involved in counseling although many could be doing a better job.[12]

In another book Collins answers the argument that counseling is not an appropriate work for a pastor and stresses the vital place of the congregation as a healing power in the lives of people.[13]

---

12. Collins, *Effective Counseling*, p. 10.
13. Gary R. Collins, *Christian Counseling* (Waco, Tex.: Word, 1980), pp. 13-21.

Danger in secular methods. Not only is there danger in the denial of demonic involvement in genuine cases of oppression or demonization, but some of the treatment administered by professionals may actually be harmful in such cases. Those therapies that rely heavily upon hospitalization and/or drugs run the risk of perpetuating the problem while only treating the symptoms. In fact, they may aggravate the problem by seeming depersonalization, by isolation, by misunderstanding the root of the problem, by denying the reason and the experience of the person who judges his problem as demonic, by prolonging the demon residence, and by disabling the mind with drugs from full capacity to submit to God and resist the devil. They may play into the scheme of demons who work on mental passivity.

Ensign and Howe have a good treatment of the place of proper nutrition and the dangers of drugs therapy.[14]

DANGERS INVOLVED

Some reject counseling the demonized because of the dangers attached. They fear hurt to those involved, imbalance or extremism, brainwashing, loss of reputation, delving into something akin to spiritism, the amount of time spent, and failure with its discouragement. We must briefly answer these objections.

Hurt to those involved. "This is just too dangerous to handle. We know so little about demons. The whole thing is so eerie. We might get hurt or hurt the person oppressed."

To answer this, we must say that when proper precautions are taken and the situation is conditioned by asking for God's protection, the ministering presence of His angels, and wisdom for the task, there is nothing to fear. In fact, the demons tremble when we take our stand in Christ and in His authority. All of their resistance and activity can be restrained by prayer and command in the name of Jesus our Lord. There is no magic involved; no special gifts are needed. Our heavenly Father guards and controls the situation even when we do not know all that we should do. I have seen prayers almost instantly answered when we asked that wicked spirits would cease their momentary attack upon a counselee.

14. Grayson H. Ensign and Edward Howe, *Bothered? Bewildered? Bewitched?* (Cincinnati: Recovery, 1984), pp. 206-18.

"But what of spiritual harm?" Ensign and Howe comment on this matter:

> In every case of those who continued through to the end of a series of deliverance sessions we can say each was most beneficial. No spiritual harm has come to those who were willing to let the Lord work through their lives until He was finished with His work.[15]

"But wouldn't the shock of hearing that there might be a demon problem present or inhabiting his body cause damaging trauma to the person?"

We must face reality with reality, but we must do it tactfully. Not to honestly and tenderly tell the person with a life-threatening or disabling malady so that he might recognize it and properly handle it is to deprive him of his needs and his rights. God can help us to face reality and to cast all our concerns upon Him, for He controls and He cares. Alfred Lechler speaks to this point:

> While it is true that one must initially show great restraint when investigating a case of suspected demonic subjection, if it becomes transparently clear that the demonic is present, then the person concerned must be told quite definitely, but in love, that Satan has bound him to himself. Even if the patient is unwilling to accept this or shows signs of alarm, one must still not withhold the truth from him, and any resulting shock will only have a wholesome effect in the end. The patient must be made to realize who the enemy of his soul really is, and then together with the counsellor and if possible a group of praying Christians he must set out to ⁻esist this enemy.[16]

Of course, no one should rush into this brashly depending upon his own wisdom or strength. We should not discount the trickery or power of demons. However, they are no match for the Lord. He gives the victory.

Common sense, calmness, trust in the Lord, and exercise of our authority in prayer and command can handle the dangers involved. There are dangers in many enterprises. I have never

15. Ibid., p. 186.
16. Alfred Lechler, "Distinguishing the Disease and the Demonic," in Koch, pp. 189-90

been hurt nor have my counselees in hundreds of sessions.

Imbalance or extremism. "Aren't you in danger of going off the deep end, centering your interests in this ministry, seeing a demon behind every bush?"

Extremism may be found in any area of pursuit. Not all personalities are suited to this type of counsel. But then, not everyone is suited for psychological counseling or pastoral work either. Each person must face his own propensities and weaknesses. However, those who walk a balanced life with the Lord, enjoy normal relationships, and have a healthy mental and emotional life should not fear becoming extremist. This label is often used to deter Christians from any kind of devoted lifestyle and ministry.

There must be balance in our lives in everything, particularly in the realm of spiritual warfare. We must distinguish the natural and the supernatural, but both must be recognized. And as we said before, for everyone who sees a demon behind every bush, there are many more who can't even recognize a bush. It is my opinion that few if any should ever undertake a ministry completely devoted to counseling the demon oppressed or "enter a deliverance ministry" full-time. We need to live well-rounded lives and teach the whole counsel of God. I am so glad that I have had that opportunity from God for so many years.

Brainwashing. "But aren't you in danger of 'brainwashing' people, causing them to park their minds and follow your authoritative approach to their personal problems?"

This is a danger in any field of counseling or of interpersonal relationship. It occurs all the time in improper advertising and with manipulative persons. But such is not in keeping with the concept of personal dignity and responsibility and of the individual priesthood of the believer. The authoritative or the magical approach used by some is inconsiderate and wrong. The counselor needs to involve the counselee at every level of the procedure and inform him as much as needed of every step in the process. We pray that the Lord will give the counselee recognition of what is transpiring and awareness of his own thoughts and feelings. We pray that the Lord will help him distinguish between his thoughts and the demon's and be able to voice his own thoughts at any time.

Though psychiatrist Scott Peck may have witnessed "an exorcism" that was "a form of brainwashing" that left the individual "simultaneously feeling relieved, profoundly grateful, and raped," yet he may not have witnessed the proper procedure with the preparation and consent of the individual. He follows with this point:

> In the years since then the feelings of gratitude and relief have, if anything, increased, and the sense of rape has faded—as does the trauma of surgery.
>
> What prevents exorcism from being true rape is that, as with surgery, the individual consents to the procedure. . . . They should know exactly what they are letting themselves in for.[17]

I do not like the term *exorcism,* since it denotes a ritualistic attempt to remove spirits. I prefer "casting out," "removal," "dismissal," or "delivering." I have never known any of my counselees to have felt mentally "raped" after our sessions. This is because I seek to treat them with all biblical and spiritually based dignity and respect, keeping their physical and spiritual welfare in the foremost of my thinking. There is no "brainwashing," nor should there be. God has honored that balanced approach, according to the counselees' testimonies.

Loss of reputation. But what will people think of us, of our church, or of our counseling ministry if we actually start dealing with the demonic? Will not this affect our reputation and ministry in other areas?

Those who enter "new fields" are often misunderstood and maligned by others who do not understand the facts or the need. Many medical doctors and scientists have had to face this, even those who called for sterile conditions in operations and in hospitals. Even the thought of the biblical truth of the existence of demons will cause the eyebrows of many to lift in unbelief. However, we must face reality with the sense of devotion to obeying God and serving others despite the cost. We might be too concerned about our reputation instead of our character and conduct. The apostles were set forth as fools in the sight of unbelievers, but they risked their lives as well as their reputations for the cause of Christ and the good of others.

There are proper ways of preparing people for the idea of counseling and helping the demonized, and wisdom must be

17. M. Scott Peck, *People of the Lie* (New York: Simon & Schuster, 1983), p. 187.

exercised. But with Christ, the needs of people come before the matter of personal concern about reputation. The concern about this matter might be traced to cowardice and self-preservationism. God will care for the reputation and in time build it if we obey Him.

Delving into a type of spiritism. Someone might say, "But isn't this matter of talking to demons on the edge of spiritism? Speaking to them, asking their names, asking their grounds for inhabiting, telling them to go away—doesn't the Bible warn against this?"

Yes, the Bible forbids trafficking in spiritism. But spiritism is the attempt to contact the spirits of the dead (impersonated by demons) to gain information for personal advantage and direction. This is hardly the same as determining demonic invasion (no deception or credulity involved here) and seeking information that would lead to the expulsion of wicked spirits to the pit! If that be the case, then Jesus was guilty of the same. He spoke to spirits, demanded their names, listened to their replies, and commanded them to leave. Should we not be confident that He was right and that we may follow His example?

Demanding of time. "But doesn't this take a lot of a counselor's time? Should we waste time when there are more important and acceptable things to do?"

Any counseling takes time. People will spend hour after hour telling their thoughts and sharing their inmost concerns with a professional counselor, and he will spend hours listening, evaluating, and seeking to help the counselee. To add to that there is a great deal of expense involved. Some will allow that the time may be well spent there but will not allow that confrontation and the removal of demons from a Christian is worth the time and effort. Is there not a contradiction here?

Sometimes the basic hindrance to many well-meaning Christians desirous of growing and honoring the Lord is that they have an undiagnosed state of demonization. Should we not deal with that? Is not that important to their own personal, family, church, and occupational relationships? Properly balanced counsel should be our aim, considering all the aspects of a person's needs. But we cannot neglect what has been demonstrated to be a genuine problem among many believers and still expect the persons to grow and God to bless anyhow.

There are ways of using the time most effectively. A direct

approach to determining background, personal, and associated factors helps. Asking the person to pinpoint his most serious needs, asking the right probing but considerate questions, going right to the issues that are obvious—all these things cut the time involved. Other issues and problems may surface while talking. They can be handled as briefly as possible. When checking for demonic presence and structure, go to the leading wicked spirit lest lesser ones try to sidetrack the counselor. He must know demonic ranks and tactics. Such books as the author's *Angels, Elect and Evil* are a help in these matters. Bubeck's book *The Adversary* is very practical as are several others listed in the bibliography.

Common sense in setting limits on time spent, recognizing one's own limitations, referral of complicated cases, and keeping priorities in mind are factors that keep the counselor effective.

Failure and discouragement. "But are not the dangers of failure and resultant discouragement considerations? What would this do to the counselee and the counselor?"

These are always factors to be faced in any venture. The Bible warns against the fearful mindset that says, "There is a lion outside; I shall be slain in the streets!" (Prov. 22:13). The fear of failure stems from lack of information, perspective, and trust in God. There may be failures to produce what people expect. We should not promise too much. Yet nothing ventured, nothing gained. Joshua and Caleb were not dismayed by the possibility of defeat as they faced the "giants" and "walled cities" of Canaan. They believed the promise of God: "Every place on which the sole of your foot treads, I have given it to you, just as I spoke to Moses" (Josh. 1:3). Jesus promised us, "If you abide in Me, and My words abide in you, ask whatever you wish, and it shall be done for you" (John 15:7). He also said, "Ask, and you will receive, that your joy may be made full" (John 16:24).

We can replace fear with confidence and joy if we rely upon Christ to handle our situations with His wisdom and control. We are not called to be successful but to be faithful. Success will follow if we follow Christ. He said, "You did not choose Me, but I chose you, and appointed you, that you should go and bear fruit, and that your fruit should remain, that whatever you ask of the Father in My name, He may give to you" (John 15:16).

RESPONSIBILITY FOR COUNSEL

Since the demonization of Christians is a reality, since there are good biblical and practical supports for counseling those Christians and since objections raised are not crucial or forbidding and have been answered, then the Christian community must take seriously its responsibility to handle this matter properly. We can no longer overlook this issue. Believers in biblical days did not have the luxury of passing demonized Christians on to pagan counselors. Today we have resources that the secular world cannot tap—and sad to say, we have scarcely begun to tap.

Our peculiar position. Christians stand in such a relationship to God and to the world of men and spirits that we may render service to God and men in the face of the enemy that no other group of society may offer. We have the answer to demonic oppression and demonization. Should we back away from carrying on this work of Christ?

Imagine what it might mean for those who have been so long downtrodden and subjected to the destructive and tormenting ways of demons to realize that there is hope and there are those who are willing and able to help.

Imagine the encouragement for those who are desperately concerned for family members and friends who have long been in bondage if they could find relief for them.

Imagine the testimony to the community of unbelievers who would see Christians face what many of them fear with good reason, and beholding the courage and concern of Christians they see men liberated from the enemy of the race.

Imagine what it might mean for those missionaries who operate in demon-infested cultures to face the enemy head-on with the support of mission officials and the understanding of their fellow-soldiers in the field. They might begin to make such headway against the forces of evil that the Christian and the pagan world would stand in awe of the power of Christ and turn to Him in their needs. Power confrontation is a need of the day. Missiologist Timothy Warner teaches a course entitled "Power Encounter" at Trinity Evangelical Divinity School in which he stresses the need for recognition and opposition of demonic forces in mission fields.

In this concern, I do not hold, as some, that God is reviving the miraculous gifts of the Spirit for attestation on the mission field. I believe that the normative gifts of the Spirit today do not include that which God designed to be temporary, introductory gifts of the miraculous type. I do believe that God is intervening today in both providential and miraculous ways when He so chooses, apart from giving miraculous gifts. We need nothing more than the position and authority of Christ, the Word of God, and courage to face the task before us in the power of the Spirit of God. With such resources we may stand against the enemy successfully and defeat him. He is but a creature destined for the lake of fire, and so are his henchmen. Christ is creator, controller, and judge. He is the all-sufficient head of His church. And we are His children, His servants bought with His blood and backed by His authority and the exercise of His power.

With our peculiar position in Christ, seated in heavenly places far above all demonic authority, we may face them unafraid. We may, in humble dependence upon Christ, press the battle in our day. We are on the winning side! Let us go forward with this confidence!

Our special perspective. The Christian has a world view that encompasses the reality of the natural and the supernatural. With this perspective, we may understand much of the supernatural phenomena about us. We will not assign to superstition the reality of demon activity. We will not attribute all unexplained phenomena to demonic intervention. We will not assign supernatural powers to the untapped resources of the human being, as do parapsychology and the New Age movement. We will not accept the suggestions of spiritists or Eastern religions. We will not seek psychic practitioners for counsel or relief of spirit activities in one's house. Nor will we think that secular science and pseudoscience have all the answers.

Christians can face the reality of the demonic world with confidence that God our Father controls all and that He is concerned with the welfare of all humans, particularly His own, bought by the blood of Christ. M. Scott Peck, M.D., recognized from his standpoint as a believer that demonization is "beyond standard psychopathology."[18]

18. Ibid., p. 192.

We are often in a better position because of our perspective than those who are recognized as the experts. A damaging confession comes from psychoanalyst Kenneth Mark Colby. In August 1973 he said at the Third International Conference of Artificial Intelligence at Stanford, "In psychiatry—I'll tell one of the deep, dark secrets—we don't know what we're doing. . . . We need all the help we can get and we're willing to take it from any direction."[19] Here is the place where our Christian perspective could offer help. Those of credentials ought to move to do so.

Responsible practice for the church. What responsible action should the Christian community take in this matter? The teaching and preaching ministry of the church should actively oppose Satan and his demons.

We must expose the demonic and warn against it. This is preventative counseling. Pastors and teachers must give the whole counsel of God by balanced teaching about Satan and demons and about the occult and its dangers (2 Tim. 4:1-6). They must warn Christians not to participate in sinful or false life-styles, but to oppose them (Eph. 5:11). They must preach Christ as the deliverer from darkness and bondage to demonic power (Luke 4:18-19; Col. 2:15; Heb. 2:14-15) and warn men to turn to Him in faith and renunciation of the devil and all his works.

We must exercise the ministry of testing the spirits (1 John 4:1-3), teach believers in the full expression of the Spirit-filled life (Gal. 5:16-23; Eph. 5:18), train believers to put on the full armor of God for battle with wicked spirits (Eph. 6:10-18), and train specialists who can exercise their spiritual gifts of pastoring, teaching, and encouragement in counseling those oppressed by Satan.

Finally, we must treat those enslaved by the enemy. We must encourage them to seek godly, competent counsel. We must not fear to face demonization and help those afflicted. God will help us, and God will reward us (Gal. 6:9-10).

CONCLUSION

Counseling the demonized is a proper practice for the Christian community. The supports for such are reasonable and unde-

19. R. D. Rosen, *Psychobabble* (New York: Atheneum, 1977), p. 123.

niable. Objections commonly raised do not present genuine barriers to such counsel. In fact, it is the God-given responsibility of the church—pastors, professional counselors, and laymen—to specifically come to the rescue of those who are troubled and oppressed by demonic forces, since we have the authority, the perspective, and the resources granted us by the grace of our Lord Jesus Christ, the victor and deliverer. He must win the battle, and we are on His side. Let us then move forward in the battle to free the demon oppressed and the demonized.

16

Response to the Issue

Though we have already made some general suggestions in the previous chapter regarding our responsibility as Christians in the matter of counseling the oppressed and the demonized, there remain some specific practical matters to treat. These involve some dangers to avoid and some duties to assume.

DANGERS TO AVOID

Dangers to avoid in the matters of demonization of believers and their counseling range in the areas of attitude and action.

DISCOUNTING THE EVIDENCE

It would be very easy for some to neglect the extensive evidence that has been presented and to return to a previous opinion that Christians cannot be demonized. A concept long ingrained does not change readily. This is a form of prejudice or prejudging the issue. Evidence for and against the thesis that Christians may be demonized has been considered from a large number of biblical texts and from several theological arguments. We have sought fairly to treat these texts and arguments. We have come to the conclusion that neither the Bible itself nor any logical or theological extrapolation of biblical truth can finally solve the question. We have also considered the wealth of clinical evidence available and have concluded that there is good basis for holding that believers may have inhabiting demons.

But emotions run high in this matter, and fear clouds both reason and a sense of resources in Christ. Furthermore, those who have publicly committed themselves to the position that Christians cannot be demonized hesitate to change. Reputations are involved. Nonetheless, we must face the facts and weigh them seriously with as much objectivity as possible. I have sought to do this in my research and in this volume. I hope that the readers will share in my concerns for factuality regarding the issue and for loving counsel of those oppressed.

NEGLECTING THE NEED

It would also be more convenient and less threatening not to venture into investigation of the facts and treatment of the oppressed. We tend to follow our preset patterns of ministry and to avoid those areas with which we are not familiar, especially in an area such as this that is still a question in the minds of many.

This is where we need to exercise not only concern but actual intervention. Our courage must rise to the task set before us to free the enslaved from the pressures, debilitations, depressions, and domination of demons. We have the authority and resources in Christ. We need to use them properly. Of course there are reasonable precautions to take. We do not throw caution to the wind, but neither should we let it deter us from fulfilling Christian ministry to meet an obvious need. More and more Christian pastors and professional counselors are finding persons whom they cannot help significantly with usual practice. More and more they are turning to recognize the possibility of demonization among their counselees. We need to do likewise and back those who are qualified and willing and provide for the training of more of their kind and courage.

OVEREMPHASIS

We cannot agree with those who put too high a priority on the ministry of casting out demons. There are those who each week in their assemblies deal with demonization on a mass basis in public. This turns out to be more ostentatious and superficial than helpful. Counseling is a private matter, and there are personal aspects of the problem that must be reasoned through on a biblical and practical basis with the individual. Furthermore, we need to give attention to the full range of biblical teaching, to worship, and to the needs of the whole assembly.

There are also those who make a full-time ministry out of counseling the demonically oppressed. This leads to imbalance and undue pressures upon the counselor, his family, and his church. We are to teach the whole counsel of God, and this involves balance. Those that I know who have spent an inordinate proportion of their time and ministry in this area have had their problems. There is a proper proportion to give to this area, and each counselor must listen to the advice of others concerning this matter and make that determination for himself.

One way to alleviate the pressures on those who are qualified and willing is to train others who can share the load. It does not take a specialist to give significant help to some, but there are cases that require more expertise. The Christian community must provide training and opportunity for this ministry.

OVERSIMPLIFICATION

Cases of demonization often reflect complicated background and personal problems. But it is the tendency among many practitioners—pastoral, medical, and psychological—to assume the simple-cause approach when actually there may be several concurrent causes and some of them interrelated.

In view of this tendency, we should be open to consider all factors—physical, psychological, spiritual, and demonic—when we seek to diagnose the problems of counselees. Unless there are nonpathological symptoms such as magical healing powers, speaking in languages not learned, clairvoyance, and so on, we must not presume the demonic. But there may be broader evidence indicating demonic influence is involved. Along these lines Lechler comments:

> One must be especially careful in this area, for the distinguishing between disease and the demonic is not only a very difficult task but also a very responsible one. While on the one hand one must be completely impartial when approaching the question of the demonic, it is imperative on the other hand not to diagnose demonic subjection, and even more so possession, without making a thorough-going investigation of the causes beforehand. Unfortunately there are many Christians who are all too ready to accept the presence of the demonic in doubtful cases of emotional distur-

bance. . . . The really crucial thing for this type of diagnosis is to prove after one has excluded the possibility of pathological disturbance, the presence of several of the underlying causes [of demonic influence].[1]

Dr. Lechler, for thirty-five years the medical superintendent of the largest mental hospital in Germany, also warns against glibly informing a person that he has demon problems. If such a person has been under the restraints of a pathological depression, he may fall into further confusion and depression. But when it becomes quite clear that demons are involved, the person must be told definitely and considerately. The results in this case would be beneficial if the counselor provides proper precautions and follow-up.[2]

Deliverance counseling may pave the way for other counseling. Scott Peck tells of patients from whom demons had been expelled who returned to some of their previous symptoms. He writes:

> Nonetheless, within a few hours it was possible to discern a subtle but extraordinary change. All the old complexes were back in place, but it was as if the energy had gone out of them. The change was that now these patients could listen and what they heard could now have an effect. In one case, psychotherapy became possible for the first time. In the other, more was accomplished in fifty hours of intense psychotherapy following the exorcism proper than in five hundred hours preceding it. These patients moved extraordinarily fast. It was as if they were catching up for all those lost years.[3]

This underscores the need to be aware of complex causes. Demons may cause maladies or complicate them, using whatever means they can to do their destructive work. This also points out the necessity of follow-up for those delivered from demons.

Neither must we think that a psychological diagnosis is the solution to a problem. Sometimes counselors or medical per-

1. Alfred Lechler, "Distinguishing the Disease and the Demonic," in *Occult Bondage and Deliverance,* by Kurt Koch (Grand Rapids: Kregel, 1970), p. 188.
2. Ibid., pp. 188-90.
3. M. Scott Peck, *People of the Lie* (New York: Simon & Schuster, 1983), pp. 197-98.

sonnel will place a case in a certain general category and then explain the specific case before them in the usual terms of the category. This may overlook other factors and nonconforming symptoms in the haste to come to some conclusion.

Consider the matter of multiple personalities within a human. Although there may be nonsupernatural cases of multiple personalities, perhaps created by a troubled person to be able to escape or face reality, the Christian counselor must consider the possibility that one or more of the personalities could be demonic. Demons can project themselves in that fashion. This would likely be the case if one of the personalities has occult powers, speaks in an unlearned language, or claims to derive from a previous incarnation. Ensign and Howe present such a case. "While Satan obliged by providing Evelyn, a spirit who functioned as a companion, Janet's bargain opened the door to other wicked spirits who tormented her in many destructive ways."[4]

These authors also comment:

> Once again we believe the premise has been validated that true psychological schizophrenia as evidenced specifically by multiple personality is rare and that spiritually caused multiple personality is quite common. Many forms of mental illness appear to originate, intensify, and perpetuate through the power of darkness rampant in the world.[5]

We cannot expect successful treatment and lasting healing if only one aspect of a complex set of problems is treated. Oversimplification from either the natural or the supernatural viewpoint should be avoided.

MISEMPHASIS

We must beware of expecting the immediate, magical solution to demonic problems. God deals primarily with persons, not problems. Growth and development take priority over dismissal of demons. There are many persons in this world without resident demons, but they may not be rightly related to God through Christ or, if Christians, rightly related to the Spirit of

4. Grayson H. Ensign and Edward Howe, *Bothered? Bewildered? Bewitched?* (Cincinnati: Recovery, 1984), p. 276.
5. Ibid.

God and under His cultivation. The mystical and the miraculous are not usually the way of God's dealing with us today. To expect such can easily hinder real progress and real deliverance by presuming after commanding in the name of Jesus that all demons are gone or by giving false evaluation and assurance to the counselee.

I have talked to people who have been through "deliverance sessions" and claimed to be free of spirits. But I questioned that in my mind when I saw their magical outlook on Christian life and doctrine. Others who thought they were free of demons, because some person with charisma said so, later were confused and disappointed to find the demons actually had not left. Their faith was shaken because it was placed in the wrong person—the healer rather than in Christ. The basis for their hope was the charismatic's word and not the balanced understanding and trust in the Spirit's Word, the Scriptures. How often people jump to conclusions and hope for supernatural signs and wonders just because they see some words in the Bible or take a statement out of context. Such disregard for God's Word, treating it as gypsy tea leaves or as a support for their wishes, cannot but introduce difficulty.

Of this magical outlook on life, Paul Tournier writes, "As well as in savages and children, we always find the magical mentality in neurotics and people with mental disease."[6] He continues, "But even in mild cases of nervous illness we always find traces of belief in magic."[7] Tournier's whole treatment of this problem of belief in magic is instructive, but somewhat disappointing when he touches upon what he terms "possession."[8]

Along this line we must caution against the use of what some call "the gift of discernment." Many use this term to speak of a special ability from God to tell if there are demons within someone or what sort they might be. We must point out that this was a first-century gift closely associated with the gift of prophecy. When a person claiming to have a message from God spoke in the assembly, the person with the gift of the "ability to distinguish between spirits," as the term *diakriseis pneumatōn* signi-

---

6. Paul Tournier, *A Doctor's Casebook in the Light of the Bible* (New York: Harper & Row, 1954), p. 92.
7. Ibid., p. 93.
8. Ibid., pp. 87-95.

fies,[9] could tell on the spot that the speaker was speaking either by the Holy Spirit, his human spirit, or a demonic spirit. This was a further check on the prophets who were supposed to check or "pass judgment" (*diakrinetosen*, related word) on one another to guard the assembly against deception that could originate with men or demons (1 Cor. 14:29). Since this gift was designed to operate in the early church before the completion of the prophetic word in the New Testament, it does not operate today. Its design, as with all spiritual gifts, was to operate in the assembly (1 Cor. 12:7; 14:26). It was not designed for private counseling and is not available today. Those who claim to use it today may be deceived by demons who counterfeit formerly valid gifts for the confusion and influence they may introduce through this, as with other so-called miraculous gifts of the Spirit. In my opinion, it is a form of ESP or clairvoyance. Occult practitioners claim to have similar powers today. To use the argument that the devil counterfeits what is true is not applicable to these gifts, which are not valid today. He is counterfeiting a first-century gift and passing if off as valid today. We must beware of the magical frame of mind. The enemy will use it wherever he can—especially to sidetrack and trap Christians. He is willing to exchange a piece of bait for the fish.

DIVISIONS OVER THE MATTER

There are differences of opinion over whether a genuine believer can be demonized. These have extended even to emotionally charged debates. The enemy desires to have Christians argue about the issue while he takes advantage of human emotions to cause divisions among members of Christ's Body. Just looking at the question objectively, even without the information we have considered in this study, it is absurd to let an issue that is not totally clear in the Bible or in experience (so it is said) cause interruption of Spirit control and disruption of fellowship. Demons, I suppose (on good basis), have been clapping their hands and shouting for glee at the confusion they have caused. Meanwhile they are actively continuing their full range of opposition to the saints, which the Bible spells out

9. William F. Arndt and F. Wilbur Gingrich, *Greek-English Lexicon of the New Testament* (Chicago: U. of Chicago, 1952), p. 184.

clearly. Christians need to become aware of the dangers of division over this matter.

The answer to the problem of division is first attitudinal. We must be accepting of one another despite differences of opinion. We must be forgiving where there has been hurt. We must be open to discussion without an emotionally charged atmosphere. After all, we are not talking about whether the devil can snatch a genuine believer from the hand of Christ, or whether a person can be owned by the devil and God at the same time, or whether a demonized person is the personal agent of the devil.

The second answer to the problem is to recognize that we must take some practical steps. We are talking about whether or not help should be extended to Christians who seem to fit the picture of one demonized. The question is how can we help such a person. If we find a person inhabited by a demon, are we to tell him that he is not a believer and that he must trust Christ? Or are we to tell him, if we acknowledge that he is a believer, that the voices, pressures, and threats he has felt are all hallucinations and that he should see a psychiatrist? This may not be accurate and may confuse the situation and cause the person far-reaching harm.

The third answer to the problem is to back off from our preconceived positions (often dogmatically asserted and backed by poorly exegeted Scripture or improperly constructed logic) and to investigate the question with more objectivity and less passion. We do have a responsibility to God's Word, to God's people, and to the oppressed. This is not just a theological debate or a mind game but a matter of vital concern to all involved.

We can learn to disagree agreeably. We must defuse the emotionally charged atmosphere that has sometimes surrounded this issue. We must avoid, if at all possible, causing divisions in the church over this issue. Realistically there will be divisions just as history records. But if we pursue division instead of seeking communication and unity of spirit, woe to us and glee to the devil!

PARALYSIS AND DEFEAT

Satan and his demons would just love to have us give up in dismay, either at the complexity of the problem or in the confusion of debate. He would also rejoice to have us back off in either indecisiveness or indolence. We must actively approach this question to come to biblical and practical solutions to treat the oppressed. There are so many believers suffering today at the hands of the enemy! We need to move to help them rather than debate or drop out. We should not throw up our hands in either confusion or fear but lift our hands to God in prayer and confidence that He will meet us, and those oppressed, in our needs. He has promised to give wisdom to those who are single-minded for His glory (James 1:5). The Savior rules over all circumstances, all conflicts and contenders (Eph. 1:19-21). We cannot afford to stand idle or back down in defeat.

DUTIES TO ASSUME

From what we have studied and presented throughout the course of this book, we can hardly say that information is not available on the question of whether Christians can be demonized. There is much to indicate that they can and have been. We cannot ignore the evidence, nor should we turn a deaf ear. Our motives and our actions will be evaluated at the judgment seat of Christ. Just as in reverence for God Paul sought to persuade men of his genuineness (2 Cor. 5:11), so we would do the same in this matter.

What practical response shall we take to meet the needs of the demonized? We have suggested at the end of the last chapter some practical response for the church and the Christian community. There we suggested (1) that the church warn against demonic and sinful life-styles and present Christ as victor and deliverer, (2) that we test the spirits, teach believers of true spiritual life, train them to put on God's armor for the fight, and train specialists to counsel the demonized, and (3) that we properly treat and counsel the oppressed and demonized.

Here we suggest the duties of the counselors and the duties of the oppressed.

DUTIES OF COUNSELORS

What should be the responsible practice for the counselor? How shall the counselor of the oppressed or demonized proceed?

Proper preparation. He should prepare himself for the ministry. He should avail himself of much of the good literature along this line. The bibliography suggests some materials available. He should prepare himself with biblical information and spiritual strength for the recognition and treatment of the oppressed. He should obtain intelligent and spiritual prayer backing for the task.

Proper diagnosis. He should properly diagnose those who may have demonic problems. This involves checking for (1) adequate symptoms, (2) adequate causes, and (3) adequate testing. This procedure is described in brief in chapter 9, where we treated the evidences of demonization.

He must exercise caution here. A premature diagnosis might hinder the healing process. There may not be immediate manifestation of the demonic. There may be things on the human level to care for first. There may be a complexity of causes and problems. Not all that looks demonic is necessarily demonic. Lechler adds his concern here:

> It is quite obvious therefore that each case of mental depression demands a very detailed investigation of the patient's moral and occult history. Unless this is done one will be unable to arrive at a clear understanding of the patient's problem.[10]

Lechler states further:

> Since the distinguishing between pathological and demonic disturbances involves great responsibilities one is urgently advised in all doubtful cases to call in the help of a qualified Christian psychiatrist or counsellor who has had experience in these matters (that is, he is acquainted with demonic symptoms and has treated them properly).[11]

The counselor would do well to read all that Lechler has to say about the matter of distinguishing mental illness from the demonic and their possible overlapping in some cases.

Proper treatment. He should properly treat those who come to him for help along this line. He must lovingly and firmly counsel from the biblical and practical points of view, using all

10. Lechler, in Koch, p. 190.
1. Ibid., pp. 153-90.

the skills that he has learned and developing new skills in this area. Acceptance, assurance, and direction must be given. Responsible attitude and action must be expected. He must not promise too much too soon but realistically expect growth in the battle and look for complete deliverance when God has finished the child-training process. Growth is more important than the absence of demons. The second follows upon the first.

There must be the confident and authoritative confrontation of wicked spirits, calling for their confession that Christ is victor and that the Christian is positionally victor in Christ. The demon must be made to confess that he will obey the Lord Jesus and the counselee and leave when Jesus and the counselee agree. Then there should be command for him to leave. If he does not leave immediately, the counselor must seek from the Christian or from the demon what ground (moral occasion) there might be for his staying in the person. That must be biblically judged and confessed and claimed back from the demon. Again he must be told in the name of Jesus to go to where Jesus sends him with all his host. This must be continued until the leading demon of all is gone, there is no more demonic response to inquiry or command, and the major demonic symptoms vanish from the Christian's experience. This is the approach in brief that has worked in many cases. Not all cases are the same, but the general principles pertain to all.

Proper follow-up. There should be good follow-up and continuing support of the counselee. That involves a reporting to the counselor at stated intervals with evaluation. A support community should be arranged, such as fellowship in a biblically oriented and balanced church, small group Bible study and prayer groups, and a few informed friends who have insight into this special area of concern. Deliverance is not just an occasion or short process. It also involves a way of life thereafter to maintain spiritual health and freedom.

Proper referral. Finally, there should be in some cases responsible referral. Each counselor must recognize his limitations and know when he is involved beyond his expertise. His responsibility is to refer to adequate resources in such cases. This involves having a list of qualified persons to meet the need and sharing with that person what the counselee permits. Cooperation with the other resource person should be offered.

DUTIES OF THE OPPRESSED

What would be the responsible practice for the oppressed or demonized? The counselee has his own personal responsibilities, and these are basic to his spiritual well-being and progress. These include several key factors. Chapter 13 outlines the defense of the believer in spiritual warfare and against demonization particularly. These are also spelled out in some detail in my book *Angels, Elect and Evil.*[12] Briefly stated, they include the following responsibilities.

Receiving Christ. If there is doubt that the person is a genuine Christian, he must hear, understand, and accept the gospel. The gospel of our Lord Jesus Christ includes these very simple but profound truths, presented in God's Word, the Bible, and substantiated by the death and resurrection of the Son of God, our Savior: (1) God is the personal creator and judge of all, (2) man has sinned against his creator and now stands under the guilt of sin and God's condemnation, (3) God's eternal Son also became man and as the God-man paid the penalty for our sin by His death on the cross as our substitute, (4) Jesus rose again from the dead, and (5) man must trust Christ by receiving Him personally. Receiving the Savior meets the requirements of God for total forgiveness and total acceptance. God also raises the believer to a position that includes having the righteousness of Christ and authority to fellowship with God and carry on His work as we submit to Him in practical obedience to His revealed Scriptures, the Bible. God also creates within the believer new spiritual life that is legally identified with the risen and exalted Christ and includes authority to resist the devil.

Confession and renunciation. Any possible ancestral involvement must be renounced. The demonized must take a stand against the devil and all his works. There must be a breaking of any allegiance given explicitly or tacitly. Personal sins must be confessed, especially those that were likely to have led to bondage.

Removal of occult objects or connections. Possession of such objects or the continuation of friendships that are occult or sinful must be broken. Willful refusal is rebellion that Satan can use as ground.

12. C. Fred Dickason, *Angels, Elect and Evil* (Chicago: Moody, 1975), pp. 206-9.

Resting in Christ and resisting the devil. Christ has promised to forgive and help those who turn to Him. Confidence in His love and power is fundamental. We must understand and rest in His victory over the evil ones and stand against them in His name.

Submitting to Christ and cultivating spiritual life. The Christian must yield his new life to Christ for His cultivation. The devil is the destroyer; Christ is the creator of life and joy. We must submit to God, resist the devil, and he will flee from us. We must understand our position in Christ and obey the command to be filled with the Spirit. This means obeying His Word in the Bible, confessing our sins, and depending upon Him to control our lives, not magically but reasonably through logically and willfully following the commands of Scripture. No one can successfully resist the devil unless he first submits his entire person and the direction of his life to Christ. No rebel can oppose properly the great rebel, Satan; instead, he is to some degree siding with him against God.

The person must cultivate new habits of thinking properly about God, about himself, and about others. He must exercise the means of growth: reading and memorizing appropriate Bible passages, praying for God's will and his growth and deliverance, participating in Christian fellowship, serving Christ in the fellowship of the church, and sharing the gospel. He must be sure to put on the armor of God (Eph. 6:10-18). He should seek specific prayer support from understanding Christians and seek out a qualified counselor to aid him in his quest for deliverance.

Practicing these things will assure growth and deliverance from the enemy at the proper time. He must exercise trust and patience and keep on keeping on, developing right attitudes and actions.

There is hope for the demonized. Christ the victor and deliverer stands ready with all authority in heaven and on earth to intervene for the rescue. He wants the believer to grow in his trust and commitment to Him. He seeks to develop the believer's spiritual life and will even use the presence of the enemy to accomplish this. Demons are invaders, squatters, defeated by Christ and subject to expulsion to the pit. If they are allowed to continue for any length of time in the demonized, it is only for the glory of God and the good of the believer. When the believer's attitudes and actions are sufficiently developed under the tender but firm hand of the Father, when the Father's loving child-training has run its course, then the believer will recognize all the good that has been accomplished and profit from the development of holiness in his life (Heb. 12:5-11). In the meantime, he needs to recognize that demons are the unwilling catalysts for his growth. He needs also to lay hold on the promise "Submit therefore to God. Resist the devil and he will flee from you. Draw near to God and He will draw near to you. . . . Humble yourselves in the presence of the Lord, and He will exalt you" (James 4:7-8, 10).

CONCLUSION

In counseling Christians who are demonized, there are some dangers to avoid. These include discounting the evidence that Christians actually can be demon-inhabited, neglecting the need to treat them properly, overemphasizing this ministry to the neglect of other ministries, oversimplifying the problems by improper diagnosis, misemphasis upon "miraculous gifts" or "magical cures," causing division in the church over this issue, and withdrawal in confusion and defeat.

There are definite duties to assume for the church and Christian community, particularly for the counselor and the oppressed. These have been outlined and explained in brief.

17

Conclusion

We have sought an objective approach to these questions:
(1) Can Christians be demonized? and (2) If so, what should be done for them?

Our basic and final authority has been the inspired and infallible Scriptures of the Christian Bible. We sought from a proper interpretational and exegetical approach to examine the evidence presented in the Bible. We sought evidence also from clinical experiences taken from reliable sources.

REVIEW OF APPROACH

Part 1, Preliminary Considerations, included a biblical study of the reality and activity of demons, the definition and description of demonization, the definition of a Christian and his relationship to Christ, and a description of the various aspects of spiritual warfare.

Part 2, Major Considerations, involved investigation and statement of evidence from biblical, theological, and clinical sources.

Part 3, Related Issues, treated the dynamics of demonization, our defense against demonization, perspectives in warfare, deliverance from demonization, the propriety of counseling the demonized, and a suggested response to the issue.

RESTATEMENT OF FINDINGS

A rather thorough examination of the biblical evidence leads us to conclude that it neither clearly affirms nor denies the reality of demonization of believers. There is some weight of evidence leaning toward the affirmative. But to be fair, we must say that with biblical evidence alone, we cannot reach a definite or dogmatic conclusion.

The commonly expressed theological arguments for and against demonization of believers were subjected to careful biblical and logical analysis. They also were found to be indefinite. What may be regarded as the strongest argument against demon inhabitation of a Christian is that it is impossible for the Holy Spirit and an evil spirit to live in the same human body. We have examined the argument and found it to be lacking from both biblical and logical standpoints. In fact, it is impossible, from the very nature of evidence, to prove that no Christian has ever been inhabited by demons.

After establishing the validity and limitations of evidence from reason and clinical experience, we set forth an analogy in treating the question Can a Christian have cancer? We demonstrated how that question might be resolved, since the Bible does not specifically support the affirmative or the negative. In resolving it we must use both biblical and clinical guidelines and information.

At this point we introduced case studies from widely separated and reliable counselors that attest to the reality of demonization of Christians. This type of evidence cannot be dismissed on the basis that it is nonbiblical any more than can other factual, reliable, investigations. This approach is the basis for many accepted scientific and sociological studies or surveys.

In treating the dynamics of demonization we sought to describe (1) the results of demon control from biblical and clinical information and (2) the probable mechanisms or processes that occur during demonization. We considered demonic mind-control methods and the relation of mind, brain, and body. We paid particular attention to the susceptibility of Christians. Again we introduced case studies from reliable sources to illustrate the dynamics of control.

There is a positive defense against demonization in a proper approach to the whole subject of spiritual warfare from a biblical and practical point of view. We emphasized that we must have a proper perspective in spiritual warfare and in the deliverance. Our established priority should be to honor God through worship, fellowship, and spiritual growth and service. We sought to give perspective on the "miraculous gifts" and the proper place of deliverance ministry.

In presenting deliverance from demonization we looked at biblical terms and results. Then we considered clinical results using the testimonies of involved counselors and counselees.

There is a proper place in the Christian community for counseling the oppressed and the demonized. We considered the biblical and practical supports for counsel, the commonly raised objections, and our responsibility to counsel those under demonic bondage.

A final section suggested a fitting response to the issue, including dangers to avoid and duties to assume.

Reassurance of Victory

It is encouraging to know that Christians have been delivered from demon oppression and demonization in the past and are being delivered today as well. No one need think his case is helpless or that help cannot be found for those we see in bondage. We do not hold that God uses "miraculous gifts" or specially gifted and empowered leaders for this ministry. We hold that such gifts ceased with the apostolic age or shortly thereafter. But the source of our encouragement and authority for ministry is the risen and exalted God-man, the Lord Jesus, who stands as victor over the enemy and supernaturally intervenes today for those who look to Him, obey His Word, and take an active stand against the enemy. Those who prepare themselves for spiritual warfare will be able to help, at least in measure, those in bondage. Often just a word of well-founded encouragement and a firm stand and prayer specifically against the enemy will save a life from total disaster. We have good basis for expecting victory in the battle.

CHRIST'S VICTORY OVER SATAN AND DEMONS

Strong, scheming, and relentless as the enemy may be, he is no match for the risen, exalted Lord Jesus. Satan and his demons are but creatures. Depraved, destructive, and full of devices as they are, yet they have been soundly defeated, stripped of much power, and paraded to open shame by the victor, the God-man, our Savior. By His cross and resurrection He realized the purpose of God to lay the basis for our salvation and God's glory in extending His grace. He released the prisoners of Satan, He routed the powers of evil, and ratified their punishment. Wicked spirit beings shall be bound at Christ's second coming and after the kingdom will be cast into the lake of fire to suffer eternally under the hand of the Righteous Judge. They shall be forever banished from any display of their wickedness whatsoever for all eternity. And God's people will forever be with their loving and gracious Savior in the new heavens and new earth.

OUR POSITION OF VICTORY

Every believer has been baptized into Christ and so owns the position of being "in Christ." We are raised to new life in the resurrected Christ, we are seated with Him in the heavenlies where He is exalted, and we share in a position of authority far above all classes and ranks of wicked spirits, even above Satan himself. We need to claim that position and exercise that authority in the whole range of Christian life and service and particularly in spiritual warfare. We are, by our God-granted position, victors in the Victor. He leads us in the train of His triumph, and we operate out of a position of victory. The Christian must never lose that perspective, whether he be one that is oppressed or one seeking to help the oppressed.

THE PRACTICE OF VICTORY

Some might fear the unknown and particularly the dark and devious enemy of our souls, but we have the sovereign Lord as the captain of our salvation who has overcome the devil and promises that we will overcome as we trust Him and tread on the enemy. Joshua and Caleb did not overlook the tall and strong people of Canaan or their walled cities, but they trusted in the promises and the power of God. They were not paralyzed or hindered by fear but trusted God's power and promises. He had demonstrated His care and intervention in the deliverance from Egypt and all the enemies in the past. Now they were trusting in Him and His promise: "Every place on which the sole of your foot treads, I have given it to you, just as I spoke to Moses" (Josh. 1:3). The faithful and courageous Joshua and Caleb, with the host of those who followed them, did take the land on which they trod.

In like manner, we must trust the promises and the power of God in this matter of spiritual warfare. He will never leave us or forsake us, and He will see us through to victory. Our job is to submit to God and to resist the devil; then he will flee from us. Submitting to God demands total allegiance. We cannot toy with sin and the world or hold onto anything the devil supplies. If we do, we are rebels ourselves and are siding with Satan in his rebellion. We must take sides in the battle, as did Joshua. He challenged the people in his day, "Choose for yourselves today whom you will serve. . . . but as for me and my house, we will serve the Lord" (Josh. 24:15).

We must actively resist the devil. This demands a recognition of his reality and his influence, even of oppression or demonization of Christians. It also demands a firm stand in the power of the Lord and in His might. He alone has the resources against the hosts of wickedness. It demands an aggressive defense and a courageous offense. No battle is won only by a good defense, and there is no indication that spiritual warfare is only defensive. Jesus spoke of the inability of the gates of hades (authorities of the unseen world of spirits) to stand against the extension of the church and her authority (Matt 16:18). The Word of God and prayer are great offensive weapons ʋ use in our firm stance and advance (Eph. 6:12-18). We must confess and renounce all known sin and ground given to the enemy in any way. We can verbalize our stand in allegiance to Christ and in opposition to Satan. We can tell our enemies that they must back down and flee. And the promise is that they will (James 4:7).

There may be degrees of submission and degrees of resistance, some of which is normal with growth of understanding and obedience. There may be degrees of deliverance or freedom from the power of the enemy. The battle may not fade overnight, but we must continue fighting until daybreak, when the sun of God's righteousness breaks through and there is full deliverance. Our job is to keep on keeping on with the Lord, depending upon His power and obeying His command until the battle is fully won.

RESPONSE OF THE FAITHFUL

Faith is the victory that overcomes the world and the devil. But what shall the faithful do in light of the reality and intensity of the battle in oppression and demonization? I respectfully and humbly but firmly urge the reader and the Christian community to hear my final words in this matter.

RESPOND WITH OPENNESS

I am grateful to my readers for their following the presentation of my research and findings in this matter. I would urge Christians to (1) consider seriously the contributions of this study, (2) evaluate objectively the matters discussed, (3) determine from a biblical world view what should be their stance about demon oppression and demonization, (4) participate in meaningful and open discussion with others, and (5) do their part as God gives opportunity to ease the affliction of those in dire distress and bondage.

RESPOND WITH COMMITMENT

If you agree to any degree with the major concern of my findings and recognize that Christians stand in need of specific counsel that deals with the demonic, then I urge you to prepare for helping them. This is not the time to flee the conflict but to face the foe. This is not the time for indecision but for determination to help the afflicted.

There is need for counselors who will invest study and time in such counseling. Churches need to allow and encourage spiritual warfare counseling. Seminars and classes can be held for the presentation of spiritual warfare and counseling. I am glad to note that some centers for treatment and rehabilitation have been established. I would urge caution that those centers be evaluated according to biblical and professional standards.

Beware of the "miraculous ministry," "reprogramming," the psychic, and the "holistic healing" approaches. They can further complicate matters. Some of the charismatic community claim to cast out demons by the laying on of hands and the speaking in tongues. We must credit them with recognizing the reality of spiritual warfare but object to their lack of thorough biblical

basis and emphasis upon special gifts, which may be counter-
feited by Satan. They have in some cases helped and in other
cases just played "musical chairs" with demons, moving out
some and replacing them with others. I have found fifteen cases
of false tongues that invaded Christians through the laying on of
hands, a technique used often in the occult for the transference
of power. Those in reprogramming often fail to recognize the
person's worth and right of self-determination. The psychics are
for the most part demonic mediums, and Satan does not cast out
demons. The holistic health approach recognizes that the whole
person must be treated in the healing process, but they proceed
from the wrong basis. Their world view is often akin to Eastern
religions and the occult. The Lord warned us against wolves in
sheep's clothing (Matt. 7:15), and Paul warned about ravenous
wolves even from within the church (Acts 20:29-30). Such men
and such approaches we must avoid (2 Tim. 2:15-16).

RESPOND WITH CONFIDENCE

A word to leadership and counselors. You will face many
questions, misunderstandings, and opposition ranging from
mild to strong. Wicked spirits themselves will seek to oppose
you in this matter, for they fear your taking this seriously and
pressing the battle. They know they will be defeated and deprived of their activity and freedom. Do not back down! The
Lord will encourage and strengthen you and give you wisdom in
the battle. Who will meet the urgent need if we fail in the face
of criticism? God will hold us responsible.

Hesitancy to advance in the spiritual battle to aid the oppressed and the demonized in the Body of Christ may stem
from ignorance of the realm of the spirit world. This can be
remedied from the study of what God has revealed in the Scriptures. Those who fear to study what God has wisely revealed in
His Word are really falling back in distrust and self-preservation.
Proverbs 24:10-12 says:

> If you are slack in the day of distress,
> Your strength is limited.
> Deliver those who are being taken away to death,
> And those who are staggering to slaughter, O hold them back.
> If you say, "See, we did not know this,"

Does He not consider it who weighs the hearts?
And does He not know it who keeps your soul?
And will He not render to man according to his work?

This is at once a warning and a challenge to meet the task set before us.

A word to the oppressed. Friends, there is hope and help in the Savior. There is no reason to continue in confusion, doubt, depression, and isolation. God has better things for you. You need not grovel in the face of adversity and at the hands of the adversary. God has helped others, and He will help you. But you have to make the move to trust and obey. "There is no other way to be happy in Jesus, but to trust and obey." Follow through on what has been suggested in this book. Read part 1 for the facts and perspective in the warfare. In part 3, read and apply the principles of defense in chapter 13; and in chapter 16, read and follow through on the duties you must assume.

Do not give up. Commit your case to God, just as Peter said:

> Humble yourselves, therefore, under the mighty hand of God, that He may exalt you at the proper time, casting all your anxiety upon Him, because He cares for you. Be of sober spirit, be on the alert. Your adversary, the devil, prowls about like a roaring lion, seeking someone to devour. But resist him, firm in your faith, knowing that the same experiences of suffering are being accomplished by your brethren who are in the world. And after you have suffered for a little, the God of all grace, who called you to His eternal glory in Christ, will Himself perfect, confirm, strengthen *and* establish you. To Him be dominion forever and ever. Amen. (1 Peter 5:6-11)

This refers primarily to our ultimate deliverance from opposition and suffering when we inherit glory, but the principle of our trust in God's care and His intervention at the proper time and in the proper way pertains even today.

Do not give up hope. Do not withdraw in amazement and hurt that most people do not understand or care. There are those who care and will seek to help you. Pray that you might be led together. Perhaps you need to pray that eyes will be opened to the reality and hearts be moved to aid in the battle. There are more and more solid Bible-believing and balanced Christians who are realizing the truth, seeing the need, and moving to help those in distress. Be patient, be forgiving, be faithful in obeying the Word and claiming all that is rightfully yours in Christ. God's Word is forever settled in heaven. You need to let it settle in your heart that God is good, that you are the object of His love and care, and that He will intervene for you as you diligently seek Him, obey His Word, and trust Him to see you through. "Weeping may last for the night, but a shout of joy comes in the morning" (Ps. 30:5).

One of the most helpful books I know to help you in this matter is *The Adversary,* written by my good friend and fellow-soldier, Mark I. Bubeck, and published by Moody Press. You will profit from the perspective, encouragement, and warfare prayers suggested in this book.

For those believers who might previously or after reading this book have feared the invasion of demons, I say, "Relax in the Lord." No one walking in fellowship with Christ—that is, obeying His Word, walking in the Spirit, and seeking to honor Him in moral life, spiritual growth, and good interpersonal relationships—has anything to fear about becoming invaded. God guards His own (Ps. 27; 90; Isa. 41:10). We have been talking about those who have been invaded through grounds given in ancestral involvement or personal involvement in things contrary to the Word of God—such as occult, immoral, or religious practices—by which demons took opportunity. If these factors do not pertain to you, fear not.

We can all enjoy the powerful hymn from Martin Luther:

> A mighty fortress is our God,
> A bulwark never failing;
> Our helper He, amid the flood
> Of mortal ills prevailing.
> For still our ancient foe
> Doth seek to work us woe;
> His craft and power are great,
> And, armed with cruel hate,
> On earth is not his equal.
>
> Did we in our own strength confide,
> Our striving would be losing,
> Were not the right Man on our side,
> The man of God's own choosing:
> Dost ask who that may be?

Christ Jesus, it is He;
Lord Sabaoth His name,
　From age to age the same,
And He must win the battle.

And though this world, with devils filled,
　Should threaten to undo us,
We will not fear, for God hath willed
　His truth to triumph through us.
The prince of darkness grim—
　We tremble not for him;
His rage we can endure,
　For lo! his doom is sure;
One little word shall fell him.

That word above all earthly powers—
　No thanks to them—abideth;
The Spirit and the gifts are ours
　Through Him who with us sideth:
Let goods and kindred go,
　This mortal life also;
The body they may kill:
　God's truth abideth still,
His kingdom is forever. Amen.

A FINAL, FINAL WORD

I trust the Lord will use this sincere attempt, even with its limitations, to stir Christians to face reality, trust the Lord Jesus, resist the enemy, and find the freedom for themselves and others that God has designed through the deliverance from sin and Satan that is found in Christ the exalted Victor and Sovereign.

What better words on which to end a presentation of spiritual warfare than those penned at the close of such a section by Paul in Ephesians 6:18-19?

With all prayer and petition pray at all times in the Spirit, and with this in view, be on the alert with all perseverance and petition for all the saints, and pray on my behalf, that utterance may be given to me in the opening of my mouth, to make known with boldness the mystery of the gospel.

I pray for my readers.

Selected Bibliography

REFERENCE WORKS

Arndt, William F., and Gingrich, F. Wilbur. *Greek-English Lexicon of the New Testament.* Chicago: U. of Chicago, 1952.

Chamberlain, William Douglas. *An Exegetical Grammar of the Greek New Testament.* New York: Macmillan, 1957.

Dana, H. E., and Mantey, Julius R. *A Manual Grammar of the Greek New Testament.* New York: Macmillan, 1948.

Davidson, Gustave. *A Dictionary of Angels.* New York: Macmillan, 1967.

Geisler, Norman L., and Nix, William E. *A General Introduction to the Bible.* Revised and expanded. Chicago: Moody, 1986.

Kittel, Gerhard, and Friedrich, G., eds. *Theological Dictionary of the New Testament.* Translated by G. W. Bromiley. Vols. 1 and 2. Grand Rapids: Eerdmans, n.d.

Robertson, A. T. *Word Pictures in the New Testament.* Nashville: Broadman, 1930.

Thomas, Robert L., and Gundry, Stanley N. *A Harmony of the Gospels.* Chicago: Moody, 1978.

EXEGETICAL STUDIES

Findlay, G. G. "St. Paul's First Epistle to the Corinthians." In *The Expositor's Greek Testament,* edited by W. Robertson Nicoll. Grand Rapids: Eerdmans, 1951. 2:729-953.

Godet, F. *Commentary on the First Epistle of St. Paul to the Corinthians.* 1886. Reprint. Grand Rapids: Zondervan, 1957. Vol. 2.

Kent, Homer A. *Ephesians, The Glory of the Church.* Everyman's Bible Commentary. Chicago: Moody, 1971.

Knowling, R. J. "The Acts of the Apostles." In *The Expositor's Greek Testament,* edited by W. Robertson Nicoll. Grand Rapids: Eerdmans, 1951. 2:3-554.

Ladd, George Eldon. *A Commentary on the Revelation of John.* Grand Rapids: Eerdmans, 1972.

Meyer, H. A. W. *Critical and Exegetical Handbook to the Epistle to the Corinthians.* Translated by David Hunter. *Critical and Exegetical Commentary on the New Testament.* Edited by William P. Dickson and William Stewart, vol. 2. Edinburgh: T. and T. Clark, 1879.

Ryrie, Charles C. "The First Epistle of John." In *The Wycliffe Bible Commentary,* edited by Charles F Pfeiffer and Everett F. Harrison. Chicago: Moody, 1962.

Wuest, Kenneth S. *In These Last Days.* Grand Rapids: Eerdmans, 1954.

SPIRITUAL WARFARE, DEMONOLOGY, AND THE OCCULT

Alexander, William Menzies. *Demonic Possession in the New Testament.* Edinburgh: T. and T. Clark, 1902.

Baker, Roger. *Binding the Devil.* New York: Hawthorne, 1975.

Baldwin, Stanley. *Games Satan Plays.* Wheaton, Ill.: Scripture Press, 1971.

Barnhouse, Donald Grey. *The Invisible War.* Grand Rapids: Zondervan, 1965.

Bilheimer, Paul. *Destined to Overcome.* Ft. Washington, Pa.: Christian Literature Crusade, 1982.

Bubeck, Mark I. *The Adversary.* Chicago: Moody, 1975.

———. *Overcoming the Adversary.* Chicago: Moody, 1984.

Chafer, Lewis Sperry. *Satan.* Chicago: Moody, 1942.

Demon Experiences in Many Lands. Chicago: Moody, 1960.

Dickason, C. Fred. *Angels, Elect and Evil.* Chicago: Moody, 1975.

Dobbins, Richard. *Can a Christian Be Demon-Possessed?* Akron, Ohio: Emerge, 1973.

Ensign, Grayson H., and Howe, Edward. *Bothered? Bewildered? Bewitched? Your Guide to Practical, Supernatural Healing* Cincinnati: Recovery, 1984.

Ernst, Victor. *I Talked with Spirits.* Wheaton, Ill.: Tyndale, 1971

Hammond, Frank, and Hammond, Ida Mae. *Pigs in the Parlor: A*

Practical Guide to Deliverance. Kirkwood, Mo.: Impact, 1973.

Koch, Kurt. *Between Christ and Satan.* Grand Rapids: Kregel, 1962.

———. *Christian Counseling and Occultism.* Grand Rapids: Kregel, 1965.

———. *Demonology, Past and Present.* Grand Rapids: Kregel, 1973.

———. *The Devil's Alphabet.* Grand Rapids: Kregel, 1969.

———. *Occult Bondage and Deliverance.* Grand Rapids: Kregel, 1970.

———. *Satan's Devices.* Grand Rapids: Kregel, 1978.

———. *The Strife of Tongues.* Berghausen, Germany: Evangelization Publisher, n.d.

Lechler, Alfred. "Distinguishing the Disease and the Demonic." In *Occult Bondage and Deliverance,* by Kurt Koch. Grand Rapids: Kregel, 1970, pp. 133-98.

Lewis, C. S. *The Screwtape Letters.* New York: Macmillan, 1956.

Lindsey, Hal. *Satan Is Alive and Well on Planet Earth.* Grand Rapids: Zondervan, 1972.

Manuel, Frances D. *Though an Host Should Encamp.* Ft. Washington, Pa.: Christian Literature Crusade, 1973.

Matthews, Victor. *Growth in Grace.* Grand Rapids: Zondervan, 1971.

McLeod, W. L. *Demonism Among Evangelicals and the Way to Victory.* Saskatoon, Sask.: Western Tract Mission, 1975.

Montgomery, John Warwick. *Demon Possession.* Minneapolis: Bethany Fellowship, 1973.

———. *Principalities and Powers: The World of the Occult.* Revised edition. Minneapolis: Bethany Fellowship, 1975.

Murrell, Conrad. *Practical Demonology.* Pineville, La.: Saber, n.d.

Nevius, John L. *Demon Possession.* Reprint. Grand Rapids: Kregel, 1968.

Newport, John P. *Demons, Demons, Demons.* Nashville: Broadman, 1972.

Penn-Lewis, Jessie, and Roberts, Evan. *War on the Saints.* Abridged edition. Edited by J. C. Metcalf. Ft. Washington, Pa.: Christian Literature Crusade, 1977.

Pentecost, J. Dwight. *Your Adversary the Devil.* Grand Rapids: Zondervan, 1969.

Peterson, Robert. *Are Demons for Real?* Chicago: Moody, 1972.

Philpott, Kent. *A Manual of Demonology and the Occult.* Grand Rapids: Zondervan, 1973.

Rockstad, Ernest B. *Demon Activity and the Christian.* Andover, Kan.: Faith and Life, n.d.

Rockstad, Ernest B., and Chessman, Lulu Jordan. *From the Snare of the Fowler.* Andover, Kan.: Faith and Life, 1972.

Schneider, Bernard N. *The World of Unseen Spirits.* Winona Lake, Ind.: BMH, 1975.

Unger, Merrill F. *Biblical Demonology.* Wheaton, Ill.: Scripture Press, 1957.

————. *Demons in the World Today.* Wheaton, Ill.: Tyndale, 1976.

————. *What Demons Can Do to Saints.* Chicago: Moody, 1977.

Watson, David. *How to Win the War: Strategies for Spriritual Conflict.* Wheaton, Ill.: Harold Shaw, 1972.

Wilson, Clifford, and Weldon, John. *Occult Shock and Psychic Forces.* San Diego: Master, 1980.

RELATED SUBJECTS

Adams, Jay E. *Competent to Counsel.* Nutley, N. J.: Presbyterian and Reformed, 1974.

————. *Matters of Concern to Christian Counselors.* Phillipsburg, N.J.: Presbyterian and Reformed, 1978.

Armerding, Hudson T. *Christianity and the World of Thought.* Chicago: Moody, 1968.

Benner, David G., ed. *Baker's Encyclopedia of Psychology.* Grand Rapids: Baker, 1985.

Bobgan, Martin, and Bobgan, Deidre. *The Psychological Way/ The Spiritual Way.* Minneapolis: Bethany, 1978.

Bilheimer, Paul. *Destined for the Throne.* Ft. Washington, Pa.: Christian Literature Crusade, 1975.

Burdick, Donald E. *Tongues: To Speak or Not to Speak.* Chicago: Moody, 1969.

Collins, Gary R. *Christian Counseling.* Waco, Tex.: Word, 1980.

————. *Effective Counseling.* Carol Stream, Ill.: Creation House, 1972.

————. *Fractured Personalities.* Carol Stream, Ill.: Creation House, 1972.

————. *How to Be a People Helper.* Santa Ana, Calif.: Vision House, 1976.

Crabb, Lawrence J., Jr. *Effective Biblical Counseling.* Grand Rapids: Zondervan, 1977.

Custance, Arthur C. *The Mysterious Matter of the Mind.* Grand Rapids: Zondervan, 1980.

Flynn, Leslie B. *Nineteen Gifts of the Spirit.* Wheaton, Ill.: Victor, 1977.

Geisler, Norman L. *False Gods of Our Time.* Eugene, Ore.: Harvest House, 1985.

Harner, Michael. *The Way of the Shaman.* New York: Bantam, 1980.

Kallas, James. *The Significance of the Synoptic Miracles.* SPCK Biblical Monograph Series. Greenwich, Conn.: Seabury, 1961.

Little, Gilbert. *Nervous Christians.* Lincoln, Neb.: Back to the Bible, 1956.

Michaelson, Johanna. *The Beautiful Side of Evil.* Eugene, Ore.: Harvest House, 1982.

Morris, Henry M. *The Scientific Case for Creation.* San Diego: Creation Life, 1977.

Narramore, S. Bruce. *The Integration of Psychology and Theology: An Introduction.* Grand Rapids: Zondervan, 1979.

———. *No Condemnation.* Grand Rapids: Zondervan, 1984.

———. *You're Someone Special.* Grand Rapids: Zondervan, 1978.

Narramore, Bruce, and Counts, Bill. *Freedom from Guilt.* Santa Ana, Calif.: Vision House, 1974.

Nee, Watchman. *The Key to Experiencing Christ—The Human Spirit.* Los Angeles: The Stream, n.d.

———. *Release of the Spirit.* Indianapolis: Sure Foundation, 1965.

Peck, M. Scott. *People of the Lie: The Hope for Healing Human Evil.* New York: Simon & Schuster, 1983.

Nelson, Marion. *Why Christians Crack Up.* Chicago: Moody, 1960.

Ramm, Bernard. *Protestant Biblical Interpretation.* Revised edition. Boston: W. A. Wilde, 1956.

Rosen, R. D. *Psychobabble.* New York: Atheneum, 1977.

Ryrie, Charles C. *Balancing the Christian Life.* Chicago: Moody, 1969.

———. *What You Should Know About Inerrancy.* Chicago: Moody, 1981.

Schaeffer, Francis A. *A Christian Manifesto.* Westchester, Ill.:

Crossway, 1981.

Sire, James W. *The Universe Next Door: A Basic World View Catalog.* Downers Grove, Ill.: InterVarsity, 1976.

Thomas, Robert L. *Understanding Spiritual Gifts.* Chicago: Moody, 1978.

Tournier, Paul. *A Doctor's Casebook in the Light of the Bible.* New York: Harper & Row, 1960.

Trask, Willard R. *Shamanism, Archaic Techniques of Ecstacy.* Princeton, N.J.: Princeton U., 1964.

Virkler, Henry A. "Demonic Influence and Psychotherapy." In *Baker's Encyclopedia of Psychology,* edited by David G. Benner. Grand Rapids: Baker, 1985.

Wagner, Peter. *On the Crest of the Wave: Becoming a World Christian.* Ventura, Calif.: Regal, 1983, pp. 123-42.

Warfield, Benjamin B. *Counterfeit Miracles.* London: Banner of Truth, 1972.

Weldon, John, and Bjornstad, James. *Playing with Fire.* Chicago: Moody, 1984.

Weldon, John, and Levitt, Zola. *Psychic Healing.* Chicago: Moody, 1982.

Wenham, John W. *The Goodness of God.* Downers Grove, Ill.: InterVarsity, 1974.

Wright, Norman H. *Crisis Counseling: Helping People in Crisis and Stress.* San Bernardino, Calif.: Here's Life, 1985.

PERIODICALS

Berends, William. "The Biblical Criteria for Demon-Possession." *Westminister Journal* 37 (1975): 242-65.

Brand, Paul, and Yancey, Philip. "A Surgeon's View of Divine Healing." *Christianity Today,* 25 November 1983, pp. 14-21.

Clapp, Rodney. "Faith Healing: A Look at What's Happening." *Christianity Today,* 16 December 1983, pp. 12-17.

Clark, Gordon. "God and Logic." *The Trinity Review* 16 (November/December 1980).

Cottrell, Jack. "All About Demons: Who? What? When?" *The Lookout,* 27 January 1980, p. 7.

Crews, Frederick. "The Future of an Illusion." *The New Republic,* 21 January 1985.

Dickason, C. Fred. "Demons—Our Invisible Enemies." *Fundamentalist Journal,* October 1984, pp. 21-23.

"Expanding Horizons: Psychical Research and Parapsychology." *Spiritual Counterfeits Project Journal,* Winter 1980-81, pp. 3-44.

Glasser, Arthur. "Culture, the Powers and the Spirit." *Missiology* 5 (April 1977): 1931-39.

Gundry, Robert H. " 'Ecstatic Utterance' (N.E.B.)?" *Journal of Biblical Literature* 13, no. 2 (October 1966).

Hohensee, Donald. "Power Encounter Paves Way for Church Growth in Africa." *Evangelical Missions Quarterly* 15 (April 1979): 87.

"Holistic Health Issue." *Spiritual Counterfeits Project Journal,* August 1978, pp. 3-51.

"Occult: A Substitute Faith." *Time,* 19 June 1972, pp. 62-68.

Otis, Gerald E. "Power Encounter: The Way to Muslim Breakthrough." *Evangelical Mission Quarterly* 16 (October 1980): 217.

Scott, Steve, and Alexander, Brooks. "Inner Healing Issue." *Spiritual Counterfeits Project Journal,* April 1980, pp. 12-15.

Smith, Charles R. "The New Testament Doctrine of Demons." *Grace Journal* 10 (Spring 1969): 26-42.

Thomas, Robert L. "Tongues Shall Cease." *Bibliotheca Sacra* 17, no. 2 (Spring 1974): 81-89.

Virkler, Henry A., and Virkler, Mary B. "Demonic Involvement in Human Life and Illness." *Journal of Psychology and Theology* 5, no. 2 (1977): 95-102.

Weaver, Gilbert. "Tongues Shall Cease." *Grace Journal* 14, no. 1 (Winter 1973): 12-24.

Whitcomb, John C. "Does God Want Christians to Perform Miracles Today?" *Grace Journal* 12, no. 3 (Fall 1971): 3-12.

Zuck, Roy B. "The Practice of Witchcraft in the Scriptures." *Bibliotheca Sacra* 128 (October-December 1971): 352-60.

UNPUBLISHED WORKS

Hillstrom, Elizabeth. "Altered States of Consciousness and Their Relationship to Demonic Influence." Class notes for course on Counseling: Demon Oppression, presented at Moody Bible Institute Graduate School, 7 January 1986.

———. "Near Death Phenomena as Altered States." Class notes for course on Counseling: Demon Oppression, presented at Moody Bible Institute Graduate School, 7 January 1986.